ENDORSEMENTS FOR RATCLIFF'S WORK

JJ Abrams (Director & Writer of *Lost, Alias, Fringe, Star Trek, Super 8, Star Wars: The Force Awakens*):

"Trey's images are other-worldly, mind-blowing creations that, at first glance, appear to be some digital trompe l'oeil; a Photoshop trickery post-production creation. But no, Ratcliff's photographs—through techniques he freely shares —are inspiring and real. Something which makes them all the more incredible."

Hans Zimmer (Composer for *The Lion King, Gladiator, Inception, Interstellar, Batman*):

"Trey's pictures are a daily source of inspiration for me. I can't count the times that I've gotten stuck in my writing and, as I sit there staring at my computer screen desperately trying to think of the next idea, the screensaver kicks in with one of Trey's images, and the shapes and colors triggered something in me that got me to the next note..."

Patrick Rothfuss (Author of *The Name of the Wind, The Wise Man's Fear, Doors of Stone*):

"Someone once told me that a photographer is an artist that paints with light. I never understood what that meant until I saw Trey's work."

Hugh Howey (Author of *The Wool Trilogy; I, Zombie; Beacon 23*):

"Trey's art not only captures the soul of its subjects and environment; his body of work reveals the depth of the man behind the camera. I aspire to see the world with as much grace, humility, and wisdom as Trey. He is more than a photographer; he is an observer of the human condition, and he relates what he sees in stunning prose, with biting wit, and with soaring images."

Tina Guo (CEO of Guo Industries; Grammy-nominated acoustic/electric cellist; recording artist; composer):

"I love Trey's beautiful imagery, his body of work and I've even been lucky enough to go on a photo walk with him in Budapest, traveling around the city taking pictures and listening to words of wisdom on both life and photography matters! This book takes an all-encompassing look at the world of social media and specifically Instagram, analyzing what it truly means to connect with your following and the importance of building a real and loyal fan base as opposed to a mere numbers game. As with all things, quality over quantity!"

Lisa Donchak (Technology Consultant, Behavioral Scientist):

"Trey has been deeply involved in social media since long before most of us knew what it was. Through his art, he's been able to reach millions of people across social media networks, in some cases redefining the engagement model between an Influencer and their followers. As he's made his name across these platforms, Trey has delved deeply into their inner workings, through his own experimentation, his conversations with other thought leaders in the space, and his discussions with the founders of many of the most popular social media companies. In this book, Trey shares his unique insights on the topic of the darker side of social media—perspectives that will shift the broader conversation about how we interact with each other on the web."

Kevin Kelly (Founder of WIRED and Author of *The Inevitable* and *What Technology Wants*):

"You can often learn how something works by how it breaks. The thing I really like about the book is way Trey shines x-ray beams into a broken system and thereby illuminates how it works. Once one understands how the system works, the reader can then optimize it for good. While Trey educates us on how to fake influence, this book is really about how to create genuine positive influence—and why it is more powerful and sustainable. This is also a tremendous resource for those who employ Influencers, because it gives you different smell tests to discern the genuine from the imposters, protecting your own reputation and money. I'd go so far as to say the discernment and media skills entailed in this book should be a required literacy in every high schooler's education. You've heard of critical media skills? This is critical Influencing skills."

JOIN THE CONVERSATION

Do you find these topics interesting and timely? Take a photo of the image below and share it with your friends on social media with the hashtag #UnderTheInfluence. I mean, assuming they are real friends and not bots.

I also invite you to join the conversation inside our Facebook Group. And hey, be nice, eh? That's a good rule for life.

https://www.facebook.com/groups/UnderTheInfluenceBook

UNDER THE INFLUENCE

HOW TO FAKE YOUR WAY INTO GETTING RICH ON INSTAGRAM

UNDER THE INFLUENCE

HOW TO
FAKE
YOUR WAY INTO
GETTING RICH
ON INSTAGRAM

INFLUENCER FRAUD,
SELFIES, ANXIETY, EGO
& MASS DELUSIONAL BEHAVIOR

TREY RATCLIFF

Cover Design by @stephanbollinger.
Interior layout and design by www.writingnights.org.
Book preparation by Chad Robertson.
For information about permission to reproduce selections from this book, email business@stuckincustoms.com.

ISBN: 9781091586550

This book may contain suggestive themes, crude humor, and strong language. Content may not be suitable for anyone who is easily outraged or offended.

Real Instagram handles and names are used throughout as examples. In this book, I provide my personal opinion on what may constitute fraudulent behavior on social media, based on the evidence and data available to me. The reader is welcome to draw their own conclusions.

Printed on acid free paper in the United States of America.

24   23   22   21   20   19   18   17 8   7   6   5   4   3   2   1

Dedicated to my dad. Dude, I am sorry you're gone, but thanks for the inspiration and that awesome DNA. Also, speaking of acronyms, I wish we had done MDMA together!

*"In the beginning, the Universe was created.
This has made a lot of people very angry and
been widely regarded as a bad move."*

— **Douglas Adams**

CONTENTS

PREFACE

I invite you to read this book in its entirety, especially if you're dreaming of fame and fortune as a Social Media Influencer. For those with different aspirations, and those who are hoping I'll get to the interesting parts quickly, I've handpicked some juicy bits that I think you'll find most relevant.

For Marketing Managers, Advertising Directors, Brand Managers, and their Bosses: Immediately read the first half of the book about Instagram-related fraudulent behavior so you can spot the fakes before you waste another dime on doomed Influencer marketing campaigns. You'll probably want to be sitting down.

For Sociopaths: I can't stop you from using this book to fake your way to getting rich on Instagram, as thousands have before you. Follow the recipes inside if you're an asshole who thinks fraud is kinda cool.

For Techies and Social Media Insiders: There are plenty of graphs and objective technical analyses to geek out on. There are also a few bold conclusions that you might be surprised to see in print.

For Instagram Employees: You probably already know all the scams and tricks I'm about to expose in chapter 3. So, I've also provided some solutions in chapters 4 and 7 that might make you a hero at the next company brainstorm.

For Parents: Go straight to the part about selfies and anxiety in chapter

5, right after you fail to force your child to replace Instagram on their phones with the Headspace meditation app. I may never convince you that mindfulness is better for their lives—and yours—than selfies, but I'll try.

For those of you who think Social Media might be causing your anxiety: It probably is. Read chapter 5, about selfies and anxiety to understand why this is. Then check out chapter 8, where I talk about some solutions.

For Technophobes: If you've managed thus far to not be tempted to live your life online, congratulations! If you're into *schadenfreude*, this is the book for you.

For Artists and Creatives: Even if you don't believe you belong in this category, I hope I inspire you to create in some way, whether it's online or IRL. Along the way, don't take social media or yourself too seriously. There is an extensive section on how to have actual influence rather than faking it.

For those who don't skip ahead to the "About the Author" section in Appendix A: I, Trey Ratcliff, am an artist and professional photographer. I run the #1 Travel Photography blog in the world. I'm also a bit of a computer geek, so I jumped on social media back in the early days. I regularly communicate with heaps of friends I haven't met yet (I now have over 5 million followers, including 170,000 on Instagram). I guess that makes me a Social Media Influencer. To be clear, I haven't purchased any of these followers using the fraudulent means I will soon describe in this book. You can read more about your new author friend in Appendix A.

ACKNOWLEDGEMENTS

Special thanks to my editors Lisa Donchak (Instagram - @therainbowgoat) and Pamela Bramwell (Instagram - @pbramwell) and contributors including, but not limited to:

Aaron Lammer (Instagram - @aaronlammer)
Amber Colle (Instagram - @ladycolle)
Amelia McGeorge (Instagram - @amelia.mcnugget)
Amie Yavor (Instagram - @amie_yavor)
Annika Beer (Instagram - @annika_beer25)
Baz Macdonald (Twitter - @kaabazmac)
Beatrice Onions (Instagram - @beatriceonions)
Ben Calvert (he's too old and grumpy to use Instagram)
Brian Brushwood (Instagram - @scamschoolbrian)
Carla Munro (Instagram - @blackrobincreative)
Chad Robertson (does not understand Instagram's value proposition)
Christa Laser (Instagram - @christa.laser)
Clayton Morris (Instagram - @claytonmorris)
Cliff Redeker (Instagram - @mcrsquared2)
Curtis Simmons (Instagram - @curtissimmons)
Danny Garcia (Instagram - @danmiami)
Dave Gent (I asked for his Instagram but he wanted a beer)
David Maxwell (Instagram - @davidewtmaxwell)
Dean Burrell
Elizabeth Carlson (Instagram - @youngadventuress)
Erin Keeble
Frederick Van Johnson (Twitter - @frederickvan)

Gary Beller (Instagram - @garybeller)

Georgia Rickard (Instagram - @georgiarickard)

Gino Barasa (Instagram - @ginobarasa)

Graham Woodyatt

Hans Mast (Instagram - @hansmast)

Hugh Howey (Has quit all social media)

Jared Polin (Instagram - @jaredpolin)

Jason Silva (Instagram - @jasonsilva)

Jeffrey Martin (Instagram - @gigajeff)

Jim Pollard (Instagram - @jimpollardgoesclick)

John Tierney (Twitter - @johntierneynyc)

Johnny Jet (Instagram - @johnnyjet)

Josh Whiton (Instagram - @joshwhiton)

Julie Wolf (Instagram - @whygeorgia)

Kevin Kelly (Instagram - @kevin2kelly)

Kevin Rose (Instagram - @kevinrose)

Kiersten Rich (Instagram - @theblondeabroad)

Kirk Strawn (Instagram - @kirkstrawn)

Lauren P. Bath (Instagram - @laurenepbath)

Leo Laporte (Has quit all social media)

Lindsay Adler (Instagram - @lindsayadler_photo)

Matt Hackett (Twitter - @mhkt)

Matt Mullenweg (Instagram - @photomatt)

Matt Ridley (Twitter - @mattwridley)

Meagan Morrison (@travelwritedraw)

Miranda Spary (Instagram - @mirandaqueenstown.co.nz)

Nicole S. Young (Twitter - @nicolesy)

Niki Shmikis (Instagram - @nikishmikis)

Olivia Wensley (Instagram - @liv_wensley)

Om Malik (Instagram - @om)

Patrick Rothfuss (Twitter - @patrickrothfuss)

Peter Ruprecht (Instagram - @peterruprecht)

Rene Smith (Instagram - @renejsmith)

Rick Sammon (Instagram - @ricksammonphotography)

Robert Scoble (Instagram - @scobleizer)

Ruby Wilson (Instagram - @rujean)

Sally Rutter (Instagram - @seesallyeat)

Serge Ramelli (Instagram - @photoserge)

Sofia Jin (Instagram - @_sofjin)

Stephan Bollinger (Instagram - @stephanbollinger)

Stu Davidson (Instagram - @veridian3)

Susan Ratcliff (Instagram - @calinapa)

Tane Gent (His real Instagram - @tanegent)

Thomas Hawk (Instagram - @thomashawk)

Tina Guo (Instagram - @tinaguo)

Tobi Innes (Instagram - @tobi.innes)

Tom Anderson (Instagram - @myspacetom)

Tracy Cameron (Instagram - @ican_models)

Will Scown (Instagram - @daysrun)

Zeeshan Kazmi (Instagram - @zshankazmi1)

INTRODUCTION

Lacie is constantly on her phone. An app dominates her attention—one where people are giving ratings on a scale of one to five, but not of her photos.

People are rating *her*.

Lacie's ratings are based on everything she posts online as well as how she behaves in the real world. Her quotidian barista gives her a nice rating and she gives one back. She greets her coworkers while gliding through the office as they merrily flick high ratings at one another.

But all is not sunny for Lacie. She rates a 4.2 out of 5, and she's desperate to get a higher rating. She contorts her behavior in ways she believes will earn her good reviews from other, more highly rated people. Her self-worth is tied to that score, and it fills her with anxiety. This app is no longer just an app. It's her whole life.

"It's easy to lose sight of what's real," Lacie laments. Things begin to go awry for Lacie as a series of events injure her rating and her sanity spirals downward. Showing that her life, directed by the app, is hollow and meaningless outside of it.

Black Mirror fans will no doubt recognize Lacie from "Nosedive" (Season 3, Episode 1) of the Netflix sci-fi drama.[1] Charlie Brooker, the writer and creator of *Black Mirror*, called the episode a "satire on acceptance and the image of ourselves we like to portray and project to others."

Of course, Brooker's unflinching portrayal of social hacking leading to mass delusional behavior is fiction. But the episode is uncomfortable to watch because this is the world many of us, to varying degrees, actually inhabit.

Now, let's take it one step further. Imagine if the highest-scoring users of this app could cash in on their scores and receive luxury perks—even cold hard cash—in real life. In 2017 according to *The Atlantic*, brands paid an estimated $2 billion to popular Instagram users—also known as Influencers—in exchange for an Influencer mention on social media, the latest form of celebrity endorsement.[2]

Unfortunately, the world of *Black Mirror* is no longer fiction. Before we dive into the bewildering world of social media, where a 7-year-old made $22 million in 2018 for reviewing toys and an alarming number of fake Influencers swindled companies out of mountains of cash and luxury goods, let's take a brief step back.

CHAPTER 1
UNDER THE INFLUENCE

"There can be no progress without head-on confrontation."
— **CHRISTOPHER HITCHENS**

BEFORE I WALK you down the primrose path that begins with innocence on Instagram and ends with a polemical analysis of dystopian mass delusional behavior, let's start with the basics of social media.

CONNECTING THE WORLD

Many great things have come from connecting the world on social media platforms. Due to the advent of social media, large-scale charity has been accomplished. Promising programmers in a remote village in India can get a job in Silicon Valley. Yogis can find and plan retreats.

Political protests can spread and gather momentum to create meaningful change. Artists can collaborate. Inspirational videos (as well as ones about cats) can be shared. We can easily share birthday photos with loved ones on the other side of the world, get people to turn up for our community bake sales, and form gardening clubs with other people who like to talk about flowers.

While social media can enable some of these marvelous activities, it also acts as a platform and a megaphone for some of the worst aspects of human nature. Fear, violence, narcissism, hate, and bullying have all found homes on social media.

There are all kinds of crazy things happening on the internet. Based on a Pareto distribution, about 80% appear to be negative. In this book, I'll not only talk about the bad activities but also the bad actors who are contributing to the creation of an unstable online world that can't be trusted.

In the following chapters, I use Instagram as my case example. That said, most of the content you'll read about is applicable to most social networks.

WHO USES INSTAGRAM?

In 2010 a photo sharing app called Instagram launched bringing back the nostalgia of Polaroids with a trendy square photo crop. The platform quickly gained a massive user base due to its user interface. It provided a simple way to edit a mobile photo directly on your phone, allow you to add fun filters to make it look cool, and share it instantly with your friends. Two years later Facebook acquired Instagram for a cool $1 billion helping Instagram skyrocket into one of the world's most popular social networks. Today it has about a billion users worldwide. It's an obvious place to hang out if you're into photography but people use it for nearly everything.

Number of monthly active Instagram users from January 2013 to June 2018 (in millions)

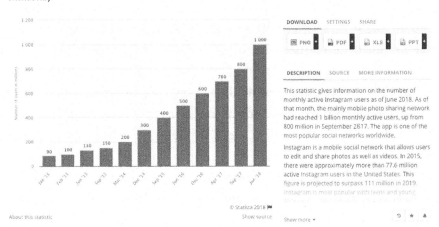

Instagram just passed 1 billion users, and it shows no sign of slowing down.[1]

WHAT ARE INFLUENCERS, AND WHY DO THEY MATTER?

I'll never forget the time I first met an Instagram "Influencer." It happened several years ago. I was speaking at a social media conference about travel photography. Later that evening, at a dreadful cocktail party, a woman came up to me with eyes as large as saucers. She squealed, "Are you an Influencer, like us?"

In my mind, I was thinking, "What the hell is an Influencer?" If I can't even influence my besetting kids to clean their rooms, how could I possibly influence anyone else?

Advertising has changed a lot in recent years. We no longer wait until 6 p.m. to watch the news, which is interrupted by advertisements. As print media declines in circulation, it becomes less relevant as an advertising platform. The paid services that we use, such as Netflix and Spotify, don't even have advertising. And many online users make use of ad blocking software.

Because of these shifts, advertisers have had to look for novel ways to put their products in front of eyeballs.

Celebrity endorsements are not a new phenomenon. There have always been famous people who promote products or services and are paid to do so. Traditionally this promotion happened overtly, in a video or print advertisement, or perhaps via product placement in a movie or TV show.

Since the advent of social media, a new type of celebrity has arisen. These new celebrities are the social media users with the most followers and they are most commonly called "Influencers." Often, because these Influencers are so popular on the Internet, they are paid by brands to mention products or services in their social media posts. The general idea is that when an Influencer endorses something their followers will definitely take notice, especially if the endorsement is authentic. Additionally, Influencers typically have a well-defined niche such as running, fashion, baking, or in my case, travel photography. Brands think they can more easily target their intended audience—for example, aspiring bakers—by working with Influencers in that space.

What's the threshold to be considered an Influencer? Generally, on Instagram, an Influencer is someone with over 25,000 followers. Influencers with over 25,000 followers are now being pursued by companies who are not only offering their products and services for free to Influencers but often paying cash for the exposure, much like a traditional advertising contract.

To be clear, these sponsorships are different than the paid "Sponsored ads" that you see in your feed. Sponsored ads are deals that brands broker directly with Instagram. Influencer deals, on the other hand, happen behind the scenes—between the Influencer and the brand.

When your favorite celebrity is selling something in a magazine ad, most of us take it with a grain of salt. We know she's getting paid to be associated with that product. But when a social media star touts a Prada bag as an essential accessory for a particular lifestyle she's promoting, most of her followers will take it as a genuine endorsement because it deliberately is not redolent a traditional advertisement.

An enthusiastic endorsement by an Instagram star could be worth many times what companies pay for a mention in a post because the endorsement looks authentic to a captivated audience. It's as if the star really believes the product is great. The endorsement looks so real that Influencer love now comes with a pretty hefty price tag.

In general, the more followers you have the more money you can make on your posts. Some of the most-followed Influencers, with millions of followers, can easily ask for over $100,000 for a post or for a series of posts across a campaign.

There are also "micro-Influencers," with over 10,000 followers in a particular niche, who are also attractive to advertisers. These rates can vary wildly from a few hundred dollars to a few thousand. Using our baking example—instead of paying just one very famous Influencer, Betty Crocker could do deals with 100 different micro-Influencers in the baking space who mostly just post photos of cakes and muffins.

Instagram doesn't require sponsorship transparency. They don't require that a lifestyle Influencer disclose they received a bag for free or that Prada negotiated a deal to be featured in three of her posts in exchange for a handsome paycheck. The Federal Communications Commission does require this sort of disclosure. However, on social media, it's very difficult to know just by looking if someone is just being showy with their Prada bag or if they were paid to show off their Prada bag.

WHO ARE INFLUENCERS?

Some of these Influencers are quite well known and they make quite a bit of money. Among the top ten highest-paid influencers in 2018 are Selena Gomez, Beyoncé, and Justin Bieber.

IMAGE	RANK ▲	NAME	LOCATION	NICHE	FOLLOWERS	COST PER POST
	1	Kylie Jenner @kyliejenner	USA	Celebrity	110,000,000	1,000,000
	2	Selena Gomez @selenagomez	USA	Celebrity	138,000,000	800,000
	3	Cristiano Ronaldo @cristiano	Europe	Celebrity, Sport	133,000,000	750,000
	4	Kim Kardashian @kimkardashian	USA	Celebrity	113,000,000	720,000
	5	Beyonce Knowles @beyonce	USA	Celebrity	115,000,000	700,000
	6	Dwayne Johnson @therock	USA	Celebrity	109,000,000	650,000
	7	Justin Bieber @justinbieber	USA	Celebrity	100,000,000	630,000
	8	Neymar da Silva Santos Junior @neymarjr	South America	Celebrity, Sport	101,000,000	600,000
	9	Lionel Messi @leomessi	South America	Sport	95,300,000	500,000
	10	Kendall Jenner @kendalljenner	USA	Celebrity	92,400,000	500,000

Here's the top ten highest-paid Instagram Influencers in 2018, according to Hop-perHQ.com.[2] Imagine being able to make $1M USD with just one Instagram post.

However, post sponsorship extends far beyond the most obvious stars. For example, there's a good chance these twin 2-year-olds, Tay-tum and Oakley Fisher, make more money than you. According to Fast Company, they command $15,000 to $25,000 per post. Their manag-ing parents say they can get bigger deals but it's difficult right now "because the girls can't really follow directions."[3]

View More on Instagram

100,130 likes
kcstauffer

#ad They are my little Wreck-It Ralphs...believe me this was a joy to clean up but I rewarded my hard-working self with a little game play. If you haven't already, check out @disneymagickingdoms. Now that Ralph and friends are in the game, you can WRECK IT with endless fun of your own!

view all 213 comments

Two enterprising out-of-work Hollywood actors have created a goldmine Instagram account for their twin daughters.

This is just one example of the impact social media is having on kids growing up with it. Around the world, becoming a social media Influencer has skyrocketed to the #1 career aspiration for kids. Mediakix released a study that said that 75% of kids aged 6 to 17 want to become an online personality, whereas just 1 in 15 want to be a boring doctor.[4] In New Zealand, where I live, the number is even higher—9 in 10 children said they want to be an Influencer.[5] Why spend ten long and expensive years in medical school when you can get a lot of free stuff, go on trips to exotic places, and party all the time while being adored by fans around the world?

For comparison, when I was growing up in the '70s, I wanted to be an astronaut or President of the United States. I still want to be an astronaut.

OPPO, a mobile phone company, recently announced they were looking for an Influencer to go on a paid gig to travel for free for 3 months to take photos with their new phone. Who wouldn't want that?

The announcement, coincidentally, came on the heels of a study they conducted on the effectiveness and desirability of being an Influencer. According to OPPO's study, "36% [of Influencers] say they've tried to build up their Instagram following, with 39% admitting they get anxious about the number of likes they'll get when posting on Instagram."[6] Their study also showed that 1 in 6 aspirational Influencers said they would gladly take a course that teaches them how to be a more successful Influencer. Many already take expensive courses as referenced later in the book.

HOW WIDESPREAD IS THIS PHENOMENON?

The sponsorship of Instagram posts is a quickly growing trend. There were about 10 million brand-sponsored Influencer posts on Instagram in 2016 and that number is expected to break 30 million in 2019. That's a growth rate of almost 50% year-on-year.

Number of brand sponsored influencer posts on Instagram from 2016 to 2019 (in millions)

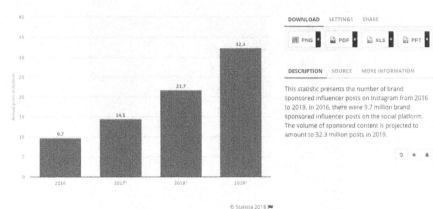

© Statista 2018

About this statistic · Show source

Over the last few years, the number of brand-sponsored Influencer posts has grown by almost 50% every year.[7]

At the individual Influencer level, the prices brands are willing to pay are astronomical. Kylie Jenner (@kyliejenner) makes $1M USD per post on Instagram. Selena Gomez (@selenagomez) makes $800K per post. Kim Kardashian's desultory posts are bringing up the rear. Take a look a few pages back to see the top ten list.[8]

Successful Influencers can make millions per year on social media deals alone. The top YouTube Influencer, Ryan ToysReview, made over $20 million last year.[9] Ryan's channel, you may not be surprised to learn, features reviews of toys. On the other hand, you may be surprised to learn that Ryan is seven years old.

1		Ryan ToysReview	$22m	↑+7
2		Jake Paul	$21.5m	↑+6
3		Dude Perfect	$20m	=
4		Daniel Middleton	$18.5m	↓
5		Jeffree Star	$18m	●
6		Markiplier	$17.5m	↓2
7		Evan Fong	$17m	↓5
8		Jacksepticeye	$15.5m	NEW
9		PewDiePie	$17m	↓3
10		Logan Paul	$14.5m	↓

Source: Forbes   BBC

This is a list of the earnings of some of the top Influencers from YouTube.[10] You may not recognize many of these names, but I can guarantee your children probably would. It is important to note that I am not suggesting any of them are fraudulent, but rather illustrating how these massive paychecks can be very alluring. Sidenote: Ryan ToysReview, in the #1 spot, is seven years old. There was no way I could have come close with my paper route or any afterschool job when I was a kid. Actually, good for him, because there is some good stuff that happens on the Internet and brings good fortune to creative content. Personally, I find his YouTube channel to be unwatchable, but it just shows how many types of audiences are out there.

Many brands feel like advertising in this way on social media is no longer an optional channel—it's required. For example, there was a recent article in WIRED about a new eyelash company, called Lashify. Lashify's founder, Sahara Lotti, said, "she was told to expect to shell out $50,000 to $70,000 per Influencer just to make her company's name known." When she didn't get in the Influencer game, she alleges a competitor paid a top Influencer to give her Lashify product a brutally negative review. Lotti compared the system to the mafia.[11]

WHAT'S THE SECRET?

If you have played around with Instagram at all you'll know it's not as easy as it sounds to get 25,000 people to click on the "Follow" button. It takes a lot more than posting a few pretty pics. So, how are so many newly minted Influencers appearing seemingly overnight, boasting huge followings and an enviable engagement rate that qualifies them for cash and free stuff?

Hey, pssssst, wanna know a secret? You can buy followers. You can buy comments. You can buy likes. And, to the casual observer, this interaction appears to be legitimate.

But these followers, commenters, and likers are not real. Purchased post engagement is actually generated mostly by bots. That's right— these followers, comments, and likes are non-human scripts running on a remote computer. They aren't real people. And hardly anybody is checking to see if they are.

And hardly anybody is checking to see if they are.

Why would someone buy fake followers? Some users simply buy followers for clout, so they can appear more popular than they are to their friends. These social media addicts may also buy likes and comments for their photos, just to show off. I think this is a very silly and egotistic reason, but it's not fraud.

However, there is a more unscrupulous reason for buying followers.

Influencers use the methods described in this book to get cash and free stuff for their own benefit. Once they hit the thresholds we discussed above (10,000, 25,000, or more followers), brands start approaching them (or vice-versa) to make business deals. So, some Instagram users are doing just that. They've created a fake following— mostly consisting of fake people—and now are reaping real rewards.

Anything that can be counted online can be faked. And more people than you think are faking it.

Besides the people that are faking it by using the fraudulent techniques outlined in the book, we also delve into that unusual cadre of Influencers who pretend to have a perfect life. As you'll see, their seemingly virginal nobility is more likely an immaculate misconception.

WHAT IS REALLY HAPPENING TO US ON SOCIAL MEDIA?

Why is it important to know that some of the most popular users on social media are deceiving us? We are currently experiencing one of the most significant sociological upheavals in history and it's impacting almost everyone on Earth. The social media phenomenon has only taken a few short years to significantly impact society, and yet it has created more mass anxiety than almost any other social change in history.

Our minds and lives are being hacked by social media. The algorithms that choose what you see online are engineered to maximize the time you spend looking at your screen rather than time away from your screen. These algorithms have figured out what you like, what you don't like, what gets you outraged, and what keeps you interacting.

There is a saying that fish cannot see the water in which they swim. They're too used to its ubiquity. In this way, humans also "swim" in something we don't completely understand—our consciousness. Consciousness is definitely real, but it's difficult for us to discern or describe. If you practice mindfulness, meditation, reflection, or if you spend time in nature, then you do get a glimpse of it. However, in a short space of time, social media has taken humans away from a more mindful and conscious state of mind.

How has this happened? Have you noticed the little boost you get from seeing you've got a new comment, "like," or follower on a social media platform? What about the disappointment in finding no new notifications and feeling that craving to check all over again a few moments later?

When you find those comments, likes, or followers, your body generates dopamine—a chemical that signals to us that something good has happened. It's part of a built-in reward system that, when abused, can be very addictive.

Our brain gets a squirt of dopamine when something good happens—like eating a good meal or having sex. However, the apps on our phones are capable of triggering the same chemical response in our bodies.

By introducing positive reinforcement on a randomized schedule, through notifications, these apps can create addiction-like behavior in users. It's the same mechanism that drug or gambling addicts have been subject to as part of their hobbies or activities, and it can lead to very unhealthy behaviors.

Just like gambling, these social media notifications are addictive. Millions of people are getting hooked. A 2018 study from Nielsen estimated the average American adult is spending over 11 hours per day listening to, watching, reading, or interacting with media across all devices, and about 10% of that time is devoted just to social media.[12] The Washington Post reported that teens spend nearly nine hours every day on their phones alone, and much of that time is on social media.[13]

There have been many studies that have concluded that social media addiction is real. Mark Griffiths and Daria Kuss are psychologists at Nottingham Trent University in the U.K. They specialize in studying the impact of technology and social media on cognitive and social behavior. Back in 2011, they were the first academics to systematically review the existing scientific literature on excessive social media use. They found that for a small minority of individuals, social media had a significant detrimental effect on many aspects of life including relationships, work, and academic achievement. They argued that such signs are indicative of addiction and are similar to what people experience with alcohol or drugs.[14]

It isn't just the academics who have noticed. The movers and shakers in the technology space know this is happening, as well. Marc Benioff, the

CEO of the popular sales platform Salesforce, likened social media addiction to smoking. Even Mark Zuckerberg, Facebook's CEO and founder, has admitted that social media sits "at the intersection of technology and psychology, and it's very personal."[15]

Robert Lustig, a professor of pediatrics who wrote the book *The Hacking of the American Mind*, says even kids can be addicted to social media. "[Social media] is not a drug, but it might as well be. It works the same way… it has the same results."[16]

The social media drug has side effects too. When you flip through Instagram, instead of feeling inspired by seeing beautiful people living seemingly perfect lives, you may notice discomfort, unease or even a sense of anxiety. This is not your imagination.

One of the ways social media can cause anxiety is by introducing irrational standards of beauty to the user. Matt Mullenweg, the founder of WordPress, told me in an email exchange, "I think the picture-perfectness of photo posting to social media creates unrealistic expectations for life." What he describes is part of a "social media hangover"—an undue anxiousness in viewers that I'll unpack for you a bit later in the book.

For now, I'll just share what I think: someone who leads a perfect life has no need to tell anyone else because the telling of it does not increase its perfection.

An Ego-Fueling Social World

All social media platforms are built to reward one of the most sneaky parts of the human mind: the ego. Those of you who have studied mindfulness, presence, and consciousness know the very essence of this word "ego," but let me break it down in case you've never dissected it.

You've probably heard people say, "Oh, a guy with a big ego likes to show off his car and money and stuff." Well, that's certainly true. Colloquially we do use the word "ego" to mean arrogance or self-centeredness.

However, the word "ego" stands for so much more. In traditional psychology, the word signifies the part of the mind that goes between the conscious and the unconscious. It's responsible for reality testing and creating a sense of personal identity.

The ego's job is to create an identity for you, which is a story about you that you tell yourself over, and over, and over again, even if it's a false narrative. The ego also encourages you to repeat that story to other people so that they might help reinforce it. The unconscious part of the ego can have a tremendous amount of control over your entire life if you allow it.

This isn't always a good thing. Reinforcing a story in this way can lead to inflexible thinking and to the generation of narratives that may not be true.

This is where the zen part comes into it: the ego's story is a fictional identity. It only has power over you when you let it take charge. The pictures you're seeing on social media can only bother you if you let them.

The real you is the silence behind your thoughts. You can watch those thoughts go by as an independent non-judgmental observer. If I'm confusing you, Eckhart Tolle explains this concept beautifully in his books such as *The Power of Now* and *A New Earth*. In it, he explains how clever the ego is into tricking you into thinking all you are is a jumble of random, often contradictory, thoughts.

For my nerdy friends, the ego is glitchy software that takes up an obscene amount of processing power if you leave it running in the background of your mind. It can't be disabled completely, but once you discover it's open source you can pause it and turn off notifications to free up your mind in all sorts of delightful ways. Even better, you can choose to not use your mind at all sometimes and to let it just rest. Imagine going all day and not being bothered by anything. Now doesn't that sound pleasant? We'll get into how to do this a little later on.

We're Being Hacked

If you believe Artificial Intelligence (AI) is the stuff of science fiction, then I can assure you it's already seeping into every part of our everyday lives. Does that mean robots will exterminate humans and take over the Earth? Probably not.

Well, maybe. We have no idea what an AI that is ten times smarter than us would want to do with itself on Earth (or beyond). For example, a horse can look at humans and have no idea why we would want to build a hospital or go to a respected sushi restaurant. Horses can't even conceive of things like this, so how could we possibly conceive of things that AI might like to do with their time?

AI is a big concern for major thinkers in this space, primarily because some AI will be able to reprogram themselves so they are hundreds or thousands of times smarter than humans. The gap in intelligence can easily be much greater than that between a mosquito and a human. Maybe these uber-smart AI will ignore us, the way we ignore Bonobo monkeys. But maybe not.

The current concern is that as we march forward towards AI—a march that is impossible to stop—we are starting to see how some of the most clever algorithms in the world are already manipulating human behavior.

How Do They Do It?

Social media networks collect an immense amount of data from the activities of millions of users and have to figure out what, from all of this, to show you. Algorithms are the rules that help to sort and prioritize this data.

Instagram, while they employ thousands of people, doesn't have nearly enough employees to sort through all the photos uploaded every minute and decide which ones *you* might be most interested in seeing and interacting with. So, they use algorithms—mathematical rules that decide what content to show you.

A team at Instagram decides what rules the algorithm should follow to slice and dice all of this data to create your feed. Your feed is composed of the images and posts that this team, through these hugger-mugger algorithms, calculates will be the most relevant and interesting to you. Then they present this information in a way that keeps you and me, the viewers, coming back for more. The algorithms are creating opportunities for more and more engagement without worrying if this increased engagement is unintentionally harming user psyche. With each new notification or post, we're getting that little squirt of dopamine.

Social media algorithms are infiltrating our minds and manipulating our behavior by hacking our ego software, causing us anxiety and stress. They've gained access to our attention and time by knowing how our minds and egos work, better than we ourselves do.

THE BLACK MIRROR NOSEDIVE

On Instagram, it's quite common to feel inadequate if your photo does not get as many likes and comments as other photos. This measurement is a very public scoreboard that encourages you to compete for the approval of absolute strangers you will never meet and who will never have any material impact on your life. It sounds silly when you put it like that. I'm sure you know that people's reaction to your photo should have no impact on your well-being, but it's an easy trap to fall into.

The Royal Society for Public Health, in the United Kingdom, recently surveyed 1,500 Britons aged 14 to 24. These young people associated Instagram with many negative attributes as well as low self-esteem. The outcome? An increase in poor body image and a decrease in sleep.[17] Because of social media, we feel worse about ourselves.

As we discussed in the previous section, social media content is fed to you using specific algorithms which decide which content is the most relevant to you or will keep you on the site for longer. These algorithms can be optimized to show you a variety of different types of content, and someone is making choices regarding what that content is.

Historically, feeds would show you posts chronologically. So you would see all, or at least most, of the posts of people you're following, in order of most recent to oldest. This seems like it would be okay, but most social media sites don't do this anymore. They changed that algorithm for a few reasons.

Firstly, Instagram decided it can give you a better experience on the site by showing you posts that you are more likely to engage with. It determines which posts those are by looking at how quickly other people are clicking "like" or commenting on these posts. The goal is to keep you engaged with Instagram as long as possible so that you see more ads.

Secondly, the non-chronological feed helps make Instagram more money. How? If you want to be sure your post is seen, you have to pay Instagram advertising dollars to make sure it appears in more people's feeds.

So, what happens to the user? There you are, lounging on the couch in your comfy pants and eating a tub of Ben & Jerry's ice cream, and you can't help but compare yourself and your life to all those filtered, edited, beautiful snapshots from your friends and family. And look at how many likes they are getting! Now part of you knows there's absolutely no need to compare yourself to anyone. But try remembering that when you go online to browse some photos and you suddenly find yourself sucked into the beautiful, glamorous, heavily-edited lives of your peers, right?

Since most of the trendsetters on Instagram are Influencers with lots of followers, now more than ever, we're bombarded by updates on what the popular kids are doing. We see these posts, compare ourselves to them, and find ourselves lacking. Hence, anxiety and stress.

These social networks just keep that game going, while taking innocent minds further and further from true mindfulness and peace. Some people's entire self-identity is made up of the social media groups they are in or the sorts of photos they post, manipulated by a set of rules in a game they don't even know they're playing.

IS THERE ANOTHER PATH?

Okay, let's wrap up this multi-headed hydra of a chapter so we have a solid foundation going forward.

- Instagram magically appeared and created the first major, predominantly visually-based, photo-sharing social network. Cool.
- Some Instagrammers became very popular, with tons of followers.
- The intentionally inscrutable institute of the Influencer was born and Influencers started making money.
- Other Instagram users figured this out and some of these sneaky aspirational Influencers started to buy robotic followers, likes, and comments.
- These deceptive Influencers use fabricated engagement numbers to create a false narrative—a life of perfection and popularity—all whilst getting freebies and cash from unsuspecting brands.
- Influencers are clever at making the sorts of beatific and aspirational posts that are preferred by the algorithm which itself has been engineered to elicit responses from you.
- This often causes us—the users—undue anxiety even when we don't realize that's what's happening to us.
- In addition, the algorithm is designed to maximize your screen time while minimizing the opportunities you have for daily mindful moments of true meaning in your life.

You'll come to know that I find the idea of zen and consciousness to be particularly fascinating. I am extremely interested in how these social networks have accidentally taken us away from being a more conscious state of mind by encouraging our worst instincts. In this book, I talk a lot about my philosophy—my zen approach to social media.

Maybe, just maybe, I can help a few people out there who are experiencing social-media-induced anxiety by showing that, indeed, there is another path.

CHAPTER 2
SOMETHING FISHY IS GOING ON

"Yeah, well, you know, that's just, like, your opinion, man."
— THE DUDE

HOW DID I FIGURE ALL THIS OUT? About 18 months ago, I started noticing strange patterns inside Instagram—users with a strange number of followers, who made comments that didn't seem quite human. Upon further investigation, I found a burgeoning Instagram black market where users could buy fake followers, likes, and comments.

I was curious how big a problem this was so I thought it might be interesting to set up some experiments myself and help expose a few cracks in the system.

What I found was jarring, even to me. Through the course of these experiments, I discovered just how easy it was to cheat, and the scale on which it's happening.

Why would anyone bother to buy followers, likes, and comments? Not only is it often annoying and egotistical, but in some cases, it's outright fraudulent.

Instagram users buy these followers, likes, and comments to attract brand sponsorship. Brands are spending hundreds of millions of dollars to woo Influencers to promote their brand—in the same way these brands use perks to woo celebrities. This sponsorship often arrives to Influencers in three ways.

- **Unsolicited free stuff.** In the first, this wooing shows up, unsolicited, in the form of free products—from designer clothes and first-class airplane tickets to status-symbol purses and free hotel stays. In the hope that the Influencer will spontaneously gush about the brand online.
- **Formal agreements for free stuff.** In the second, which occurs more often, brands (or agencies that represent the brands) will negotiate a formal agreement with an Influencer. Influencers may be given expensive cars to drive, resort stays, spa treatments to try, gadgets to test, lavish meals at posh restaurants, you name it, in exchange for name-dropping that brand in a post.
- **Money, money, money.** And then there's the *cash money*! In the third method, on top of or instead of free products, a brand would lay down cold hard cash to buy Influencer love. This happens in just about every industry and is especially common in fashion, travel, entertainment, fitness, food, music, and beauty. This is perhaps the biggest reason, as people will do most anything to end their state of protracted penury.

In this last method, incentives start at about $1,000 to buy a mention of a product or service from a small-time Influencer and can range up to $1 million for a major Influencer. The exact figure varies based upon how competitive a market is but is typically linked to how many followers an Influencer has and their history of follower engagement (a measurement of likes and comments on a post).

We'll follow the money to see who is winning by cheating the system and who the injured parties are. We'll also talk to Instagram to find out what is being done, if anything (hint: not a lot). I will give you examples in the photography and travel industry, an area where I have some authority. But keep in mind that fake followers aren't confined to this one industry. They are everywhere.

Also, if you skipped the preface, this bears repeating: I have not employed any of these devious methods to grow my own following.

SOCIAL NETWORK MEASUREMENTS AS A FICTIONAL CONSTRUCT

Let's talk about Social Networks on an abstract level for a moment before we dive into the sordid details. We'll use Instagram as an example but you could plug any other social network into its spot. In many ways, the Instagram platform itself acts like a country with its own economy. It has citizens. It has a currency in the form of followers, likes, and comments.

Now that we've established that the most meaningful currencies on Instagram are followers, likes, and comments, let's take a deeper look. It turns out that these three currencies are being commodified and now have real monetary value outside of Instagram.

For example, over the past few years, I've had an agreement with the Ritz-Carlton—I stay at their hotels and take destination photos that they can use to promote these locations. Annually, this relationship was worth over six figures, on top of free rooms and food for me and my team. What a deal, eh? We didn't ask for free air travel in this situation, but it's usually a given for Influencers entering into this sort of agreement.

I would often post photos of Ritz-Carlton properties using the hashtag #rcmemories. My contract with the hotel chain was related to me providing destination photos and hosting live events such as art talks to invited guests. In this specific partnership, I also retained the rights to the photos, which isn't always true in agreements of this nature. In any case, I believe I over-delivered in terms of the imagery. I'm admittedly a bit of a people-pleaser (perhaps psychologically related to my parents' divorce and the inevitable self-blame!) and want to keep my partners more than happy.

Please understand that I am not using this example to "show off," but instead to illustrate that I have significant and first-hand authority not only observing, but participating in, the Instagram economy. Just as you can trade Euros or Yuan for the US Dollar, you can now in essence trade Instagram followers, likes, and comments for real money.

People need to believe in the veracity of a currency for it to have any utility in an economy. It's impossible to have agreements, do business, or make any progress if nobody trusts the framework. If you could photocopy $100 bills and spend them freely, you could contribute to destabilizing an economy. If there are a million people doing it, no rational person would believe in the strength of the currency.

There are billions of dollars flowing into Influencers on social networks. On Instagram alone, brands spent $2 billion in Influencer sponsorship in 2017. That figure is expected to grow to $10 billion by 2020.[1] Brands are spending some of this money on Influencers who are using counterfeit currency—fake followers, likes, and comments. Because fraudulent Influencers are earning money, other Influencers are incentivized to further partake in this bad behavior. This feedback mechanism threatens to destabilize the entire system.

It may seem like I have a hidden personal motive for uncovering Influencer fraud, since it's true that I have made some lucrative deals with major brands as an Influencer myself over the years. It could be perceived that I'm defending my turf because these fakes are jeopardizing my business. But in fact, Influencer deals are a minor (albeit enjoyable) part of my fine art business revenue, accounting for less than 10% of my revenue pie chart. So, I don't mind taking the heat. Besides, who wants to live in a world where many of the numbers you rely upon have no basis in reality? Not me.

The follower, the like, and the comment are becoming as important as the meter, the hour, and the pound for measuring and making agreements. In Instagram's case, if you can't trust any of its metrics, how can anyone believe what they see, make agreements, and have a trusted economic exchange on the platform?

I started meeting more and more of these "Instagram Influencers" in real life at luxury travel destinations, five-star hotels, banquets, yacht parties, and the like. Something seemed a bit off with some of them. When I met some of these Instagram Influencers, there was occasionally a hollowness, a lacking, a missing of the gravitas that one might expect from someone with experience engaging with tens of thousands of people on a daily basis.

Out of curiosity, I looked into their follower counts and many exceeded mine even though they had been on Instagram for a fraction of the time. Similarly, engagement (likes and comments) seemed out of mathematical proportion. Curious.

So how did these Influencers grow such big audiences so quickly, I wondered?

To find out, I spoke with a variety of legitimate Influencers about these sorts of scams. One of them was Johnny Jet (@johnnyjet), travel blogger from www.JohnnyJet.com. He told me what I already suspected, which is that some of these "successful" Influencers are buying their engagement. Jet said, "I do know people who have bought followers, likes and comments, and I think it sucks. It worked for some early adopters; they essentially followed the advice 'fake it until you make it.' But it's going to bite most scammers, as both users and brands are getting savvier. So, while it may have worked for them in the short-term, it won't in the long-term." He said he personally knows someone that he suspects "has bought followers and comments, and they're traveling the world in style, thanks to fake engagement."

When I talked to the famous photographer Lindsay Adler about this topic, she also knew something was up. She said, "I absolutely know people that have purchased their Instagram following, and I was dismayed because they used these fake followers to convince brands of their 'influence.' Times are certainly changing—I hope!—but a lot of brands still look purely at numbers as a way to select people to work with. It was more than a bit questionable when this person attracted brands with their following, and then suddenly lost 30% of their followers in a day, when Instagram did a purge of bots. Unfortunately, it seemed that the brands didn't notice or didn't care."

Lauren Bath (@laurenepbath), the well-known Australian Instagrammer with over 450,000 followers, said she knows many people who buy followers to defraud big brands. "I have a lot of proof that a scary number of users, businesses, and Influencers are hacking the system in one way or another." She also said she knows of many people who bought hundreds of thousands of followers a long time ago and then stopped. Of people who buy followers, she said, "I'd say that a large percentage of working Influencers, that are directly benefiting from businesses, are cheating. The worst is the brands that know their Influencers are cheating but are prepared to look the other way because it makes their bottom line look better. And yes, I have first-hand information about this happening."

I asked Liz Carlson (@youngadventuress), another well-known Travel Influencer, if she knew anyone on Instagram who buys followers/comments/likes. She said, "Yes, I know of a lot of people that do that and suspect many more. I think it's really shit. You can't fake genuine influence, and it damages everyone when you don't organically build a community and then sell yourself as an Influencer. You're defrauding the brands you're working with and deceiving the real followers that you do have."

I take my hat off to the New York Times for recently publishing a well-researched, in-depth article, *The Follower Factory*, about people who buy Twitter followers. The article describes how people from all walks of life, including, for example, politicians, buy fake followers to pad their numbers and make it appear as if they have significant authority or extreme fame.[2]

Many creatives jump on Instagram because they are told they must have a social media presence to promote their businesses. They see that their competitors are ahead by tens and sometimes hundreds of thousands of followers, and it leaves them feeling hopeless. They feel it's too late to even get started.

I see desperation. They are putting in a lot of time and working hard to create great content yet it seems they can't grow their following organically fast enough to keep up. Their wedding photography business, hair salon, yoga studio, bakery, boutique B&B, or their band is spinning its wheels. Meanwhile, the duplicitous thrive.

Top Influencers who fraudulently buy their popularity create an illusion of success that causes a tremendous amount of anxiety for millions of "normal" people on Instagram—especially those who have their own business to promote and who are using legitimate means to do so. These normal Instagram users are playing by the rules—at least as they see them—and are often unaware that the game is rigged. So, naturally, people that play by the rules are flummoxed by how some of these other people are so successful. This causes a deleterious emotional impact on those people who believe that what they see is real and that the rewards are based on merit.

FAKES ARE ON ALL PLATFORMS

Although I've been picking on Instagram, this dynamic isn't limited to a single platform. Many people are surprised when they discover that anyone can buy fake engagement numbers on any and all social platforms. Instagram is not the only social media platform where its users can mislead—and be misled. Any social media "currency" metric you see may be inflated—from followers, to likes, to comments, to retweets or reblogs, to shares … you get the idea.

For example, in my testing, I discovered I could buy almost anything I wanted, on any platform.

Platform	What I could buy
Facebook	• Post likes • Post comments • Video views
Instagram	• Followers • Likes • Comments • Story Views • Video Plays • "Verified" blue tick
LinkedIn	• Connections (btw, what loser would buy random LinkedIn connections??)
Music.ly	• Subscribers • Plays
SoundCloud	• Plays
Spotify	• Followers • Plays
TikTok	• Subscribers • Plays
YouTube	• Views • Subscribers • Comments • Thumbs up / down

This phenomenon isn't just restricted to traditional social media sites, although that's what we're focusing on here. Engagement metrics can also be bought to bolster accounts or business on other online tools, such as ratings on the iTunes App Store to reviews on Yelp.

Basically, anything that can be counted online can be faked. In this book, we'll focus on Instagram to keep things simple. Instagram is also one of the most popular games in town, and the acceleration of money flowing into the ecosystem makes it one of the most important social locations for Fortune 500 companies with cash burning a hole in their pockets.

WHAT'S WRONG WITH PURCHASED FOLLOWERS?

Some people may think purchasing followers isn't such a big deal. It's just a shortcut to the same place. However, aside from the ethical considerations, there are monetary implications. For example, a brand who's investing in an Influencer because they think the Influencer has 500,000 real followers won't actually be getting that same "bang for their buck" if those followers are fake.

Purchased followers are not valuable to advertisers because they aren't real people. They are non-human bots running as scripts on a computer somewhere.

Case Study: The Mega-hit Band Threatin

If it's still not obvious why purchased followers/likes/comments/YouTube plays/etc. are worthless, there was a recent article about a new band, Threatin, that illustrates the point quite plainly. For publicity, the band shot some videos at home, then doctored those videos to look like they were recorded during live performances.

Threatin then purchased followers, likes, comments, and YouTube plays for these videos. With all of this social media engagement, Threatin looked like a popular up-and-coming band. Based on their apparent online popularity, Threatin then was booked for a big concert tour overseas.[3]

'Fake band' Threatin just played a UK tour to... pretty much no-one

Tom Connick
Nov 9, 2018 1:16 pm

This "band" bought likes, comments, and YouTube plays, before having a concert in London. No actual humans appeared, despite claims of high ticket sales and lots of RSVPs on their Facebook event.[4]

To keep up the ruse, they even faked the ticket sales.

In the end, only the tour manager showed up to see the concert.

Remember that empty hall when many "Influencers" claim that their purchased followers are simply a shortcut to getting real followers. Bought followers are not real. They are vapor.

OTHER INSTAGRAM SCAMS

A quick side note: there are many other types of scams on Instagram and other social platforms. Unscrupulous users may try to trick you into:

- Paying them money
- Entering spurious contests
- Sending them nude photos, then blackmailing you
- Giving up valuable personal information to hijack your account
- Hiring fake escorts
- Anything else they think you'll do that might allow them to extract money from you

I think a lot of these scams are very obviously scams, and therefore, not quite as interesting to discuss.

A quick rule of thumb for the uninitiated: don't fall for any of the scams I just listed above. Also, don't give money to random strangers on the Internet. There's a reason these scammers are still out there—it's because these scams are lucrative, and people fall for them. Don't let yourself be taken advantage of.

WHY THIS IS IMPORTANT NOW: BACKLASH AGAINST INSTAGRAM

Social entropy is a measure of the natural decay inside of a social system. Attorney Nicole Shanahan has used the phrase to describe a growing trend of public loss of trust in social institutions.[5] We can see social entropy occurring in many arenas, as people continue to lose trust in constructs like government, lawyers, marriage, corporations, and many other structures we deal with on a regular basis.

Even if you are an avid social network user, you probably have a bit less faith in the social media framework than you did in the beginning. The more you use it, the more you see it has its flaws.

Amidst the tech literati, there is also a growing negativity around Instagram and many social networks.

Leo Laporte, host of The Tech Guy and TWiT.TV, sent me an email saying that he's disconnected completely from social media. In it, he explained, "I recently deactivated my Facebook, Instagram, Twitter, and Tumblr accounts. I considered keeping Instagram because I do enjoy the images, but I decided not to, because of all the things you mention. I also did not like the ads in the feed. Most of all, I don't want to support Facebook."

It's not just the negative and poisonous comments that drive people off these platforms, but many see it as a breeding ground for the worst aspects of human nature. Laporte went on to say, "I am increasingly of the opinion that social media is a malign influence on us all. I prefer to put my pictures on my blog, Smugmug, [or] Flickr—where photos come first."

Each month, I have more clever high-tech friends leaving these networks. They may be the canaries in the coal mine.

I firmly believe that we can use social networks to do great things in the world. Humans are amazing at cooperating to accomplish great things. Unfortunately, these same tools can also allow us to do terrible things.

WHY HAS NOBODY WRITTEN THIS BOOK BEFORE? (OR: RETRIBUTION-BOTS AND REVENGE-BOTS)

Why hasn't anyone written a book quite like this before, and why aren't people talking about this issue if it's as widespread as I claim?

The main reason none of the major players have spoken up is simple. Most people who know about this stuff derive the majority of their income from their Instagram followings, and they don't want to threaten that revenue stream. And I'm not just talking about people who are earning their income fraudulently. A lot of legitimate users I spoke with asked me not to quote them in the book because of the fear of retribution.

What do I mean by retribution? Let me explain. About a year ago, one brave Instagrammer did attempt an exposé of this underground black market. Retaliation was swift. The bots and fraudulent networks turned on her and ruined her Instagram account by adding a massive number of fake followers. These bad actors spread many lies about her, ruining any future possible Influencer deals for her. Will the same happen to me? Without a doubt! I expect my account to get trashed. But I don't depend on my Instagram for my life so I don't mind. I'm sure people will spread all kinds of lies about me.

I've included my smooth organic follower growth chart below, as a baseline, to compare with any future spikes or dips that will likely be caused by revenge-bots. I hypothesize that they will try anything to discredit me, in order to deflect from the main issue—that there's a black market for engagement metrics on Instagram and other social media platforms. Such responses from retribution-bots and upset people are expected, especially considering how much money is at stake. People like me, who practice the subtle art of not giving a f*ck, are dangerous to the status quo.

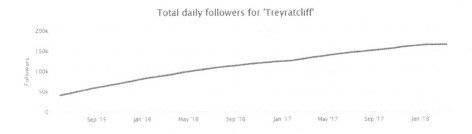

This shows my smooth follower growth over time as opposed to big jumps you will often see with scammers. Socialblade.com is often changing its website, and historical data may not be available. Source: Socialblade.com

For the time being, it's up to all of us to stay vigilant to keep the bots and fake Influencer population under control.

CHAPTER 3
THE INSIDE SCOOP (OR: HOW TO BUY YOUR WAY TO FAKE INTERNET FAME)

"Lies are the social equivalent of toxic waste: Everyone is poten-
tially harmed by their spread."
— SAM HARRIS

L **AST YEAR WAS THE YEAR OF "FAKE NEWS".** Perhaps this is the year of "fake followers."

The tricks that fake Influencers employ include, but are not limited to, buying followers, buying likes, buying comments, podding, follow/unfollow schemes, buying video/story plays, and beyond. I'll explain how all that works, but no matter the tactic or latest tool, the effect of the con is the same. I expose 99% of the tricks fake Influencers are using on Instagram and other social platforms to commit fraud. I wish I could claim I knew 100% of the tactics, but I think these ne'er-do-wells probably have a few more tricks up their sleeves I don't know about yet.

In this chapter, I'll walk you through how, exactly, these fraudulent Instagram Influencers are plying their trade. Where do they go to trade for followers, likes, and comments? How do they actually do it, and how much does it cost? Can they do it for free?

MY EXPERIMENT:
I BUILT A FAKE INFLUENCER ACCOUNT

For testing (and a bit of hilarity), I started a new Instagram account for one of my assistants, Tane Gent, who is a good sport. His first name is pronounced "TahnAY," if you were wondering. It's a Maori name.

Anyway, I started this risible Instagram account, @genttravel, to test how quickly we could grow a significant following by mimicking the methods I suspected people were using to mislead their followers and potential brand sponsors. To be more scientific, I also started a second, control account, @genttravelnz, at the same time. I posted the exact same photos, but only using legitimate methods, to grow engagement organically. That way, we could compare the results of each account to determine what differences, if any, we observed between the accounts.

The idea of the experiment was to compare and contrast the follower numbers for the two accounts over time and, if the cheater was successful in getting over 100K followers, to approach agencies and brands to see if they could spot the fake.

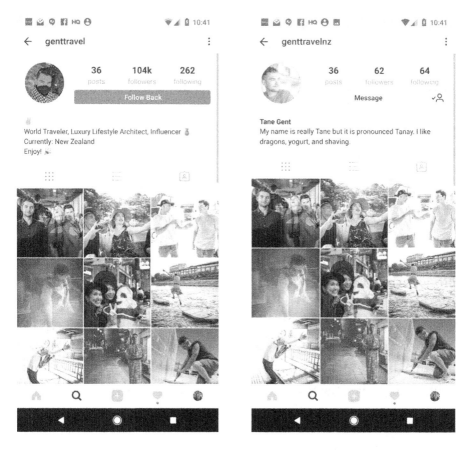

Two mostly identical accounts. On left account, we bought followers, likes, and comments. In our research, we were able to buy 30,000 followers for as little as $40 and 500 custom comments for $3.99.

How did we do it? Read on to find out.

STEP 1: OPEN THE ACCOUNT AND MAKE SOME CONTENT

As luck would have it, besides being a very capable assistant, Tane is a good-looking kid. I have about a thousand photos of him taken in cool places all over the world. We filled his accounts with a bunch of photos of him in demigod mode. We would often include silly, self-important captions, often referencing brands, like, "I'm not often on the open seas, but when I am, I am on million-dollar yachts hosted by Blue Azure," and other deep thoughts in this vein. I actually had a little too much fun creating this fake persona.

genttravel • Follow

genttravel Live from Ozone in Hong Kong, the highest bar in the world

clithmeltrabvie1985 Perfeito

laa_gabrielly Chocolate doesn't make inquiries, chocolate gets it

brunaah_diias_ By and large, the easy way out appeals. Additionally, I am fantastic at parallel stopping.

biiancchii God favors this chaotic situation

omundodetheodoro God favors this chaotic situation

roseane.reporter Travel man Gent - Here to serve. the feline overlord

Liked by curtissimmons and 1,519 others

MARCH 13, 2019

Add a comment...

The amazing thing about Tane is he actually travels with a steamer trunk full of sparkly pillows that he seductively arranges around his manboy body whenever he assumes a semi supine sprawl.

Look at Tane fondling that mango. Those sweet, soft, boyish fingers know no bounds.

STEP 2: GO TO THE INSTAGRAM "BLACK MARKET" AND BUY SOME FOLLOWERS

The next thing we needed to do was buy some followers for his account. There are countless options on the web and via apps to buy followers. Below I've listed just five I found.

This is from igreviews.com and it only represents a mere fraction of the thousands of websites where you can buy followers, likes, and comments.[1]

What's surprising is when you want to buy followers from any of these providers, you're not always required to provide Instagram login details for the account you want to fill. That's right, you can, right now, go buy followers for *any* Instagram user you choose. It doesn't have to be your own account.

This is one of the services called Tweetangels.com. These services are getting smarter in that you don't buy 10,000 followers all at once, for example. They trickle them in over a month, so it looks less suspicious. Many of the more astute fake Influencers now prefer to use this technique as it makes their historical growth appear more organic.

By paying third party services, we were able to amass over 100,000 followers for our fake Influencer, @genttravel, in only 30 days.

Meanwhile, the control account, @genttravelnz, had difficulty getting over 100 followers in the same 30 days. I even mentioned it several times from my own personal account, @treyratcliff, to try and help it catch up. Being attractive, featuring exotic settings, and even getting a genuine shout out from a big account can all help build a following organically, but it's not enough these days and it wasn't enough for @genttravelnz.

Get Free Refills

The Instagram black market is getting competitive enough that many follower-buying companies offer a customer service guarantee. They promise to "refill your wine glass" if you don't get the full delivery of the 10,000 drops you ordered. If you look closer at the data, you'll often see these refills come in later days.

Instagram knows full well there are automated scripts and services that perform these actions en masse. Emily Cain, from Instagram's communication team, shared her thoughts with me over email. She said, "This type of service requires no technical skill, and while almost all services claim to operate within our terms of service, they most certainly do not, as they turn to automation to perform all actions."

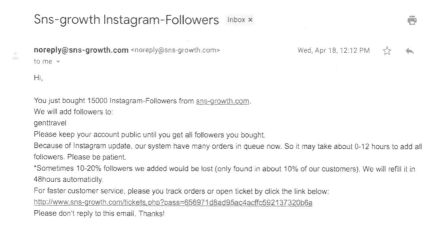

Here is an email we received from another company after we bought 15,000 followers for our test account, for just a few pennies. Notice they mention how you will lose followers, but they will backfill them for you. Bloody nice blokes there!

Buy Legitimate Advertisements to Attract Followers

It bears mentioning that there's actually already a system in place for you to legitimately get more eyeballs and interaction on your photos, that also grows your followers: Instagram advertising! I mean, this may be very obvious, but it is worth pointing out. Anyone can pay Instagram itself to make sure a particular photo gets shown to more users. Instagram lets you get quite specific about which people you'd like to see it. Also, far fewer of these users are bots.

All of these other sketchy systems out there are undercutting Instagram's own advertising system by skirting around it. This seems to be another good reason for Instagram to go after these third parties since there are millions of dollars going to these unscrupulous sites that might otherwise be spent directly with Instagram.

Use the Follow/ Unfollow Method of Gaining Followers

Say you see a notification that a brand, such as @amazingthailand, or a stranger who you don't know, just started following you. If you've ever paid any attention to your Instagram notifications and wondered *why* certain people or companies might want to start following you out of the blue, let me burst your bubble yet again. Yes, they could have found you organically because you happened to have posted a particularly eye-catching photo of a tree in your garden in Brooklyn. It's possible they had a look at your other photos and decided they had to follow you. However, neither of these scenarios is that likely (not to say that your garden snaps aren't great).

They're probably following you in hopes you'll automatically return the favor and follow them back. Then, they'll unfollow you and repeat the process with another unsuspecting Instagram user.

This is a popular method to gain followers. Following users en masse can be done manually and not cost anything besides your time. However, it's much easier to go through an automated service on a large scale for a very inexpensive price.

How does it work? Basically, an automated service follows about 7,500 random people. These may be potters in Bangladesh, tire companies in Portland, a farmer in Uruguay, fake bots, or maybe you. Some of those people, a very small percentage, will see a notification that they have a new follower and they'll follow back out of politeness. Some of these accounts, which are also run by bots, will see the new follow and will also follow back. Days later, the original account unfollows you and the thousands of others they started following. Some of those people will unfollow them too, but some will stick around because they don't know it's a ploy. So, net-net, the original account has more followers than they did at the beginning of this exercise.

It's a numbers game. Over time, these accounts will slowly accumulate followers. It should be noted that this activity is against Instagram's Terms & Conditions, but it still goes on all the time.

STEP 3: BUY SOME LIKES

We've talked a lot about followers. What's the next step?

The other metric on Instagram that gets a lot of attention is known as engagement, which is counted in likes and comments. It's measuring how engaged your follower base is.

Marketing companies are especially interested in engagement because high engagement indicates how readily your followers can be influenced to take an action. Action-oriented followers might, down the line, turn into buyers for these brands.

Fly high with BuzzDayz Instant Instagram likes

MICRO	MINI	STARTER	STANDARD	MEDIUM	PREMIUM
$2	$6	$13	$22	$40	$70
One Time Fee	One Time Fee	One Time Fee	One Time Fee	One Time Fee	One Time Fee
100 LIKES	1000 LIKES	2500 LIKES	5000 LIKES	10,000 LIKES	20,000 LIKES
High Quality	High Quality	High Quality	High Quality	High Quality	High Quality
100% Safe	100% Safe	100% Safe	100% Safe	100% Safe	100% Safe
Super fast delivery	Super fast delivery	Super fast delivery	Super fast delivery	Super fast delivery	Super fast delivery
Buy Now	Buy Now	Buy Now	Buy Now	Buy Now	Buy Now

There are countless places to buy likes, including this one—BuzzDayz. You can put all your likes all on one photo or spread them across a selection. Delivery is usually within a few minutes.

Buying likes is extremely simple and commonplace because it's an effective way for fake Influencers to impress both agencies and brands.

We found at least two dozen services for buying likes. We tried five of them to build up our @genttravel fake Influencer account. They all worked perfectly. We were shocked when the first one we tried delivered the 10,000 likes we ordered, across 16 photos, all in less than 10 minutes. It's obvious these likes have to be automated—there's no way humans could do this so quickly.

You have a lot of options when buying likes. You can dump them all on a single photo or spread them out over a group of photos. Currently, there is no way to look at a historical graph of likes (as there is for followers, which you will see in the next chapter). If you could see a historical graph of likes, the mathematical anomalies over time would be obvious, as a few posts would show much higher engagement than others.

Because there's no way of checking "like" trends over time, brands and agencies have a difficult time testing the veracity of likes. A typical post that a brand might pay for could garner as many as 20,000 likes or more. In the Instagram app, you can look at who liked a post and even click to view their account, to check if they're a real human. However, taking these steps 20,000 times to verify that these people are real would take ages and would result in some serious Repetitive Strain Injury. With "like" numbers frequently reaching into the millions across a campaign, no one is going to check the legitimacy of each and every like.

But if you did, it's easy to see when they've been purchased. We did a bit of clicking after we bought ours for the test and the bot accounts that liked our photo were pretty laughable.

How funny is this? This bot that auto-liked our photo was named "Auto Like."

STEP 4: BUY SOME COMMENTS

As far as this type of interaction goes, you can buy random comments or custom comments. Random comments are completely silly, from vague platitudes such as "Great Pic!" to a bunch of random emojis. They're also not expensive to buy.

I did somehow talk Tane into getting in the ocean to recreate this silly classic Influencer pose, but the rest is fake, including the followers who liked it and the brilliantly crafted custom comments. We created 1,000 different comments in a spreadsheet and delivered them to a service, which in turn posted them to our Instagram posts within ten minutes.
Sidenote: This would actually be a fun trick to play on your friends.

This service only offers two sorts of comments: random or custom. There are other sites that offer much cheaper comments, but they are usually poor quality.

In our first tests, we went to well-known websites for buying followers, likes, and comments for our fake Influencer account. Since those worked smoothly, we got bolder and ventured out to some edgier and less legitimate sites. They were precisely the kind of websites you wouldn't go near with your own credit card, so I borrowed the credit card of our operations guy, Curtis. (If you're reading this, Curtis, you'll probably need to torch that card pretty soon.)

A couple receipts from when we purchased random and custom comments for our experimental fake Influencer account follow.

Your order details:

Email: genttravel00@gmail.com
First name: curtis
Last name: simmons
Country: United States

Instagram	100 Custom Comments	$28.99

https://www.instagram.com/p/Bgu9NJqlEHT
Start count: 16 +11
https://www.instagram.com/p/BgP_sOOhpBa
Start count: 14 +7
https://www.instagram.com/p/BgFnlYbBU2m
Start count: 14 +14
https://www.instagram.com/p/BgAmEdEglhW
Start count: 16 +15
https://www.instagram.com/p/Bf9Q-CVAjyL
Start count: 15 +9
https://www.instagram.com/p/BfzM3zkgGzb
Start count: 14 +6
https://www.instagram.com/p/BfzMxJFAUe3
Start count: 15 +7
https://www.instagram.com/p/BfzMnNJgtyY
Start count: 14 +6
https://www.instagram.com/p/BfxArlAAWLm
Start count: 14 +5
https://www.instagram.com/p/BfxAbOHg8y0
Start count: 14 +5
https://www.instagram.com/p/BfxAOobg5Zf
Start count: 15 +6
https://www.instagram.com/p/BfujSrmAq9a
Start count: 13 +9

	Total	**$28.99**

Your order details:

Email: genttravel00@gmail.com
First name: curtis
Last name: simmons
Country: United States

Instagram | 2,000 Random Comments	$179.99

https://www.instagram.com/p/Bh46l6Gnxfe/
+250
https://www.instagram.com/p/Bh46xlgHdK4/
+250
https://www.instagram.com/p/Bh44NhZH7CW/
+250
https://www.instagram.com/p/Bh4341CHZYV/
+250
https://www.instagram.com/p/Bhut3uonVsR/
+250
https://www.instagram.com/p/Bh46OpznOzK/
+250
https://www.instagram.com/p/Bh44mR-n1Bp/
+250
https://www.instagram.com/p/Bhutaq6HXxX/
+250

	Total	$179.99

Of course, random pre-written comments can be vague enough to be applicable in many situations, but often don't make any sense in the context of the actual post. Scammers who buy these generic comments may save a bit of time generating custom comments and then have to spend time weeding out the duds afterward.

If you dive into the comments to click on the ones that look suspicious, you'll end up looking at a barely concealed bot. Someone hasn't made more than a handful of posts, yet was moved by your photo enough to comment? Seems suspicious.

That said, even when the commenting account looks like it is owned by a normal person, the comment itself may still be driven by a bot. We'll talk about how that's possible in later chapters.

One thing we did not bother to buy was comments that consist of only random emojis, the Instagram patois of the illiterate. These are the cheapest comments of all, which is why you see them on so many accounts.

In one order, we requested 2,000 random comments to be delivered across 10 different photos on our fake Influencer account, including the following five posts. Now that you know what's going on, can you spot how ridiculous the comments are?

Note: I'm going to make a bunch of captions for these photos of Tane, one of my favorite assistants. Now that we're familiar with spotting fake comments, I want you to know that all of the captions that follow are (probably) fake as well.

genttravel • Follow

taetroops Obsessed with your Fendi bag
adrianne_vasque Qm é esse baby???
marcelle_ababio Touché
arcelisapphire The colors!!
luvmiself_beemont so handsome
jstiven.sujumnong Amazing shot
curtdisbrow Liiike
dicklelacson Jdjs
godfrey_hamic Muco?

7,605 likes
APRIL 18

Log in to like or comment.

Hey, Tane—in that Stay Puft Marshmallow Man outfit in Tokyo on Halloween, re-member that time you found those guys doing pot near Shinjuku? Yeah, that was awe-some. Actually, this is the only caption that is true.

genttravel • Follow

genttravel Checking out the Coastline of Portugal
alexandriaworley LOL YOU
bpizzy.mare You are too beautiful and independent for this city!
xsridevi_bruno So cool.
youngki_takagi Perfect...
aymeebroomfield Want
xudong_csicsila Want that
dharma_pettis You have wonderful taste

7,909 likes
APRIL 23

Log in to like or comment.

Hi Tane! Remember that time at Burning Man that you woke up in the morning only wearing your blue jeans, by the trash fence with another couple? Actually, this caption is true too.

Hey Tane, remember that time in Tokyo where Curtis found you curled up in the curtains of his room at the Ritz-Carlton? You were wearing only a pajama top (with the buttons misaligned) and holding the remote control for the robot toilet? This one is actually true also.

Hey Tane, remember that time in Lisbon when you found that drug dealer named Carlos and he followed you around for days asking if you wanted to buy drugs? This story is also true.

We didn't want to let the bots have all the fun, so, as part of this experiment, we came up with 1,000 of our own custom comments for our fake Influencer account @genttravel. Check Appendix B of this book to see them all.

And, big surprise ... it worked flawlessly. For the comments we generated ourselves, we bought 5,000 more comments for $30. Some of the gems we came up with were repeated five times. We could have created 5,000 different comments or bought five separate packages of 1,000 comments. You can do whatever you want with these tools, really.

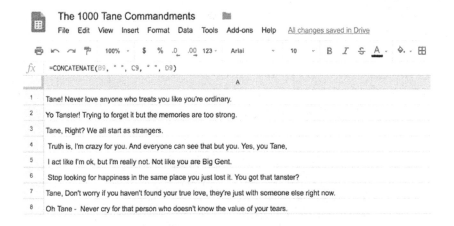

Here are some of the comments we came up with. I was obviously having a bit too much fun with Tane, because he's such a good sport. See all of the comments we came up with in Appendix B if you need some fun bedtime reading.

Hey Tane, remember that time we roofied you in my studio and the team drew all over your flawless body with Sharpie markers? No, of course you don't.

Tane used his tongue to carve out that hole in the bottom of this can and then subsequently used that same tongue as a proboscis to suck out and swallow the can's mysterious innards.

One can see how a savvy social media scammer might create a bunch of custom comments that speak specifically to a particular brand or product. Hopefully, they would do a much more effective job than me, with my obviously ludicrous comments. Influencers know what their clients want to hear. With custom comments, they can make sure the bots deliver those talking points perfectly.

The brand managers, visiting the post, often never suspect a thing. Even if they did, and had the time and inclination to analyze thousands of comments individually, they would have great difficulty figuring out if the comments were real or not. It would still be almost impossible to prove.

All of those followers, likes, and comments we had purchased for Tane came from bots, not real people. But no one seemed to notice. The account of @genttravel soon started receiving queries from several "Instagram Influencer" agencies who wanted to represent him to make deals with Fortune 500 brands.

STEP 5: BUY INSTAGRAM STORY VIEWS

Many regular Instagram users are familiar with Instagram Stories. These are short 15-second videos or photos that appear at the top of your feed. They only last 24 hours before they disappear, but these are also commonly used tools for Influencers, who can promise their brands to do X number of stories in exchange for some number of dollars.

Buy Instagram Story Views at Cheap Price $ 1.30

500+ Story Views	1000+ Story Views	2500+ Story Views	5000+ Story Views	10000+ Story Views	20000+ Story Views
$ 1.30	$ 2.70	$ 6.70	$ 13.70	$ 22.70	$ 44.70
500+ Organic Story Views	1000+ Original Story Views	2500+ Organic Story Views	5000+ Organic Story Views	10000+ Organic Story Views	20000+ Organic Story Views
Authentic Provider	Authentic Provider	Authentic Provider	Authentic Provider	Authentic Provider	Authentic Provider
Views for All Stories	Views for All Stories	Views for All Stories	Views for All Stories	Views for All Stories	Views for All Stories
Brand Engagement Booster	Brand Engagement Booster	Brand Engagement Booster	Brand Engagement Booster	Brand Engagement Booster	Brand Engagement Booster
Delivery: Within 1 Hour	Delivery: Within 1 Hour	Delivery: Within 1 Hour	Delivery: Within 1 Hour	Delivery: Within 1 Hour	Delivery: Within 1 Hour
Buy Now	Buy Now	Buy Now	Buy Now	Buy Now	Buy Now

There are many places on the web to buy story views and they are quite inexpensive, as you can see. These above options are all delivered within 1 hour. Of course, these views are all coming from automated bots, because the company doesn't have 10,000 people sitting in a big room telling everyone which stories to view.

It should go without saying that if you can buy one type of number to fake influence, you can buy almost any kind of number.

There is another feature on Instagram, called Instagram TV, where people can upload much longer videos. Those videos can be more interactive, allowing people to comment and like while the video is playing. Many websites allow you to buy IGTV views, impressions, comments, and likes.

STEP 6: BUY THE VERIFIED BLUE TICK

Counterfeit social media accounts have been around since the beginning. Many users started creating accounts to impersonate famous people. Instagram and other social media platforms needed a way to indicate which accounts were the real deal, so they created the blue tick. A group within Instagram now bestows that blue tick on verified profiles to indicate those accounts are a real person, of some importance. These ticks are generally reserved for celebrities or for someone who achieved a certain amount of success in one area or another.

Since the verified blue tick lends legitimacy and credibility, it can also be used to trick brands and agencies into thinking the blue tick account is influential. At this stage, you won't be surprised to learn there are now several companies online which claim to be able to supply a coveted blue tick outside of official channels. I did not attempt to do this for the fake Influencer account we built for @genttravel, but I found many services online that claim to be able to make this happen.

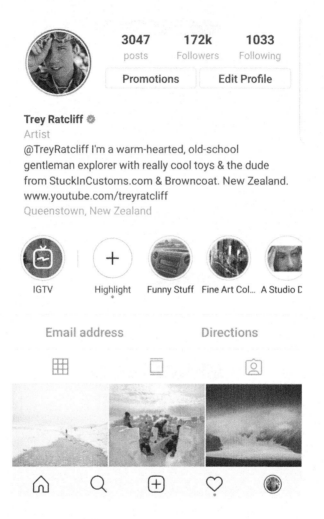

You can see I have earned the "blue tick" that indicates I have been verified.
However, sometimes people get this tick through clandestine maneuvers.

Many of these blue tick offers are actually phishing scams, where the perpetrator attempts to steal Instagram details from desperate wannabe Influencers. An email my friend @linneaberzen received from a company offering to get her a blue tick for her Instagram account follows. I'm not saying this particular offer is an attempt at phishing, but it might be.

Here's an example of a phishing email, trying to either get information or money from the target, while they claim to be able to get you a blue verified account tick.

Many people are probably fooled by this scheme. But look at the official email address they've supplied—Instagraamhelp2018@gmail.com. Hopefully common sense will prevail.

STEP 7: EXPLORE EVERYTHING ELSE

So, now you've created your account, generated some content, attracted some fake followers, drummed up some fake engagement, and maybe even verified that you're a legitimate actor. What else can you do?

Join a Pod or a Megapod

A pod is a group of a few dozen, hundred, or thousand people who agree to like and comment on one another's photos within the first few minutes of those photos being posted. This activity tricks the Instagram algorithm into assuming a photo is extremely popular. When this happens, the algorithms kick in and the target post is more likely to show up in other followers' feeds or on the popular page. It's also often used as another way to pump up the number of comments and likes to impress a brand who has paid the Influencer to generate interest in their product.

I have been invited into many "pods," but have never joined one, because pods essentially are groups of people who are collaborating to game the system. They do not encourage authentic interaction. Pods are unscrupulous because they are a very poor facsimile of genuine engagement.

Most pods can also be quite draconian, demanding that all pod members comment and like for many hours a day. If you don't comment and like back immediately, you are kicked out of the pod. The biggest pods often require people to be on their phone for over 10 hours a day.

Lauren Bath, the popular Australian Instagrammer (@laurenepbath), knows many Influencers who use pods to make their posts seem more popular than they actually are. She told me over email that several Influencers "buy engagement through sophisticated (very sophisticated) automation (and) via niche superpods." According to Bath, huge pods "are still going strong and some of the biggest Influencers in the world have been at the forefront of this craze. To make money, yep!"

How does it work in practice? Let's say you're part of a pod. Whenever you make a new post, you notify your pod inside of a group chat. Then, everyone in the group chat is required to go like the post and make a fawning comment immediately. Yes, these comments are technically made by real people who *could* be interested in the brand you've been paid to promote, but it is improbable since they're just other Influencers. And if they're playing with pods, their followers are probably not worth targeting for a genuine Influencer.

Members of the pod comment on your post solely to get the same engagement benefit on their own posts. Some pods are huge and have thousands of members who have to adhere to stringent guidelines, which often involve actively being on their phone for over ten hours a day. If they do not, they are excommunicated from the group and blackballed forever. It's all rotten.

I have a photographer friend in Austin named Gino Barasa (@ginobarasa) who was invited into a pod. He told me all about it.

> Quite a while back, a friend of mine was in a podding group with some Influencers with 6-digit followers. He got me into the group and my followers did, in fact, grow by a few thousand in the few months that I was involved. It was mind-numbingly tedious, and you had to stay at it every day, and in the end I was bored out of my mind having to think of new ways to say something nice about all of their posts every day. After I dropped out of the group I steadily lost almost all of the gains over a 3 or 4 month period. I was convinced that I could replicate the growth without podding if I just put up good content with funny stories. But I couldn't. The dream of legitimately "earning" a large following proved more elusive than self-esteem itself.
>
> So, how did I feel about podding? Not awesome, but it felt more real than buying followers or likes. I was hoping that by having accounts with 25K - 200K in followers comment on my images I could earn my own following. Make a few connections that I would

not otherwise have ever gotten in front of. But, the burning question in the back of my head was always, "Why are these big accounts doing this for me? I get what's in it for me. What's in it for them?" What I came to realize is that these other accounts were frauds, that had bought their following and they were no more influential than I was. The entire process was a huge circle jerk and a waste of time and energy.

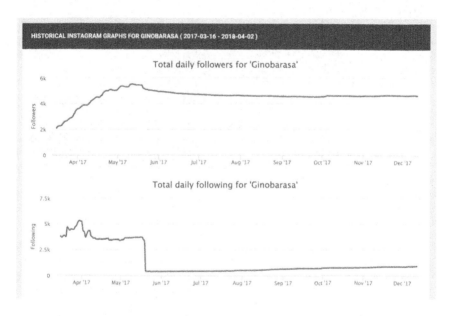

Here, we can see when @ginobarasa joined and left the pod. His followers did grow a lot during the period he was in the cabal. Source: Socialblade.com

Joseph Harper, social media lead for Kellogg's, found some surprising results when he looked at one of their more "successful" campaigns. They worked with an advertising agency on this campaign and it turned out that most of the comments that resulted from this campaign actually came from pods. He described his findings: "One agency we work with said a campaign was a success because it generated loads of comments, but when we dug deeper into the report, we realized that the Influencers we'd paid had just gone to a WhatsApp group of other

Influencers and asked them to make all of those comments."[2]

WhatsApp, the group messaging app, is one of the top ways for pods to communicate because the app does not keep a record of conversations. WhatsApp's conversational data is also encrypted in transit, which makes it a more secure communications platform.

It's important to note that pods can communicate using many different methods. The screenshots below illustrate Facebook groups that are used for pod communication.

Here's an example of a pod that communicates via a Facebook group. I found about 100 of these by just searching for "Instagram Pod" through the Facebook search bar.

Recently, Facebook deleted 10 Instagram podding groups after a

Buzzfeed article exposed them. One clandestine group, in particular, had over 200,000 people who had all agreed to fake engagement by liking and commenting on one another's photos.[3]

What is troubling is that it took third parties to report the problem to Instagram and Facebook. The Facebook podding groups had incredibly obvious names, such as "Instagram Like & Comment" and "Daily Instagram Engagement," and yet neither Instagram nor Facebook had noticed. Instagram's PR director Gabe Madway wouldn't comment, except to confirm to me that this behavior is against their Terms and Conditions, and is the reason for shutting these groups down.

*These are just some of the groups on Facebook that people join to get
more activity on their Instagram posts. The biggest and most effective pods
use private group chats in Telegram or WhatsApp, which are much
harder to detect than a simple Facebook group. Source: Buzzfeed*

Instagram is truly playing whack-a-mole with these pods. With no real structure or approach, these efforts appear to be mostly ineffective in slowing down the corrupt behavior.

However, podding activity should be straightforward for Instagram to detect. Since there is a network of ten to thousands of people working together, they should be able to map out increased network activity that interconnects those people. For example, I have many friends on

Instagram, but I don't comment on all their photos within the first hour. People in pods do. Therefore, it's a pattern of behavior that's extremely easy to detect with statistical analysis.

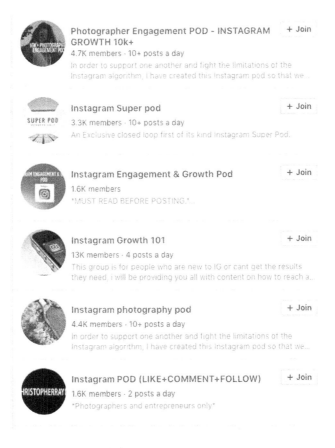

Even though the Buzzfeed article says that Facebook/Instagram deleted 10 of the groups, there are still a ton out there. And, again, these are some of the sloppiest pods. The more sophisticated ones do not use Facebook groups but rather less easily detected communication techniques that ensures everyone follows the rules or else they get kicked out.

TRADE SOME CLICKS—CREDIT CARD NOT REQUIRED

We've talked about numerous ways some people can buy more followers, likes, or comments, but buying engagement doesn't always have to cost money.

If you don't have time for a pod and don't want to buy followers outright, you can use a "token" system. There are countless apps for iOS and Android that allow you to, in essence, trade followers, likes, and comments with other users based on quantity rather than quality. You provide the app your username and password for Instagram and then you earn tokens by using the app to follow other users randomly and to like their photos. The more you follow and like, the more tokens you get. You can then use those tokens to buy your own followers, likes, and comments. The example below is an app called Fame Boom, but there are hundreds of others I could have chosen.

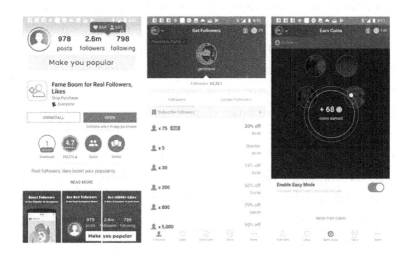

This is an app called Fame Boom. It has over 1,000,000 downloads from the Google Play store, and it is one of hundreds of similar apps. On the right, you can see I selected "Easy Mode," and this began an automated process of following other users and liking photos at random.

After I had a bit of fun playing along and collecting tokens, I deleted the app on my phone. To make sure that it was completely disconnected from my Instagram account, I then logged into Instagram's website to check the "Authorized Applications" in the settings. Fame Boom didn't appear. However, because I had previously given them my username and password, they could still have been storing my login details on their servers. Because these third parties have my credentials, they do not even need to use the Instagram API to act on my behalf. So, how were they doing it?

Like some websites we used to buy followers, likes, and comments for our test, we were required to give our Instagram username and password when we signed up for Fame Book. These credentials provide the company with ongoing access to our account, letting them follow, like, and comment on my behalf, even when I choose to stop playing.

Instagram claims to have robust automated services that automatically monitor and remove this sort of activity. "With new apps launching all the time, our abuse-fighting team builds and constantly updates a combination of automated and manual systems," Instagram said. "We already have about 10,000 people working on safety and security, and we're planning to double that to 20,000 in the next year." Alas, while they are willing to admit that podding is a problem, they are still missing the mark when it comes to policing their own system, despite what seems like quite a few humans currently on the task. We talk more about what Instagram can do to stop this behavior later on.

Despite Instagram's claims of its ability to discover fraudulent behavior, they seem to have little or no power to prevent us from building up our fake Influencer account @genttravel so quickly or the hundreds of other fraudulent accounts we examined.

Do It at Scale Through Farming—Marketing Automation

Why make one fake account, when you can make 10, or 100? Think big!

Farming refers to the idea of managing many accounts at once. Managing one account can be quite time consuming. Uploading photos, making stories, writing, commenting, liking, etc. can all take quite a long time. I personally spend about 30 minutes a day on my Instagram, but I know others who spend hours upon hours daily.

So, it would make sense that there are now services to help make this process more efficient. In fact, there are a variety of online tools where you can utilize all the benefits of scripting and bots for yourself. They can multiply efficiency by allowing you to have maximum interaction on multiple accounts at once.

How does this work? Next, I walk through a couple of websites that allow you to do this.

Jarvee

My first example is the website Jarvee.com. First, you create an account on Jarvee.com. As part of this process, you provide them with your Instagram login credentials. Then, on your behalf, the Jarvee.com scripts will mimic the behaviors of a human being, using some of the techniques we discussed above, to increase engagement on your account. These scripts will do everything from leaving realistic looking comments to liking comments that people (or bots) leave on your photos.

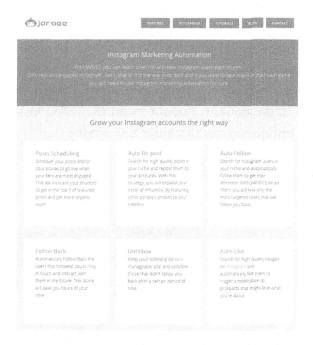

These are only a few of the features that Jarvee.com offers.

The Tutorials page on Jarvee has many friendly videos, including one called "Learn how to automatically grow your social media accounts," with a rather conniving pitch. The voiceover says, "Why would you follow other people?" Oh, good question, you have me hooked. Then it explains, "It's based on the reciprocity principle, which is a basic law in social psychology."

What this means is Jarvee is one of many services that offer follow/unfollow automation. After you set it up, your account will follow a bunch of people (and often bots) at random in the hope some of them will follow you back. What the video fails to explain is these are entirely useless followers because either they are bots or they are completely random individuals who have no interest in the subject matter you post. But if all that matters to you is that your follower count goes up, it's a success.

The video goes on to explain why Jarvee will helpfully "unfollow" for you automatically. On Instagram, since you're only allowed to follow 7,500 people at a time, after you reach that maximum you need to then unfollow a whole bunch of folks in order to follow 7,500 more. Rinse and repeat.

This is the same pattern we will analyze with the @amazingthailand account later in the book. It doesn't mean they used Jarvee, but there are countless online services that offer this service.

Jarvee allows you to manage up to 150 accounts at once,
creating a situation called Bot Farming.

Instagram has a steady stream of public announcements to say that they are attempting to crack down on services like Jarvee. However, in a recent article on WIRED, "Jarvee said there was 'nothing to worry about' and dismissed claims that Instagram's crackdown had any effect on its services."[4]

InstaBoostGram

InstaBoostGram is another such service and one that looks to be pretty popular. It's on the first page of Google search results, which I found particularly interesting since their marketing speak isn't all that convincing in making the practice sound legitimate.

I invite you to read some of the stellar marketing copy in the screenshots below, including such gems as: "One of the most important business chunk is a website. You can get a hype of traffic on your site through Instagram."

A screenshot showing the homepage, including some of the services you can buy.

Need More Followers? Click Here

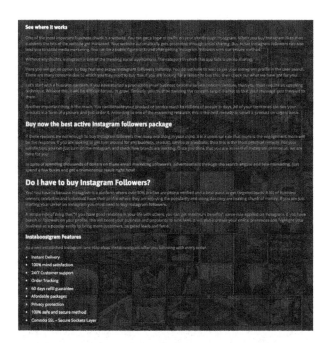

Some of the follower packages offered.

Some of their excellent marketing copy.

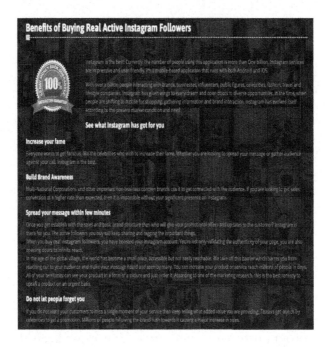

Are you convinced yet?

What they are not telling you, of course, is your purchased followers, likes, and comments are worthless because they either come from bots or via compromised accounts.

Followadder

Another one of the thousands of sites where you can buy followers is Followadder, who encourages you to "Save time and money by putting your Instagram network building on auto pilot."

Another one of the many auto-follow sites out there. This one requires you to download a program that runs on your computer all the time so that you can be part of the cabal.

When you sign up and pay money for this one, you are required to download a program to your computer. You must keep that program running in the background. The program is, of course, doing automated things and running bots. It allows your computer to pretend to be multiple accounts, and then follow, like, and comment on countless other accounts. This technique is employed by many other sites as well and, by any objective analysis, it's quite a sketchy tactic.

Instajool

Naturally, when you see there's a tool that lets you manage over 100 accounts at once, you know there is some crazy stuff goin' down. Or at least I hope you do. Instajool allows you to do just that.

Some sites, like Instajool, allow you to manage the automated activities of 100 accounts at once.

The number of these sites operating on the Internet is unbelievable. They don't even attempt to hide what they are up to, which makes many people believe it must be legitimate.

These services are not necessarily built solely for scammers, but also for regular people who simply want a lot of followers to feed their ego and impress their easily-impressed friends. Many of these sites have free sign-ups, so you can try it out before you buy.

The most active fraudsters on Instagram don't just use one site like this one, but regularly use multiple. They often justify this behavior as a tribute to their cleverness and their ability to figure out the system. Humans are able to justify a wide range of activities, even if they aren't ethically sound.

There are indeed a few agencies that use tools to manage multiple accounts for their clients. However, hopefully, these agencies would not actually use a tool like Instajool, because a tagline like "Get unlimited free Instagram followers using the best instagram bot liker," should let professional agencies know to stay clear. Or does it? We'll find out more in chapter 4.

Oh wow. If this model knew that her stock photo was being used to help Influencers mislead, she would not be so happy.

As you can see in the reviews above, people are able to justify their behavior in a ridiculous manner.

Teach Others How: "Sign Up For My Instagram Follower Course!"

Here's another outrageous trend: Instagrammers selling online courses to teach others how to cheat the system.

Why? Well, many people, especially YouTubers, make money by recommending different services for users to buy followers, likes, and comments. These Influencers make money this way because whenever anyone clicks on their link to a service, the Influencer gets a kickback.

One highly recommended site is Followadder because Followadder pays a 50% share of the revenue they generate to the person who provided the affiliate link. If someone wants to buy followers, and they click on your link to Followadder and buy $1,000 of followers, you'd get $500 of that money. Pretty sweet deal.

Here you can see the "type-ahead" suggestions on YouTube. If you click through, you find that some of these websites share free advice, but some are selling a paid online course.

I have never personally paid to take one of these courses, because I'm already, like, totally to the max, a super expert.

While some of these courses are legitimate, some of these courses are absolute scams, designed to swindle both you and your friends out of money.

There was a recent article by an Instagrammer on Medium who claimed she was roped into one of these Influencer classes. The class was run by celebrity Influencer Aggie Lal (@travel_inhershoes). The swindled author described the class, saying that, while Lal claimed to have earned their Influencer status legitimately, some of the numbers just didn't add up. "I watched [Lal] hit the benchmarks of followers: 200k, 400k, 500k. Hell, I even witnessed her hit 890k and then weirdly drop to 840k in ten minutes…"[5]

The author continued, "I have been playing at this Instagram game for a while. I know the tricks, I know the deep dark secrets. I've done the pods, I've played the Follow/Unfollow game, and I know all about the growth methods most of these 500k+ follower girls do. I also know that this particular Instagram Star did a lot of those same techniques. I saw her name on the lists of Secret Giveaways. I saw her in the same pod circles as many of my friends, I knew she was doing the same things we all were. But was she going to be honest about it?"[6]

According to the article, this course was, in fact, a scam. The main point of the course was to get as many of your friends as possible to sign up for the course. It was a thinly-veiled pyramid scheme. But hey, as P.T. Barnum said, "there's an Influencer born every minute."

Another article about the scam explained how @travel_inhershoes promised to illustrate how she went from "being a broke traveler to becoming a six figure earning travel blogger." She told Buzzfeed news that she earned $188,860 from the course. Upon learning this, most students felt swindled. One student said, "[The] videos were barely five minutes long, she was never involved with the students, and made a lot of comments that turned people off such as 'when posing for pictures try not to look pregnant' or 'people who work at Starbucks aren't living up to their potential'. The content was basic information you would find from any simple Google search. Not $500 worth."[7]

Since the purported scam of trying to "teach" other people how to be a proper Influencer has been exposed, she hasn't been getting the nicest comments.

@travel_inhershoes has a YouTube video titled, in all-caps, "I GET PAID TO TRAVEL THE WORLD - HOW I BECAME A TRAVEL BLOGGER part 1," where she attempts to explain her follower growth.

In the video, she asks a question of herself, "How did you get your numbers?" She rambles a bit and tries to explain that you have to be serious and obliquely utters, "I posted over 1,000 photos, like, easy."

She is happy to say that most travel bloggers are not that glamorous and still live with their parents, even into their 30's. Of course, she makes it abundantly clear that she does not live with her parents.

She goes on to give vague advice about how to be an Instagram Travel Influencer. "With hotels, it's very different," she bloviates. "They are ready to fly me over with a plus one. They cover everything from flights to transport to food to activities—everything included in exchange for photos—and they give you a fee on top of that." She claims to reject 90% of offers she receives.

In the video, she also vapidly says, "You really need to be as true to yourself as possible."

A Recommended Instagram Influencer Course: "How to Build Real Influence"

I will make a serious online course recommendation for those of you interested in becoming a real Influencer (instead of using all the underhanded tricks listed in this book). Obviously, there are many legitimate, financially successful Influencers. This book certainly describes many of the ways you can become a respected Influencer. However, if you want a deeper dive, there is a multi-week online course that will show you all the ropes. The course was created by a trusted friend, Lauren Bath (@laurenepbath), who also does wildly successful in-person workshops for Influencers.

If you're interested, you can sign up for the course at https://TheTravelBootCamp.com/HowToBuildRealInfluence. Also, in the interest of full disclosure, I consulted and contributed to the course. Lauren also said that she will buy me unlimited wine in addition to paying me for contributing, so I have a vested interest.

Pretend You Are Already Sponsored

In the wild, wild west of Instagram, there is another, but not often used, way to "fake" your way into getting popular. Here's how it works. Some wannabe Influencers will post photos that appear to be sponsored by a brand, like, say, a Fendi or BMW. They tag the brand and make it look like they've been sponsored. They do this to try to establish some kind of sponsorship track record, so real brands will want to work with them in the future. It's like a visual résumé filled with fake jobs.

This tactic doesn't always work. According to an article in The Atlantic, one marketing manager named Jason Wong said he was recently duped. After Wong hired one Influencer to promote his product, Wong later found out that all of that Influencer's prior brand deals were fake. Based on this experience, Wong now does his due diligence on potential partners before working with them. He cross-references all Influencers, calling up other brands they've claimed to work with to see if the work was paid.[8]

STEP 8: UNDERSTAND YOUR NEW FAKE AUDIENCE (THEY CAN'T ALL BE BOTS!)

Many of the sites we've discussed often claim that, through them, you are buying "real" followers (in contrast to bots). This is a deliberate lie, designed to lure people into the black market of this particular provider. Any followers that are purchased are either bots or scripts that have commandeered random users' accounts.

There are many ways bots operate. This is a photo of one of the countless bot-farms around the world where thousands of phones are all being controlled by a master script. Source: Random Chinese dude in China

Anyone can look into their own Instagram stats to see where their followers are coming from. There are a few geographies where these scripts are popular, like India and Turkey. I was very curious as to the type of followers we were getting on our fake Influencer account, @genttravel, so we dove into the Instagram stats to find out. Were our followers real people? Were they a mix of real people and bots? Were they just bots?

When I looked, I found they were… mostly bots. Which isn't surprising, considering that I bought and paid for most of them.

Here's an example of a few of Tane's followers. On Day 7 of starting @genttravel, when the account was at about 2,400 followers, we looked at his five most recent followers. We'll get into more around identifying fakes a little later—consider this a preview.

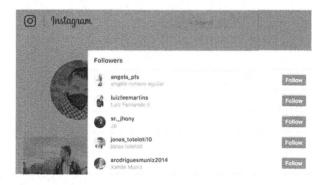

These are the five most recent followers that we purchased for @genttravel.

All five of these followers were following between 7,490 and 7,500 people. Many were following exactly 7,500, as you'll see below, which means that they are likely bots following the maximum number of accounts that they can.

jonas_toteloti10 Follow ▾ ···

5 posts   341 followers   7,500 following

jonas toteloti O corpo ta parado , mas a mente ta a milhão ,problamas eu tenho vários , mas só deus e a solução 🤙 🤙 🔱 🤙 🤙

Since these accounts are all probably fake, I like to give these bots robust personalities and ribald histories (for the ones who are of age), to fill in some of the blanks. This one seems like the kind of guy who might work in a mobile phone store. I can see my own eyes glazing over as he explains different coverage plans to me.

angela_pfs Follow ▾ ···

6 posts   151 followers   7,492 following

angela romero aguilar 12% Oringi🙋 PFS😍 💜 Jaen🏄 🏄 12💜

The one looked pretty attractive and seemed to be into some kind of kinky yoga, so I was a bit disappointed she wasn't real. And then I did a Google reverse image search and figure out this bot scraped photos from an actual account of @jenselter, who I am pretty sure does the yoga half.

arodriguesmuniz2014 Follow ▾ ···

2 posts   364 followers   7,500 following

Xande Muniz

As I write this in 2018, this kid must be four years old. He's a pretty smarmy four-year-old, so that is kind of impressive. He's no Lil' Tay, but he's trying to be a flexer, so I give him credit for that.

The only one with any history on Socialblade.com was the final one, @arodriguesmuniz2014. If you look at the pattern below, you can see the typical valleys and peaks defined by a follow/unfollow pattern.

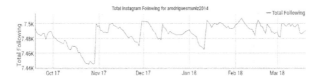

Notice the small span of follow and unfollow waves over the past two years. His count of followers never goes under 7,440 people, and yet he has a massive amount of activity. This type of pattern is a clear indication of automated bot behavior.
Source: Socialblade.com

I took screenshots of all these accounts in April of 2018. Below are screenshots taken in October of 2018. You'll see these bot accounts are still active, but the number of people they are following has been reduced in some cases.

So your girlfriend rolls a Honda, playin' workout tapes by Fonda. But Fonda ain't got a motor in the back of her Honda.

Hey, maybe I was right about this guy working at a mobile phone store!

Alas, the 4-year-old smarmy-bot was removed by Instagram. Well done, Instagram. Cue the sarcastic slow-motion golf clap.

WHERE DO BOTS GET THE PHOTOS?

No, there aren't little robots running around taking robot selfies and uploading them while having robot coffee.

So, where do the photos populating these accounts come from?

It is very easy to write a script that "scrapes" (steals) photos and text data from other people's Instagram accounts. Such a script can even scrape images directly from Google's image search. Some scraping techniques are better than others and can pull together a set of images that look alike.

Many bot accounts are sloppily assembled, like this one, which has a hodgepodge of random pictures. Other bot accounts are savvier and stick to a theme.

Above is @talaalgassem, an example of what I believe to be a bot. It is one of the bots that follows and comments on @miss.everywhere's posts (who we will meet in the next chapter), and usually comments with emojis. With many of these bots, you can see they just put any kind of picture into their feed to appear somewhat authentic. Where did the bot get the profile photo? I did a reverse Google search on this and it turns out that photo is of the glamorous Pakistani actress Mahira Khan (whose actual account is @mahirahkhan). It's very easy for bots to scrape from millions of real faces as they generate fake accounts.

Pakistani film industry extends support to Mahira Khan over troll

Published: | 23rd September 2017 06:48 PM   IANS |

Mahira Khan

Popular Pakistani actors like Ali Zafar, Humaima Malick, Mawra and Urwa Hocane have lent support to actress Mahira Khan, who was trolled over social media over a leaked photograph where she can be seen smoking.

In the image that surfaced online, Mahira can be seen smoking alongside Bollywood actor Ranbir Kapoor. Soon after the photograph went viral over social media, a lot of people started slamming Mahira for smoking and wearing a short dress.

I found this photo using Google Image search, which found the same image used in millions of places.

Many of the faces you see on bot accounts will be actual faces they've stolen from real accounts or the web, as seen above. However, some faces may not even be real people at all. NVIDIA (which is a legitimate company), recently perfected a new photo generation technique that can randomly create an infinite number of faces that look 100% authentic, as you can see below.

None of these are real people. They are all computer-generated faces. Source: NVIDIA

I added some more fake faces from NVIDIA because I think it is so interesting. Using similar technology, it's also possible to put real people's faces onto existing videos of other talking heads, making it appear as if the person is saying something they've never said. This is called "deepfake" technology, and it's getting harder and harder to detect. Soon, it will be impossible to tell if any photo or video is real or not.

Innovative Bot Techniques

Bots are being programmed in increasingly creative ways, allowing them to manipulate real accounts into following new users. The following example comes from Lauren Bath (@laurenepbath) and describes how users can set up automated programs to identify someone in their target audience and flatter that user into following them.

Let's say the aspirational Influencer wants to be a Travel Influencer. First, they'll identify a number of legitimate Influencers in that niche.

Next, they'll assign their new bot a series of tasks to target followers of these Influencers, based on the followers' activity.

Bath explained how this works. "User X (the Influencer) selects me as one of their targets. [Their] bot is set to go after all the users that engage with my posts within ten minutes of it going live. The bot can go to these accounts, like ten [of their] photos, comment on two photos, and then leave and go to the next account.

"So, the bot is targeting REAL and ACTIVE users that are already interested in travel Influencers. These [targeted] users get a big hit of engagement from the bot and the next minute, they're following back," said Bath.

They Aren't All Bots–Sometimes They Are You!

One day, I tried to follow someone on Instagram. I was surprised to be unable to follow them. The app said I had exceeded the cap of 7,500 people, which is the maximum number of users that a single account is allowed to follow.

I couldn't figure it out at first. I usually only follow friends, other photographers, and models, so I wondered how that was possible. I know I didn't follow 7,500 of them. Who were these people I was following?

To figure it out, I downloaded an app called Cleaner. Cleaner organized all the accounts I'm following into a visual view, so I could pick which ones to unfollow. When I opened it up, I was mesmerized by some of the people I was following! I didn't follow all these people... did I? How could this happen? Sure, sometimes I drunk-follow people like @seesallyeat, but not this many of them.

So how did this happen? How did my account decide to follow another account, without my knowledge?

Most likely what happened is this: as a heavy Instagram user , I use a number of "add-on" services that integrate with Instagram. Some of them show you interesting statistics, make photo books from your Instagram photos, make prints, calendars, etc. I gave my username and password to a few of these, all of which seemed legitimate at the time.

At least one of those third parties took that information and deployed a script to commandeer my account, using it to follow wannabe Influencers. Unbeknownst to me, and before I notice anything is amiss, my account is following about 5,000 other accounts, none of which I had any interest in.

What might look like an innocuous stat-tracking website may also have a side-business, where they reuse your username and password in ways you don't expect.

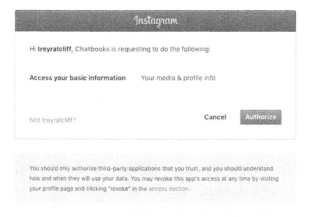

Here is an example of the secure way to log into a third-party website. With it, you don't have to enter your Instagram login details, because you're already securely logged in, perhaps in another tab. This is from Chatbooks—a good example of how to do this securely. Source: chatbooks.com

Instagram

Phone number, username, or email

Password

Log In

Here is an example of a sketchy third-party site, that is asking me to type in my username and password. I won't say what website it is, because I have no evidence they are doing anything untoward. But I can say it is from one of the biggest Instagram statistics collection websites.

After I discovered I was following 5,000+ people I had never heard of, I was annoyed enough to show Instagram security, and ask them what was going on. Instagram told me that this scenario is all too common because many people give their login details to third parties. The security team was unable to do anything about it, and I got to spend a really exciting week manually unfollowing almost everyone and cleaning up my personal Instagram account. Since the Instagram security team was also unable to pinpoint which service was responsible for the mysterious follows, they can't prevent it from happening again.

In this book, I often use websites as examples. That said, it is important to note that the vast majority of the people in the world only use their mobile phone to access the internet and are largely leveraging mobile apps to do many of the same things. Just as these websites ask you for your Instagram login details, innocuous-looking apps will do the same thing, with the same undesirable results.

I searched for "Instagram Stats" on the Google Play store. There are thousands and thousands of apps out there that can connect to your Instagram and will ask you to type in your username and password. Source: Google Play Store

Above, you can see a ton of apps that help track your Instagram stats. I installed about 10 of those above and 100% of them asked for my Instagram login details. I am not saying asking for a username and password is nefarious, but that information could certainly be used in a covert manner. Remember, any time you give access to your Instagram login details, a third party can now do anything they want with your account. It's never a good idea to share your username and password with people you don't trust.

Note—it's also possible that one of these services was hacked and my credentials were handed over to malicious actors in that way. This is absolute speculation on my part, but if hackers can gain access to some of the biggest corporations in the world with first-class security, it would be a lot easier to hack into any of the thousands of websites that contain a list of Instagram usernames and passwords.

I used an app called Cleaner to unfollow all these people I never personally followed. It didn't work that well, and over a week, I spent about an hour each day manually unfollowing about 5,000 people inside of Instagram.
It's a very slow and time-consuming process.

As the Instagram security team said, this sort of misuse of credentials is a fairly common problem. To validate, I Googled "Why am I automatically following people on Instagram?" and saw several sites where Instagrammers were discussing the issue. No one could figure out which websites were using their information in a clandestine manner, but I did find out that once these third parties have your login and password, they can even like and comment on your behalf too. Scary, right?

STEP 9: LOOK LIKE AN INFLUENCER

In business, the savvy often tell their junior colleagues to "dress for the role you want." Well, the same is true if you want to be an Influencer. I stumbled across a website a few months ago that offered all the props you need to take the perfect Instagram photo. I know, it sounds like something straight out of *The Onion*, but I wish I were being satirical. Their Instagram Influencer Starter Pack shown below includes a Mohave fedora hat, an Aztec blanket, a set of fairy lights, and a kerosene lamp. I haven't tested it, but I'm pretty sure that kerosene lamp is battery powered.

This online store offers a popular package that includes all the goodies you need to be a proper Instagram Influencer. There are a few of these stores online, including several that sell Influencer Halloween outfits.

There are lots of reviews for these packages on Tomorrowland. One reviewer, who is "verified," named K***n, gave this package five stars. In their review, they said, "I've been taking pictures for a while now but I just wanted to spice it up a little :) So, I went ahead and bought this pack and I have to say it was one of the best purchases I've done towards my hobby. I love playing around with these props to get the best shots and now I can imitate some of my favorite creator's shots too! I'm so happy. Thank you Tomorrowland!" Classic K***n.

Another review of this Wanderer pack shows how people have become fully immersed in what the reviewer described as the "Instagram game." This one from E***e—also verified—said, "I was skeptical of the pack at first but went ahead and took the leap. I have to say, it was one of the best decisions I've made. I love all four pack items. Definitely a boost to my Instagram game and now people look at me differently when I go out and shoot with these props. It's like I've become a professional. I love it!" When they say, "I have to say that," it sounds so serious, as if, perhaps, they really had to say it, otherwise it would remain unsaid.

Well-known photographer Nicole S. Young lamented the lack of originality that this sort of approach can lead to. In an email to me, she said, "Social media makes it too easy to create your own online persona, or even zap away any hint of originality that may have existed." I completely agree with this. She went on to say, "I love that more people are able to discover their love for photography and visual art through websites like Instagram. I just hope that this type of progress does not prevail at too great a cost."

My friend @harimaolee grabbed a lot of attention for using the fairy lights in an over-the-top Instagram post on a first-class seat on an airplane. The photo received a decidedly mixed reaction, ranging from, "This sort of staged nonsense is a joke. Nobody travels like this!!" to "Oh wow this is amazing! Love the lights." Personally, I think it's a creative shot and reminds me of the best kind of Saturday Night Live "commercials" where I'm laughing at the absurdity right before that moment when I'm not sure whether it's a real ad or not. Anyway, the Internet was abuzz with this photo, and soon the storm in a teacup was picked up by a bunch of reporters looking for the latest thing to be outraged about.

This could have been one of my self-portraits because this is how I usually roll on @cathaypacific. But, in all seriousness, please contact me, Cathay Pacific.

As they say, there's no such thing as bad publicity, but I thought I'd take a moment to set the record straight since this media backlash happened to a friend.

Most people, including the media, assumed that "Harimao Lee" was the model in the photo. That's some crack reporting because I've actually met "her" and taken photos with "her" all over Hong Kong—and the person behind @harimaolee is a guy. The @harimaolee Influencer account is run by a gentleman named Simon, who wakes up with his set of Y and X chromosomes, slams a beer, and then goes out to take kick-ass photos. Aside from having a cheeky sense of humor, he's a very talented photographer, and I admire his artistic eye. So, if you're going to use one of the Instagram clichés (I'll share lots more of them in chapter 7), go for it like Simon does and don't settle for trite photos, even if they ruffle a few feathers.

STEP 10: CONTACT BRANDS DIRECTLY AND SIGN UP WITH AN AGENCY THAT REPRESENTS INFLUENCERS

So, you've invested a lot of time into creating this Instagram account. You have content (probably featuring fairy lights and spandex leggings), followers (most of whom are bots), and lots of comments (probably with a lot of emojis).

Now you want to make some money. You want some brands to sponsor you. How do you do it?

Start by sending out dozens (or hundreds) of emails to brands that interest you. Ask for free products and cash in exchange for you mentioning them to your "followers."

Seem like a lot of work? If you want someone to do all this work for you, reach out to some agencies.

Agencies that connect Influencers with companies to work with, known as Influencer Marketing agencies or Digital Influencer agencies, are taking over from traditional PR firms. These agencies act as intermediaries between you and sponsoring brands. The good ones can set you up with deals and partnerships with well-known brands in exchange for money, experiences, or swag.

These agencies are not hard to find. After a short search on Google, I found at least 50 "Instagram Influencer Agency" websites. More than 420 new Influencer agencies opened in 2017, double the number that launched in 2015.[9] This is becoming a bit bigger than a cottage industry, and why wouldn't it be, with billions of dollars flowing into the Instagram Influencer system?

Most Influencers will use more than one agency. According to The Atlantic, "It's not uncommon for Influencers to be signed up for more than five Influencer-management platforms at once, and some are active on as many as 10."[10]

However, not all agencies are legitimate, and some Influencers run into trouble getting paid for their work. The article called out one agency in particular, Speakr, that has been recalcitrant in paying its Influencers. This is yet another indication of how unprofessional and fly-by-night some agencies can be.[11]

Because the importance of the Influencer is so new, it's not surprising that many brands work with agencies rather than trying to approach Influencers directly. In addition to the promise of finding suitable Influencers to work with, an agency can make reporting on key metrics, such as ROI (Return on Investment), easier for the brand as well. Agencies will often collate the collected efforts of several Influencers they have recommended and put together a marketing report for the brand to share their results internally. Well, you know how much marketing managers appreciate a good PowerPoint presentation with big numbers to show their bosses. It's quite possible that the numbers in these slick PowerPoints are based on faulty metrics, which leaves the actual ROI in question.

Are Agencies Complicit?

Fake Influencers run rampant while agencies are reaping millions of dollars in commissions. Agencies definitely stand to benefit from the Influencer game, which means that some agencies are either part of the fraud or clueless that it's happening. Neither looks good.

Are many Influencer agencies, like the ones who were scrambling to represent our fake account @genttravel, complicit? Probably. Many more have perhaps unwittingly played a role in defrauding brands out of significant marketing funds by representing fraudulent Influencers when they should have known better.

When an agency reports the results of a campaign to a brand, the agency typically rolls up all engagement metrics—views, comments, and likes—into an engagement report that paints a pretty picture to keep their clients happy. These reports are designed to be shared within the brand's company to illustrate how successful the Influencer marketing campaign has been.

The vast majority of brands involved with this song and dance don't have the time to do a deep dive into the details themselves to see if any of the numbers are legitimate. It's why they outsourced to an agency, isn't it? Most middle marketing managers nod their heads confidently and say, "Yes, absolutely" if questioned about the absolute truth of the numbers in the pretty report. But they really don't know.

I'm sure they *want* them to be true. They've probably spent months, if not years, convincing their bosses to invest in this new form of marketing. So, there's a lot at stake for everyone. It's true that social media Influencer marketing, when legitimate, has been proven to be one of the most effective ways of communicating brand messages. The trouble is that people sometimes bet on the wrong horse because the stats can't be trusted.

With real data, people can make better decisions. In business, bosses need to acknowledge the natural tendency for their employees to want to hide bad news or cover up uncertainty. When there's a culture of assigning blame, people will resort to lying, cheating, and worse to avoid punishment and failure. It's harder to create a culture where everyone is empowered to dig for and share the uncomfortable truths.

Setting tangible and relevant goals for an Influencer marketing campaign could be one way to fix the problem, but it's a slippery slope. Unlike marketing campaigns on many other platforms, with social media efforts, it's very hard to track what's called "attribution"—which marketing efforts resulted in which sales. It's not as straightforward as counting direct referrals to a lead page or relying on cookies. So, instead of sales revenue, the success of Instagram marketing campaigns is measured by tracking and reporting engagement, which, we all now know, can be very easily faked.

I wanted to do a little digging of my own to see how many agency-affiliated Influencers had used less than honest means to garner their popularity. When I visited several agency websites, I found only about half of agencies list their roster of Influencers.

When agencies publicly list their Influencers, it's easy to check these Influencers out to see if any of their metrics look suspicious, or downright obviously faked. You'll see how to check in the next chapter.

The rest of these agencies keep their Influencers behind a walled garden, so it's much harder to check. Only brands get to see the list of Influencers, and even then, it's only a partial list. The agencies will send a select number of Influencers to the client based on the job. For some of the work that I've done internationally, my company has received some of these pitch decks and gotten a peek inside the walled garden. I'll share an example a little later about when we received a pitch to work with @amazingthailand.

As an agency client, we have received plenty of agency recommendations to work with Influencers who have fraudulent accounts. Of the agencies we examined, we saw that anywhere from between 10% and 50% of their influencers were fraudulent accounts. It is important to note that some of these Influencers have only bought a portion of their following. But, for example, if you are working with an Influencer that bought 10,000 of their 100,000 followers, can you trust them? If they've proven themselves to be slightly dishonest in the past, can you trust them to represent your brand?

Wearing my Influencer hat, I've yet to be contacted by an agency that I consider legitimate. As an Influencer, I make sure that I work directly with brands when I set up a partnership. I'm not against using an agency in the future, but I am still waiting to get a proposal from one that appears trustworthy.

Agencies and Culpability

I worked with an "Influencer" (gosh, I wish there was a punctuation mark for sardonic air quotes) in Asia who was paid $4,000 to make a few Instagram posts. She had worked through an agency and was happy with the arrangement. That is, until she heard the brand had paid the agency $15,000 for the job.

In this case, the agency had contacted the Influencer, as a headhunter would, and offered her a one-time agreement. The agency had never worked with this Influencer before. A standard agency contract usually defines what percentage of the money the Influencer and the agency will each take home, but none of this was clear to this Influencer. Most Influencers are too new to the business to ask these sorts of obvious questions, and agencies take advantage of them. The agency was also at fault, as they apparently did no research into the legitimacy of the Influencer. It was apparent to us the Influencer was purchasing followers, likes, and comments.

I also talked to other Influencers that the agency hired and found out the rates they had been paid. Needless to say, the agency had been making out like a bandit.

These are comments on a post by one of the Influencers I was subjected to work with while I was in Asia. The comments appear to be mostly from bots. A usual tip-off is the vagueness of the comments, crazy emojis, and copious use of the word "dear." All these automated comments from non-humans bulk up the comment and like counters to make the "engagement" of the Influencer's posts look more impressive.

For agencies, there are a couple of competing factors at play that make this setup tricky.

- There's so much demand for Influencer attention at the moment that agencies have an obvious incentive to try and scoop up as many Influencers as they can. Quality control falls by the wayside.
- It's in the best interest of agencies to keep the financial details a secret—most of them are not transparent about who is making how much money.
- Agencies need to convince big brands that they—the agencies—are the best conduit for the brands' marketing campaigns. They do this with suitably impressive numbers—real, or "enhanced"—to back up their assertion.

These forces lead to the less-than-honest behaviors I've listed above. Personally, I've seen so much sketchy activity from agencies that I've become extremely cynical about the entire process. It seems clear to me that many big brands have strong legal cases against Influencer agencies, where they (the brands) have spent millions of dollars on vapor.

There was a recent article in The Atlantic, about the market for agencies, that does a good job of summarizing the problem.

> But this very lucrative, very new market still lacks critical infrastructure. There's no standard method of communication, no formalized negotiation process, and, often, no paperwork. Rates can range widely from brand to brand and are often hashed out entirely via direct message.[12]

So, if you're a wannabe Influencer who wants to work with an agency (or a brand), make sure you're asking the right questions, understand your compensation package, figure out who the key players are, and get everything in writing.

Automated Online Agencies

Remember our fake Influencer, @genttravel? After we built up the account, we did approach a few agencies and received interest from many.

With some of these agencies, we were able to transact entirely online, conveniently enough. Below is an example of one of the many we found. With this one, we simply applied online and waited to hear back.

Then, a few days later, we were promptly approved. This, despite having bought 100% of @genttravel's 100,000 followers, along with all the likes and comments for his posts. The agency did no diligence about our account.

The agency sent us about a dozen paid post offers right away. All we needed to do to accept the first assignment was to fill out a quick form. We went ahead and began to fill it out just to see how easy it would be. We stopped before the very end. It was just an experiment after all, and we had no intention of committing fraud.

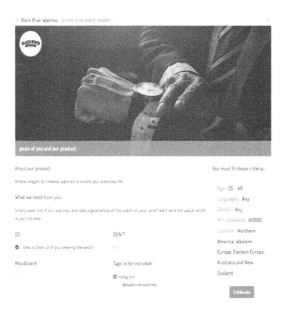

This was one of the partnership offers we received from the agency.

This is what the agreement page looked like.

As you can see, if we had accepted this offer, Tane would have gotten a fancy new watch, in addition to some monetary compensation. The suggested compensation rate was $802 for a single post, but we could have asked for more. And there were countless offers like this one on their website.

I feel bad for this watch company and for everyone else lining up to waste money like this. I frankly couldn't believe how easy it was for us to scam the system.

And this is a relatively small offer. As I've mentioned, it's not uncommon for Influencers flashing larger numbers to make thousands of dollars, or hundreds of thousands of dollars, for an extended campaign made up of a series of posts.

CONCLUSION: EVERYTHING IS FOR SALE

Currently, Instagram seems to be the most popular platform for purchasing followers, likes, and comments on the black market, and there's quite a bit of money floating around to incentivize this duplicitous behavior. The problem is not restricted just to Instagram, although that's what we've been focusing on. Users can also inflate all their other social media accounts to match, including piling on more Facebook post likes, Spotify followers, Pinterest re-pins, YouTube plays, LinkedIn connections, and more.

As we've demonstrated in this chapter, using these techniques, it's easy to deceive agencies and brands, into thinking you're the real deal. It's only a short step from there to earning money from this deception.

It should be noted that it is not only individual Influencers who buy followers/likes/comments. Some brands and companies do it as well.

Matt Hackett, one of the first employees at Tumblr and now a tech investor, says this kind of activity can be quite common. He told me that it sometimes makes sense for a less established e-commerce brand or startup to buy followers to look more legitimate as they build a following. There's a lot of pressure to do that these days, as many potential customers will go look at how many followers a brand has. If they only have a few, he says, the company doesn't appear very trustworthy.

I often wonder why so many people are engaging in this sort of fraudulent behavior. Are all these people hardened criminals who have an evil core? I don't think so. I believe they are rationally justifying their cheating behavior.

One common justification I've heard is, "everyone else is doing it, so I'm just leveling the playing field." This is actually one of the ones that make more sense to me. While it's not technically true that *everyone* else is gaming the system, it is true that many of the top Influencers are. Humans are social animals, and if they see all their friends playing a "game," they are more likely to play it the same way. The sheer volume of dodgy courses, websites, Facebook groups, and other tools available to cheat makes it seem acceptable to participate. And when you join a pod and see hundreds of thousands of others are doing the same things, it makes the justifying it to yourself a lot easier.

As we found with our @genttravel experiment, it's actually very easy to buy your way into the golden 100K (or 1 million) follower level and start getting hired as an Influencer. Once you're in the Influencer club, you'll be surrounded by a bunch of other people who are also faking it, which also makes it easier to justify.

Another justification I've heard is, "You gotta pay to play!" I hear it repeated in many YouTube videos, where hawkers encourage people to sign up for their "Instagram Follower Growth" courses. These people suggest that, if you have good content, you should pay some of these services to make sure people see your content.

While we may never fully understand the reasons, we do know how these Influencers are accomplishing their diabolic undertakings. These social media black markets make it very easy to manipulate social media ecosystems for less-than-ethically-obtained profit.

CHAPTER 4
HOW TO SLOW THE ZOMBIE APOCALYPSE (OR: HOW TO DETECT THE FAKES)

"For a successful technology, reality must take precedence over public relations, for nature cannot be fooled."
— **RICHARD P. FEYNMAN**

INSTAGRAM'S PUBLIC RELATIONS TEAM often talks about taking strong steps toward addressing the deluge of fake accounts, likes, and comments.

Way back in 2014, there was one bot purge of significance, dubbed the "Instagram Rapture." Even the @instagram account itself lost 18 million followers. Justin Bieber lost 3.5 million. Kim Kardashian lost 1.3 million. Rapper Akon even lost over 50% of his followers, as you can see in his historical chart.[1]

I am not claiming any of these people bought followers. I'm sure many of them did not. For example, as I mentioned, the @instagram account itself lost 18 million followers. It's clear to me that they would not buy followers. Bots will often follow celebrities to make the bot accounts appear more human and legitimate, and I'm sure some of these celebrities were subjected to that sort of bot activity.

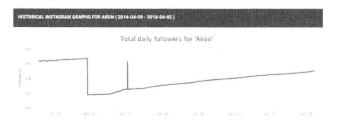

Here is the historical chart for @akon. You can see where the Instagram Rapture happened, which dropped him from about 4.3 million followers to about 2 million followers. There's also a spike in the middle of 2015. I don't know what that means, but I see that spike in many people's accounts. I believe it was a statistical reporting error. Source: Socialblade.com

Here is the historical chart for the official @instagram account. It jibes with the chart above, with the dropoff happening right before the end of 2014. This dip appears smaller than @akon, of course, but keep in mind the scale of the Y axis is in the hundreds of millions instead of singles of millions. Source: Socialblade.com

At the time of the purge in 2014, The Guardian pointed to reports suggesting that there were more bots on the Internet than there were people on the planet.[2] One can only suspect that bots have gotten smarter and more prolific since 2014.

It's doubtful that the purge of 2014 cleared out 100% of the bots.

Yet, a simple inspection of the charts above will show that there have been no serious purges since 2014. I certainly do not see any other significant dips in these charts or many of the other historical charts I've looked at. What percentage of bots did the Instagram Rapture clear out? We have no idea. Even any subsequent purge, after this book is published, is not guaranteed to clear out 100% of the bots.

In my initial conversation with representatives within Instagram in 2018, they indicated that the sort of activities I've documented are against their Terms and Conditions. When fraudulent users are discovered, they are removed. However, they don't seem to be doing a very good job of this. By looking at the charts, perhaps only minor manscaping has been achieved.

So, what can you do to detect fake accounts and Influencers who are leveraging bots to appear more popular than they are? There are a variety of tools and techniques you can use to spot the scammers. I'll walk through some of those below.

HOW TO SPOT FAKE ACCOUNTS AS A USER

In just two days of hunting, I easily found more than 200 accounts that appear to be cheating the system. I could use any of them as an example, but I'll pick one suspected fake Influencer at random, from the travel industry, and compare her account to a genuine account. I'm sure one of those two will be upset, but she should really go out and get a regular job like everyone else.

I will emphasize something I said before about the accusation of individuals. I cannot prove anything. I am looking at the trends, the data, the comments, the anomalies, etc. I believe in the intelligence of you, awesome reader, to draw your own conclusions.

Let's begin with an introduction to two seemingly very similar accounts: @miss.everywhere and @theblondeabroad. Just by looking at their Instagram feeds, which one do you think is the one who is likely buying followers and engagement? It's really hard to tell, right? Both have about half a million followers. Both are attractive blonde travelers.

Both have excellent photos taken in exotic locations. Both seem to have decent engagement on their posts.

However, I believe one of them has created an online business in a misleading way by purchasing followers, likes, and comments to pass as an Influencer.

Spot the difference? Hard, isn't it!

I really believe any average person, including someone who works in marketing, would think both these Influencers appear legitimate. You can see lots of followers, loads of likes, and heaps of comments, which are supposedly the hallmarks of legitimacy.

So, as a user, how would you go about deciding if these Influencers are legitimate?

Eyeball It

Many people think they can go look at an account and get a "sense" of how real they are as if they are using some kind of a Ouija board. This is sort of like the "sniff" test, and, honestly, it's not a terrible method.

However, doing a deep analysis of an account can take several hours, if not longer. Doing a full review of an account requires going down a series of rabbit holes, as the only accurate way to see if something passes the sniff test is to look in detail at who's making all the comments and likes and examine a significant sampling of each to see if they seem real or if they are bots. Figuring out which accounts are real people and which are bots, is becoming harder and harder, as even fake accounts will have a ton of content, great photos, Instagram stories, comments of their own, and more. In real life, it's very hard to impersonate a human with a personality. It's remarkably easy online and getting easier every day.

If you are going to analyze an account, it's good to have a few different people looking at the account, checking out suspicious comments, then drilling down and finding out if these comments are made by real people. It's challenging work that requires a lot of concentration. You may see a comment that has a pile of inscrutable emojis. You click on that person and try to figure out if it's plausible they speak emoji as a second language.

What makes it even more difficult for actual humans to find out if accounts are legitimate is that real people can make fake comments and follow accounts that they may not intend to. As we touched on in chapter 3, someone may have given their login details to a third party, and with or without their knowledge, that third party now uses bots to comment on their behalf. So the accounts may be real, but the comments and followers may still be fake.

What do you see when you eyeball @miss.everywhere? I've eyeballed many accounts now, so I've gotten a certain knack for it. When I eyeball her, I see a few things:

- She has a bunch of showy posts.
- These posts have a very high number of brand mentions.
- The account has less than 1,000,000 followers.
- But, her posts have hundreds of comments and thousands of

likes, which seems disproportionate to the number of followers she has.

That is enough to make me suspicious. So, let's do a bit more of a deep dive.

Check Their Background: Look at Their Follower Counts over Time

In every other element of society, we have background check mechanisms and trusted independent auditors to verify that people are who they say they are. There are thousands of companies that do criminal background checks during the hiring process. There are thousands of companies that do credit checks on you before you buy a car or house. There are thousands of companies that do drug testing. In traditional media, there are companies that are widely trusted to provide verified circulation audits.

But social media is still largely unregulated. Doing a quick search, I couldn't find any reliable way to verify statistics on these accounts and I can't be the only one taking a stab in the dark. As we found with @genttravel, the fake Instagram Influencer we manufactured as a test, even Influencer agencies who claim to vet Influencers can't be doing any kind of real digging—most of them didn't notice or care that our 30-day-old account was obviously a fake.

However, after rather extensive research, I did uncover a few websites that could be useful for follower and engagement background checks. Some of them do an analysis of a list of Instagrammers you provide and come back with some level of "guess" as to how many are real. I don't have confidence in any of these sites, however, because I know they don't have access to enough of Instagram's data to be completely sure—they're still guessing, just like we are.

Until Instagram opens up access to user data in a more meaningful way, the most surefire method to detect a fraudulent Influencer is based on analyzing *historical* growth patterns. The best tool to use is called Socialblade.com, which we've referenced in other places in this book.

(I hope the website doesn't crash now that I mentioned it.)

When looking up an Instagram user, it is good to click on "Historical Data" at the top, which shows older data. Currently, the site is a little strange in that it picks a random month from last year, but the chart at the bottom usually contains more historical data. Also, keep in mind that SocialBlade.come does not track 100% of users. Last, the features on the site are always in flux, so it's good to poke around and get to know the tool on your own.

So, let's start there and compare the historical growth of @miss.everywhere and @theblondeabroad.

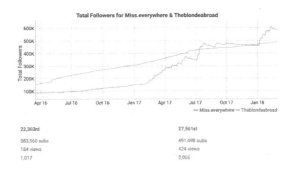

A comparative historical growth chart of followers for the two accounts we're comparing. If you're seeing this in black & white, @miss.everywhere is the jagged line. A smooth curve plots @theblondeabroad's growth. **By the way, of all the screenshots in the book, this is my favorite.** *Source: Socialblade.com Screenshot was taken on March 4, 2018.*

Those of you skilled in data analysis can already see that these curves look very different. The growth pattern for @theblondeabroad, in blue, is very smooth. The vast majority of Instagrammers will have a smooth growth curve like this. The growth curve of my own accounts looks similar to this, as do those of a variety of other trusted friends I know who also always play by the rules.

Compare this smooth growth to the staccato rhythm of @miss.everywhere's growth line. The spikes you see are very similar to

@genttravel's growth chart on the days we bought thousands of followers. You'll also notice a slight *decrease* after each of these spikes. That is abnormal for organic growth curves (you never see @theblondeabroad's follower count dip like this), but very normal to see for accounts that have purchased a lot of their followers.

If you look closely at the smoother blue line, you may have noticed two "mini-jumps," or ramps, in @theblondeabroad's curve. I asked Kiersten Rich about this. (That's her name; it's not really "theblondeabroad," as that would be a very silly name.) I met her years ago during my annual photowalk at Burning Man, so I know she's the real deal and doesn't buy followers or engagement. She works her tail off to consistently create great images with well-crafted writing and works hard to deliver quality to her clients as a genuine Influencer. She was very open to answering all of my questions.

Regarding those jumps in followers, Kiersten explained that she received three mentions on March 4th and 5th from @gopro, an extremely popular account with about 15 million followers. Kiersten sent me the three corresponding Instagram posts. She said each mention produced around 2,700 new followers for her. Remember this number because many fakers will suggest that they get much bigger spikes because they are mentioned by another Instagram account. There are not many accounts bigger than @gopro, so most of those claims are spurious at best. Each @gopro post that featured Kiersten received 200,000 to 300,000 likes.

Here is an example of one of @theblondeabroad's takeovers of the @gopro account (15 million followers). Each mention gave her an extra 2,700 followers.

People often assume that a mention from a huge account like @gopro automatically brings a windfall of followers. There are some rare exceptions, of course, but typically the conversion is quite low. Another friend, wedding photographer @jimpollardgoesclick, got a mention from a significant account when he took wedding photos of the actress @annecurtissmith, who has 8.6 million followers. She mentioned him three times and those mentions gave him a boost of about 1,700, 1,200, and 1,650 followers, respectively.

To close out this section, below is a chart from our fake account, @genttravel, for comparison. The jumps here are a little smoother, but it's still pretty clear that most of our followers were garnered inorganically.

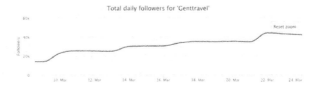

You can see from the 10th of March to the 24th of March, the account grew impossibly fast from about 18,000 followers to over 40,000 followers. This is, of course, because we bought followers from a variety of services.

Look at Where Their Followers Are Coming From

I also used a website called HypeAuditor to do some more investigating. I believe this tool's statistical analysis to be very accurate because I first ran their multi-page report on my own account and it looked pretty good. I compared it to the official numbers from the "Insights" area of the Instagram app, and it was spot on.

So, I ran the same report on @miss.everywhere. I've placed one of the most interesting sections on the following page. Now, keep in mind that @miss.everywhere herself is German and all her posts on Instagram are in English or German.

A statistical breakdown of the geography of followers of @miss.everywhere.
Source: HypeAuditor

Isn't it so interesting then how the vast majority (61%) of her audience speak Spanish, while only 25% speak English? Heck, that sure is odd. And far more of her followers come from non-English, non-German speaking countries (Mexico, Colombia, and Chile) than both her followers from the US and Germany combined.

Comparing her demographics to those of @theblondeabroad shows a stark contrast.

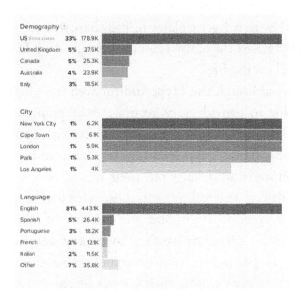

A statistical breakdown of the followers of @theblondeabroad.
Source: HypeAuditor

Here, you can see @theblondeabroad has demographic numbers that make a lot more sense given what we know about her. In contrast to @miss.everywhere, 81% of @theblondeabroad's followers live in countries that speak English, and her top five countries are precisely what we would expect. Cape Town is also a top city, which looks like an anomaly, but it makes sense because that's where she lives.

Follower demographics can be quite different depending on the Influencer's niche. In many markets, the total number of followers is less important than the demographics of the followers. For example, I don't have as many followers as, say, a 21-year-old Influencer who does beauty tutorials might have. My audience is mostly older men and women who like to travel, use expensive photography gear, enjoy reading, have disposable income, and share a love of gadgets. This sort of follower is appealing to certain types of brands—brands who wouldn't be interested in working with the more popular, young, makeup artist.

So, as you can see from these charts, @miss.everywhere has quite anomalous numbers. I made a note to talk to her about this in an upcoming interview that I get to later in the chapter. I know, this is like a thriller, right? Resist the temptation to skip ahead while I throw more evidentiary fuel on the fire.

By the way, although the HypeAuditor website where I got these reports was able to provide very accurate demographic information, you have to take some of their other conclusions with a couple of handfuls of salt. For instance, HypeAuditor also claims to be able to tell us how many followers are fake. I ran their report on several accounts, from those with very real followers to those with lots of fake followers. They weren't very good at guessing the number of fake followers an account has. Since Instagram hasn't allowed any website access to all their data yet, HypeAuditor has to extrapolate based on a very small amount of data. In my opinion, their guesses on the accounts I checked were way off.

Now, let's get deeper into unusual number patterns in follower growth.

Look for Big Decreases in Followers after Purchase Days

Earlier, I mentioned that when someone buys followers, a telltale sign that they've done this is that their follower count will jump, then drop noticeably over the next week. You see this in @miss.everywhere's growth line.

You can check out this unusual pattern in the following graphs, which show followers gained and lost on a daily basis. Organic growth, as you can see in @theblondeabroad's chart, also has ups and downs, but the variation we see in @theblondeabroad's chart is orders of magnitude smaller than the variation in @miss.everywhere's.

INSTAGRAM STATS SUMMARY / USER SUMMARY (2017-02-18 - 2018-03-03)							
DATE		FOLLOWERS		FOLLOWING		MEDIA	
2017-02-18	Sat	-1,046	187,959	+19	6,518	–	733
2017-02-19	Sun	-1,844	186,115	+2	6,520	–	733
2017-02-20	Mon	-1,054	185,061	+4	6,524	–	733
2017-02-21	Tue	-555	184,506	+4	6,528	+1	734
2017-02-22	Wed	-831	183,675	+1	6,529	+2	736
2017-02-23	Thu	+5,803	189,478	+2	6,531	+3	739
2017-02-24	Fri	+11,013	200,491	-1	6,530	+2	741
2017-02-25	Sat	+2,609	203,100	-4	6,526	+2	743
2017-02-26	Sun	+873	203,973	+1	6,527	–	743
2017-02-27	Mon	-973	203,000	–	6,527	+3	746
2017-02-28	Tue	+195	203,195	+3	6,530	–	746
2017-03-01	Wed	+18,963	222,158	+3	6,533	+3	749
2017-03-02	Thu	+2,483	224,641	+3	6,536	+3	752
2017-03-03	Fri	+383	225,024	–	6,536	–	752
2017-03-04	Sat	-4,661	220,363	–	6,536	+2	754
2017-03-05	Sun	-377	219,986	+6	6,542	+2	756
2017-03-06	Mon	-719	219,267	+3	6,545	+2	758
2017-03-07	Tue	+713	219,980	-2	6,543	+1	759
2017-03-08	Wed	-57	219,923	–	6,543	–	759
2017-03-09	Thu	+12,415	232,338	-1	6,542	+2	761
2017-03-10	Fri	+1,819	234,157	+11	6,553	+1	762
2017-03-11	Sat	-656	233,501	+3	6,556	+1	763
2017-03-12	Sun	-130	233,371	-1	6,555	–	763
2017-03-13	Mon	-541	232,830	–	6,555	–	763
2017-03-14	Tue	-482	232,348	+12	6,567	+3	766

You can see possible buying sprees by @miss.everywhere. Source: Socialblade.com

2017-07-12	Wed	+37,299	431,123
2017-07-13	Thu	+9,130	440,253
2017-07-14	Fri	+1,918	442,171
2017-07-15	Sat	+11,490	453,661
2017-07-16	Sun	+1,730	455,391
2017-07-17	Mon	**-249**	455,142
2017-07-18	Tue	**-1,908**	453,234
2017-07-19	Wed	**-69**	453,165
2017-07-20	Thu	**-837**	452,328

Over 5 days in July 2017, it appears @miss.everywhere bought over 60,000 followers. I cannot find any other logical explanation for that spike. Remember that a mention from @gopro, which has about 15 million followers, only got @theblondeabroad about 2,500 followers. So, using that example for scale, @miss.everywhere would have had to get over 20 mentions from a @gopro-sized account. Source: Socialblade.com

INSTAGRAM STATS SUMMARY / USER SUMMARY (2017-03-03 - 2018-03-03)						
DATE		FOLLOWERS		FOLLOWING		MEDIA
2017-03-03	Fri	+519	343,339	-2	490	+1	1,845
2017-03-04	Sat	+657	343,996	-13	477	+1	1,846
2017-03-05	Sun	+916	344,912	-3	474	+1	1,847
2017-03-06	Mon	+689	345,601	–	474	–	1,847
2017-03-07	Tue	+757	346,358	-4	470	+1	1,848
2017-03-08	Wed	+365	346,723	-1	469	+1	1,849
2017-03-09	Thu	+1,004	347,727	-1	468	+1	1,850
2017-03-10	Fri	+614	348,341	-2	466	+1	1,851
2017-03-11	Sat	+514	348,855	-41	425	+1	1,852
2017-03-12	Sun	+599	349,454	-4	421	+1	1,853
2017-03-13	Mon	+665	350,119	–	421	+1	1,854
2017-03-14	Tue	+634	350,753	+1	422	+2	1,856
2017-03-15	Wed	+632	351,385	–	422	+1	1,857
2017-03-16	Thu	+613	351,998	–	422	+1	1,858
2017-03-17	Fri	+480	352,478	-2	420	–	1,858
2017-03-18	Sat	+589	353,067	–	420	+1	1,859
2017-03-19	Sun	+818	353,885	-1	419	+1	1,860
2017-03-20	Mon	+549	354,434	–	419	–	1,860
2017-03-21	Tue	+787	355,221	–	419	–	1,860
2017-03-22	Wed	+544	355,765	–	419	+1	1,861
2017-03-23	Thu	+654	356,419	+1	420	+1	1,862

The smooth growth curve of @theblondeabroad. Source: Socialblade.com

Let's explore why there might be a significant decrease in followers, like the ones you can see in @miss.everywhere's daily follower chart, that you wouldn't often see in organic growth.

Here are the three likely explanations for why she loses followers after big gains:

1. Bots behave differently to humans. Many automated services, such as Jarvee, automatically follow and unfollow a certain number of people every day. Computers are much more efficient at repetitive tasks and can work without breaks and sleep. There are armies of bots out there, constantly following and unfollowing accounts with mind-numbing regularity. It's likely that many of these bot followers she purchased automatically unfollowed her in the next few days.

2. Instagram has an automated service designed to remove some

bot accounts. Some number of bots will get trapped in their automated sweep every day and removed from Instagram.

3. Sometimes, an aspirational Influencer will be followed by real people, like *you*, even if you didn't choose to follow this person. Naturally, when you discover you're following someone that you don't remember choosing to follow, you unfollow them. We discussed this phenomenon in the previous chapter.

Comparison: @genttravel

For comparison, you can see a screenshot of our fake Influencer's follower growth. It is clearly suspicious. We could have made it look less suspicious if we had paid for the more expensive services that slowly trickle in new followers over a month-long period.

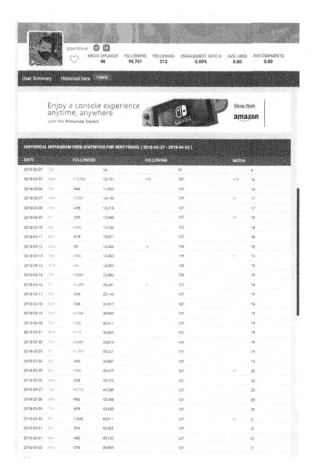

Here is an example of the daily follower count for our fake Influencer account of @genttravel. You can see, for example, that on 03-05 we bought 12,085 followers. Source: Socialblade.com

Dive into Comments

When you see questionable accounts getting hundreds of comments, it's worthwhile to dive deeply into those comments and see who's behind them. This is a time-consuming process and requires a certain concentration, but the results are often telling.

What sort of flags would indicate bot-generated comments? To identify fraudulently purchased comments, look for ones that are an arrangement of emoticons or generalized comments, such as, "Thanks dear," "Amazing look," "Soooo Perfect," and these sorts of vague sweet nothings. When you then click into those accounts, you usually find bots behind the comments. Less often, you'll find real people, who are paying a service to auto-comment for them.

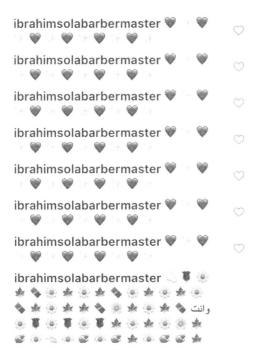

If you take the time to drop in to comment threads with 1000+ comments, you'll see many have long chains of nonsensical "engagement" like this. Many of the most popular accounts have automated services that post these emoticon-filled comments for just a few pennies.

In fact, most people who commit fraud on Instagram do pay a service to "Auto-Reply" for them to every single comment on their posts. These automatically generated comments often take the form of emojis, the classic "Thanks Dear," or custom-written replies on a rotation. These automatic responses cleverly double the total comments on the post, because, when the original poster also replies, 150 comments turn into 300, for example.

Don't think about this too much because it may make your brain hurt, but most of those 150 initial comments may be bots. And, if the Influencer is paying for automatic replies, then the replies also come from bots. This means that many comments on Instagram posts are simply bots talking to one another. What a bizarre world we live in.

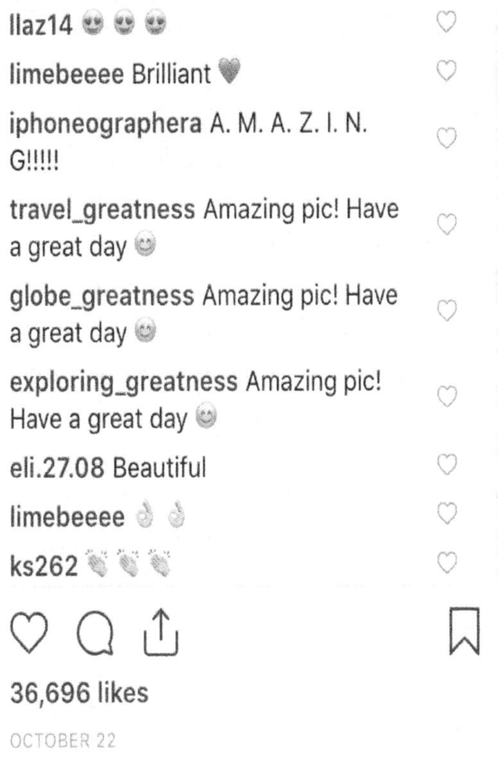

llaz14 😍 😍 😍

limebeeee Brilliant 🖤

iphoneographera A. M. A. Z. I. N. G!!!!!

travel_greatness Amazing pic! Have a great day 😊

globe_greatness Amazing pic! Have a great day 😊

exploring_greatness Amazing pic! Have a great day 😊

eli.27.08 Beautiful

limebeeee 👏 👏

ks262 👏 👏 👏

36,696 likes

OCTOBER 22

Few people in marketing have the time to examine comments on a post. I'm sure if they did, they'd quickly see the inane comments are clearly coming from scripts and bot accounts. For example, you can see above that she received the exact same comment from the rather generic sounding accounts of @travel_greatness, @globe_greatness, and @exploring_greatness.

The person behind the account that I've screenshotted above, who will remain nameless, was paid significant money to join me at a location to "boost" a project.

I have confronted many people who I thought were buying fake comments. I've even done this in person. The reactions are priceless. I'll try to describe one of these reactions here.

I was in Asia at a luxury resort and there were two Influencers who came along to collaborate by taking photos for Instagram. Husband and wife. They lived in Hong Kong, spoke perfect English as most people there do and traveled a lot for these sorts of boondoggles. Let's call them Mork and Mindy.

Like me, they were paid a lot of money and got free rooms and food. Unlike me, they appeared to buy their followers, likes, and comments. I didn't find this out until late one night when I got a bit suspicious and did some lookups on Socialblade.com.

Let's get back to Mork and Mindy. Mindy (obviously the wife) was one to wear a wide-brimmed Influencer hat, often touching it while she lords over a vast breakfast that has just been delivered by room service. Mork, her husband photographer, would help her meticulously lay out the smorgasbord. He was tall and spindly, seeming to barely know how to operate a cropped-sensor Canon. They might take one photo of Mindy lounging in bed, wearing a white robe, obviously pondering Chaucer while she sips a mimosa. The next photo might be outside on the deck of her villa while she lounges by her private pool. I know this because I had the same villa next door with the same pool. I must admit that I also ordered room service, but it was just pizza I downed with an entire bottle of Pinot Noir. I didn't take any photos because I was in a shame spiral. There was also a huge blow-up rainbow swan in the pool that I attempted to mount, with a rather embarrassing conclusion.

After looking into these two Hongkongers, I knew what was going on. I had found my quarry to query.

I sat down with Mork and Mindy for a final dinner at this resort. The meal was absolutely incredible, designed just for us by a Michelin star chef. It was a warm tropical night with a nice breeze. The breeze would blow the thick white tablecloth around while we attempted to have a conversation. I say "attempt," because I was desperate to get a polysyllabic word in response.

We were close to the beach and could see the South China Sea in the distance. Mindy sipped some champagne.

"Hey Mindy," I said, using her real name, as that reference would have definitely confused her. "I've been asked by my editor at WIRED to write an article about Instagram."

"Oh!" she said excitedly as if she could sense I might mention her in the article and possibly get her some real human followers. She leaned in with her champagne.

Tane (the actual @genttravel) was there, sitting beside me. He smiled ruefully, sensing my, now classic, rope-a-dope method.

"Yeah!" I said. "They are very interested in Influencers like you that have so quickly built up a huge number of followers and engagement!"

She was positively beaming now. Finally, someone understands how incredible she is.

"Oh!" she exclaimed with monosyllabic wonder.

I excitedly said, "Yes! They are very interested in how people like you are so successful!"

Still beaming, she now relaxed back into her chair, her champagne casually between two fingers while the three others opened. She didn't need to sip the champagne. It just languished in a dance as she began to pontificate on her methods.

"It's a lot of hard work," she said, sticking to one-syllable words. She furrowed her brows as if she was trying to put a thought together. "I had to move an ice cream truck under a palm tree for a better photo." Then, suddenly, Mork joins the conversation in a valiant manner offering, "Actually I had to move the ice cream truck!" They laughed uproariously. I couldn't get enough of their comic stylings.

The next course arrived as the intoxicating laughter slowly died down.

"So…" I began while picking up a fork, holding it in the air, tines up, "One of the aspects of the article is about people that buy followers, comments, and likes so that they can defraud honest companies. These Influencers make a lot of money and get free trips. Do you know anything about that?"

And what had begun as a most delightful dinner became super-awkward. But I love that stuff. You know that show, *Curb Your Enthusiasm*, where Larry David gets stuck in really awkward situations?

Mork's eyes got as big as Steve Buscemi's and Mindy's eyes became downcast and furtive. Now, her conversation devolved from monosyllabic to zero-syllabic. But I continued to take a schadenfreudic pleasure in pursuing this line of questioning. "Hey Mindy," I innocently asked, "Do you know anyone that buys followers, comments, and likes in order to get cash, free trips, and free food, like, for example, this amazing meal that this talented chef created for us tonight?"

Forced to respond, she said, while avoiding all eye contact, "Yes, I've heard of that." She wouldn't even look at Mork.

And then I gave Tane a knowing and seductive stare.

Look for Bots Talking to Bots

Some Influencers often try to pump up their comment counts through artificial means because having a higher number of comments looks impressive to brands. The following two screenshots are a great example of what appear to be bots leaving comments, which automated scripted bots then reply to.

OMG. One can see a common theme and pattern in these comments, not to mention the unusual names of the commenters. Note the names, because you'll see them again in the next screenshot.

Here, you can see that each of the replies from @miss.everywhere have a similar format. It appears that her replies are generated by an automated script. This particular post had over 700 comments in total, many of them like this. Remember that if you use Instagram on the web, the comments appear in chronological order, which is why you see the same names in chunks like this.

Going into these comments and doing a forensic analysis takes a lot of time and patience and this is why so few agencies and brands go through the trouble. It goes without saying that automatic responses from computers are completely worthless from a marketing perspective, as they are not actual humans and it's unlikely they'll buy your product.

Employ a Third Party "Audit" Site

There are maybe half a dozen sites out there that claim to help you analyze dubious Influencer accounts. This technique doesn't work quite as well as they claim. I tried several of them to find out if they could detect fake Influencers, and unfortunately, none of them were satisfactory.

In the experiments I ran on these audit sites, the reports were guessing in the right direction, but not with much accuracy. For example, I ran our fake Influencer account against it and it said about half the followers were fake when actually we bought 100% of the followers. Good guess though.

I also performed the same side-by-side analyses of two sizable accounts, one of which we determined was all-fake using an analysis of historical growth, and the other of which I know is authentic. You can see both of the results here.

The report on the left is an analysis of the legitimate account. It's my friend Kiersten @theblondeabroad. The one on the right is an account of someone I know who claims to have purchased 99% of his followers. Source: HypeAuditor

You can see that this website, which purports to know the difference between real and fake users, says that 17% of Kiersten's followers are suspicious, while only 8.6% of the followers for the account on the right are suspicious. This conclusion is ridiculous—when you look lower in the report, you can see that the report on the right lists India and Turkey as the two top countries from which followers hail for that account. This should automatically set off an alarm bell.

Socialblade.com appears to be one of the only sites that currently keep historical records of follower growth. Unfortunately, Socialblade.com seems to be in a constant state of flux and was even not working for a few months. As I write this, I cannot compare accounts or see a full history as I used to be able to do when I initially grabbed these screenshots a few months ago.

In April of 2018, Instagram cut off access to data for Socialblade.com (and every third-party site) to track follower count. This is either because of the Cambridge Analytica privacy debacle or because of the looming WIRED article that prompted all of my questions. About four months later, Instagram stats came back to Socialblade.com with a few changes, such as the ability to track data only if you have an authenticated business account. The features are always in flux, so it's possible things will change (or even go away) by the time you read this.

Case Study: How Valuable Are @miss.everywhere's Fake Followers?

Unfortunately, as I mentioned before, purchased followers are worthless to brands and are not valuable like organic followers. However, most brands can't tell the difference. I'll give you one more example of how ineffective @miss.everywhere appears to be in actually influencing anybody. Examine the post below from December 14, 2018.

On December 14, 2018, @miss.everywhere did a paid post from the presidential suite inside Hotel Das Central Sölden, which she tagged with the Instagram account of @dascentral_soelden. Not to add another issue in here, but you may want to take a closer look at the way those comments are repeated and the usernames.

Below is a historical growth chart for @dascentral_soelden over the time period during which @miss.everywhere mentioned their brand, which she did on December 14, 2018. One might assume to see growth around when the post was made.

DATE		FOLLOWERS		FOLLOWING		MEDIA
2018-12-04	Tue		2,977		1,190	451
2018-12-05	Wed	+9	2,986	+1	1,191	451
2018-12-06	Thu	+6	2,992	-1	1,190	451
2018-12-07	Fri	+4	2,996	+1	1,191	+1 452
2018-12-08	Sat	+21	3,017	+2	1,193	+1 453
2018-12-09	Sun	+26	3,043		1,193	453
2018-12-10	Mon	+17	3,060		1,193	453
2018-12-11	Tue	+18	3,078	+2	1,195	453
2018-12-12	Wed	+11	3,089	+3	1,198	+1 454
2018-12-13	Thu	+9	3,098		1,198	454
2018-12-14	Fri	+9	3,107	+3	1,201	454
2018-12-15	Sat	+15	3,122		1,201	454
2018-12-16	Sun	+18	3,140		1,201	+1 455
2018-12-17	Mon	+11	3,151	+1	1,202	455
Daily Averages		+9		+2		+1

Here is the historical growth chart for @dascentral_soelden over the time period of @miss.everywhere's mention. You can see on December 14, they only grew by 9 followers. Source: Socialblade.com

Now, with her 580,000+ followers and a whopping 16,000+ likes on this post, we should expect to see a sizable (or at least measurable) increase in the followers for @dascentral_soelden. However, on December 14, @dascentral_soelden only received 9 new followers, to go from 3,098 to 3,107. In fact, the daily average for their follower growth is only 9, so that's not a meaningful increase for their account. Curious. I thought at least her chatty friend @hb_889e7d72 would have followed the hotel.

Getting Fooled

Don't feel bad if you were initially fooled by these supposed invincible Influencers. For example, @miss.everywhere is convincing enough that Forbes featured her as one of *6 Female Travel Photographers You Need*

To Follow On Instagram in 2017.[3] In that article, four out of the six appear legitimate. Of course, the other two, who are likely fake, can also now use that publicity as leverage, because it makes them appear bona fide. There are thousands of articles of this nature on the Internet, ranging from *Top Fashion Instagrammers* to *How [These Guys] Got Rich on Instagram,* and so on.

I don't entirely blame the research team at Forbes. Not many people know how to audit an Influencer by looking up historical growth data. But I do hope in the future writers use these tools, and others, to do more thorough research. There are also few brands with marketing teams savvy enough to know about these problems or understand the technology enough to discern any wrongdoing.

One marketer who does realize it's a rotten game out there is Kellogg's social media lead, Joseph Harper. In an article on Digiday, Harper said, "We don't buy social media ads based on reach anymore, because it can be easily faked … Some of the agencies helping us to manage Influencers have started small but grown quickly, so they don't know how to deal with big clients."[4] Ouch. That's the nice PR way of warning other brands that hiring an Influencer agency doesn't necessarily protect you from getting conned, because many agencies are no better at separating Influencer fact from fiction.

Now, granted, @miss.everywhere takes pretty photos. However, taking a pretty photo is no longer a differentiator. Everyone seems to take pretty photos nowadays. Hey, I'm a professional photographer and I freely admit this. Saying someone has really nice photos is barely a factor in choosing an Influencer because it's a given. It's necessary, but not sufficient. So, what is the differentiator? Let's look at engagement for the following photos.

This unstaged photo had over 9,000 likes and over 110 comments.

This gem had over 20,000 likes and over 920 comments. This is quite a bit more engagement than her average posts. I mean, it's a nice looking bottle of lotion, if that's your thing. But personally, I'm a bit dubious that so many people could be stirred enough by this post to like and comment.

This fatuous pose has over 13,000 likes and over 300 comments. Art is subjective, of course, but I think most people would agree that this is a more likable and commentable photo than a product shot of a bottle of lotion, which got almost twice as many likes and three times as many comments.

In addition to the conspicuous product placement, it appears she may be using one of the many automated services (such as Jarvee) that give automated responses to comments. There are hundreds of responses with similar emoticons. It's also generally believed that the Instagram algorithm is more likely to share a post when the original creator responds

*promptly to comments. Note: If you use Instagram on the web, you can see comments in
a different order than on the app and you can see how the script dumps a ton of these
auto-responders at once.*

Based on the evidence, it appears likely that @miss.everywhere purchased likes and comments for many of her paid posts, if not all. Just as many other Influencers are doing to keep sponsors fooled until the money is in the bank. For our test Instagram account, we bought 10,000 likes for 16 photos for a mere $50, and all the likes were delivered to our account within 10 minutes. If fake Influencers can make $10,000 (or sometimes a great deal more) for an Instagram post, spending $50 to guarantee you'll get the response your client is expecting sounds like pretty good insurance. Especially if these seemingly popular posts and videos get shared outside of Instagram to YouTube, Facebook, and others.

*Many paid posts also come with videos, like this one featuring a Lenovo Yoga Book. It is
interesting to note it has only 520 views. Many Influencers typically have high volumes
of followers and views across many social networks. Of course, all of that can be bought
too. It takes a lot of effort to keep all those faux plates spinning.*

I know I'm really throwing @miss.everywhere under the bus here, but maybe she can get a paid post from a bus company before it hits.

Depending on the popularity of this book, @miss.everywhere may end up getting heaps of *actual* followers. So, I suppose, there's that. Maybe that will get me back on her Christmas Card list, but I doubt it.

Case Study: @amazingthailand

Now that you know how to validate if an Influencer is legitimate, let's use what we've learned to take a look at another account. I picked this one because I took a closer look at them several months ago in regards to a project I did in Thailand, which I talk more about in Appendix A (All about Trey). To summarize: I do fun "photo walk" events around the world to meet fans and we wander around to take photos together. A lot of times, after the walk, I also give a little art talk and do Q&As. On occasion, I invite other social media Influencers out with me to create a bit of a multiplier effect. Usually, I'll hire these people or they'll be brought on board by one of our sponsors.

For example, when I was in Vienna, Austria, I had a photo walk and invited the painter Meagan Morrison (@travelwritedraw on Instagram). She was great! Also, she's totally legit. We had a fun time leading the photo walk together, and, later, when we went back to the ballroom at the Ritz-Carlton (our sponsor), I gave a 30-minute art talk, while she did a fabulous painting. It was a lot of fun, so I decided to try to do more of this in the future.

When I was planning a visit to Thailand, an Influencer agency started recommending possible collaboration partners. You can see one of the slides they sent me.

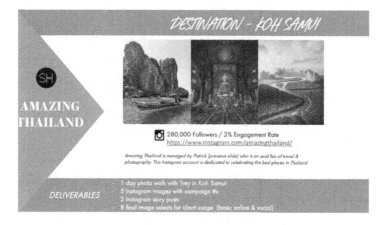

This is one of many suggestions sent to us by a supposedly trustworthy looking social media agency.

Most people don't know how to do the legwork to verify that Influencers are legitimate yet. I do. I'm actually incredibly busy working on the art business and I don't have time to do other people's work for them, but I often end up doing precisely that. Maybe you know what I mean.

Anyway, I looked up this @amazingthailand account and I eyeballed it. Nice photos, for sure. It was clearly one of those "aggregation" accounts that reuses amazing images from other people. There's nothing really wrong with that, as long as they own rights to the photo, or if those photos are part of the Creative Commons, and they give credit. That all seemed okay.

But then, when I looked into their data with Socialblade.com, I saw the incredibly obvious follow/unfollow pattern. Take a look at the follower stats for @amazingthailand yourself below. As you may remember, I am making some bold assumptions from the data. You, the reader, can decide for yourself whether you agree with my speculation.

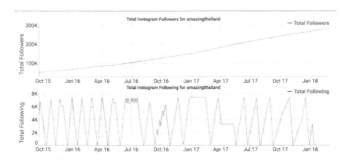

It appears that @amazingthailand has employed an automated script (or bot) to automatically follow the limit of 7,500 people and then unfollow them over time.
Source: Socialblade.com

Data-heads can see a pattern immediately. For the rest of us, I'll break it down. Look at the bottom chart first. You can see the Following count, the number of accounts @amazingthailand is following, shoot up to 7,500 (the cap) very quickly, then drop back down to zero again. Although you can see a few different shapes in the graph, all more or less follow this pattern: following, then unfollowing, as many people as possible within a short time. The sharp fluctuations and regular geometric patterns also indicate that this is an automated process.

Now if you look at the upper chart, you can see the slow accretion of followers. Obviously, this method works very well and that is why so many fake Influencer accounts employ it. It's important to remember that their followers are completely random people and there is unlikely any significant demographic overlap that would be interesting to a brand.

The Influencer agency was pretty excited to offer me the husband and wife team that runs the account of @amazingthailand as a fantastic package deal. If I hadn't run the data myself, I might have hired them. From the data, it appears evident to me that this couple was open to employing unscrupulous methods for gaining followers, so I didn't want anything to do with them. Ethics aside, their followers are also completely worthless to me. It would do nothing for me professionally and even less for the brands I work with, because the follow/unfollow tactic ends up collecting completely random people and bots, rather than building an engaged audience.

I've received countless collaboration pitches from agencies for Influencers who turn out to be fraudulent. This was just one example.

And, of course, this follow/unfollow method of gaining followers is explicitly against Instagram's Terms of Service. You'll see later in the book that, even though I presented this to Instagram security, they did nothing.

HOW TO VET INFLUENCERS IF YOU'RE A BRAND, MARKETER, AGENCY, OR BUSINESS

If *you* were in charge of finding Influencers for a big brand, would you have taken any of the steps we just discussed before engaging in a contract with either of those Influencers? Let's say you had $75,000 to spend on flying one of these Influencers to an exotic location and paying her to share a few posts on Instagram of her experience. Would you have chosen @theblondeabroad or @miss.everywhere? This is the dilemma faced by thousands of marketing people every day. Brands have to make decisions about how to spend hundreds of millions of dollars to promote their brands and they're doing it with fairly limited information.

Major brands across every industry—especially fashion, luxury travel, cars, airlines, restaurants, and entertainment—are parting with hundreds of millions of dollars in the same way. They are paying fake Instagram "Influencers" to promote their brand. These fake Influencers are deliberately pretending to be more influential than they are in order to mislead and deceive these companies.

In this section, we talk about how to avoid making this mistake, as a brand, marketing agency, or business.

Whenever you engage with a potential new Influencer, it's essential to do a deep dive in the "investigation" phase. This will not be something you can take on in about 15 minutes. Plan on spending 4-8 hours really digging and getting into the weeds.

Since none of the techniques I review in the previous section are conclusive on their own, they should be taken together to help create an informed opinion. I recommend the following steps.

Step 1: Look up Their Historical Follower Growth on Socialblade.com Or another Service

Remember that there are two main ways people buy followers:

- Buy huge swaths of followers. This is a dumb approach. You'll easily be able to detect this fraud by the big numbers that spike up in irregular patterns.
- Buy followers that are delivered in a steady stream over months and year. This is a smarter approach because these follower acquisition patterns are more difficult to detect.

When you look at historical follower growth, look for the above patterns to detect devious behavior. For more on this, check out the previous section, where I break it down in detail.

Step 2: Ask Your Influencer Lots of Questions

Another way of vetting your Influencer is by asking them some pointed questions. The answers to these questions will not necessarily indicate whether or not your Influencer is 100% authentic, but you'll get a better sense of their authenticity this way. At the very least, your Influencer will know you keep a close eye on your marketing spend and that you're a savvy buyer.

Below, I've listed a few questions you might think about asking. You should adapt these questions for the particular social network(s) you'll be hiring your Influencer to use. For instance, it's appropriate for brands or agencies to specifically request YouTube viewing statistics for all the videos concerned. My friend Jared Polin, who has a huge number of subscribers on YouTube himself, told me over email that he's seen all sorts of fishy behavior, especially when it comes to money deals.

According to Jared, a lot of less scrupulous YouTubers will buy a ton of fake views to make it seem like the brand was getting a good deal.

Here's a list of questions you might ask your future partner Influencer:

1) Have you ever purchased a follower, a like, a comment, a video play, or a story play?
2) Do you use any third party apps or software to automate your responses to comments on a post?
3) (If the user has a "verified" blue tick) Did you earn or purchase your blue tick from a third party?
4) Have you ever participated in a "pod" or engagement/follower exchange before?
5) Please send screenshots of all the Insights for your account that show audience breakdown, profile visits, countries, reach, and impressions. (I have attached an example from my personal account.)
6) Please share your media kit that illustrates your reach across the social media platforms where you engage. (For an example of this, you can look at my media kit at www.StuckinCustoms.com/media-kit)
7) Do you have references from other brands and agencies you've worked with?

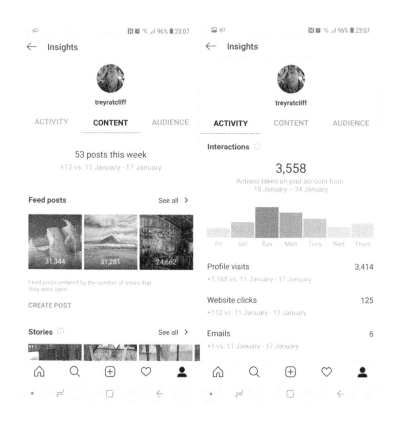

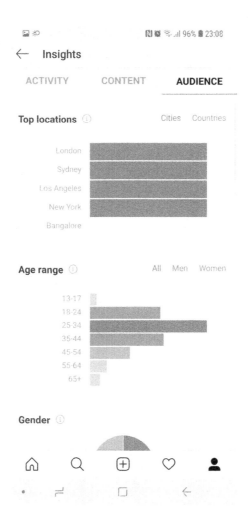

These are some of the stats that all agencies or brands should request from Influencers. These statistics are available in the Instagram app. Now, many of these numbers can be affected by bots, so they can't be trusted entirely, but this information should be included as part of the overall "investigation" phase. Note: Instagram has recently announced that even more insights and stats will become available to Top Influencers soon. Source: My Insight Screens from @treyratcliff

Step 3: Deep Dive into a Selection of Posts to Read All Comments and Likes

I'll warn you now that this will be the most time-consuming step. I recommend opening the Instagram website on a computer or laptop because it allows you to open several tabs at once for comparison.

First, look at all your target Influencer's photos over the last few years. If they appear to have built a substantial following in months, rather than years, that's a red flag. Assuming the account is more than a year old, do you see steady growth in likes and comments? Of course, it's natural for accounts to start small then gain more traction over time.

Look to see if some posts have way more comments and likes than others. Why? When Influencers mention a brand, it's usually a paid post. That's usually when they'll buy extra comments and likes to impress and achieve their KPIs (Key Performance Indicators). Sometimes a post garners more comments for innocent reasons such as they are running a contest, have a particularly awesome photo, or there is some other content inside that is more compelling than usual. Some Influencers will blame spikes in engagement on spam and bots, which might be a contributing factor, so what you're looking for are patterns.

Now, hopefully, this Influencer has made sponsored posts for other brands. You'll want to pay particular attention to these by reading all the comments and responses to comments. If you notice most responses are vague and/or a string of emojis, the Influencer is likely paying a service to auto-respond to comments. Auto-responding to comments is a bit "greyer" on the ethics scale. Many people simply believe it is good manners to reply to people personally. But that takes a lot of time on your phone, especially if you're getting a ton of comments. I can see people paying a bot to respond, but I don't think it's because of good manners; I believe most people set up an auto-response bot to deceive brands into thinking there are more comments than there really are.

Watch for reply comments that come in batches like this that appear to be automated to rack up the comment count. Note if you use Instagram on the web, you see comments in more of a chronological order and you can see when the bot scripts check in to dump auto-replies. Note that sometimes the replies are not simple emojis like this. They can say things like "Thanks dear" or empty things of this nature.

Look for common bot activity. Note the unusual comments, and note who made the comment. Also, note if other users are making the exact same comment.

Suspicious comments sometimes stick out like sore thumbs. Remember this sponsored post from Dec 14th? I'll never forget two of my literary idols, @omyma_mimo and @habiba20bc0 or their, classic catch-phrase: "Snow fairy 🌼🌼🌼☃️☃️☃️😂😂". Oh, stop it you two. Get a room. However, if you scroll further down, you'll see that same classic line, complete with emojis, repeated by the indomitable @hassanalserafy_.

There's another set of rather obvious repeats. As you can see above, @havvac508b commented, "😍😍😍I want to join you babe😍😍😍😍😍😍". That @havvac508b, he's a real charmer. But so is @shahbaa.aaa, who said the same thing, with the exact same emoticons, only a few seconds earlier. Keep track of these names, as you may see them across many posts.

The metric brands and agencies care most about is the comment count, because it indicates that people are actually taking the time to write a comment rather than just make a lazy like. Since Influencers know very few brand representatives will manually check comments, auto-responses are an easy way to inflate the number of comments. In the final marketing report about engagement on a post, it's helpful to check that the Influencer's responses to comments have been subtracted from the total number of comments. If not, the Influencer's own responses can add up to hundreds and sometimes thousands of extra comments per photo, while they shouldn't really count as new engagement.

Next, examine what kind of comments the posts are getting. Do all of them sound believable, or are there many short, vague comments that could apply to any photo such as, "What a place," "Amazing Snap," and this sort of thing? Huge strings of emojis are a telltale sign of generic comments purchased on the cheap.

Then, do many of the commenters' names look suspicious? If you are seeing a lot of names like "Create_Travel_" or "Beauty543" or "Fash.ion.Style", it's time to start popping open new tabs for each one.

I also suggest diving into the likes for each post and studying a good sample size of the accounts that made those likes. However, this approach is not always practical, since investigating a good sample size of likes for a post with, say, 5,000 likes could take days. However, if you see some fake comments above, chances are that there will be fake likes as well. Anyone that buys fake comments will likely be buying fake likes too.

Step 4: Face-To-Face

Lastly, I always suggest a face-to-face meeting, even if it has to be over Skype. You can tell a lot about a person in this way, especially if you're good at reading people. To save a bit of time, you can combine this with Step 2 by asking them those challenging questions in person and watching their expression as they respond. When I do this, I treat it like a standard job interview and ask a wide variety of questions

Also, make sure they understand that you will be asking them to turn over 100% of their data and stats for all photos associated with the campaign. It's perfectly okay for you to do this, as any first engagement should be thought of as a trial.

Bonus Step: Build a Fake Account of Your Own

Have someone at the agency or brand create their own fake account. It can be based on anything and it doesn't need to be a person. For example, make an account all about cookies and just add photos of cookies.

Why do this? Because you'll learn, first-hand, how it is done. Try several different services and you'll begin to think like the scammers. You'll become even more observant. Also, you'll be able to stay on top of the latest trends and clever ways to circumnavigate Instagram's rules and trick brands.

HOW TO SPOT FAKE ACCOUNTS IF YOU'RE INSTAGRAM— AND WHAT YOU SHOULD DO ABOUT IT

As you can see below, eight months after we bought 104,000 followers for our fake account, @genttravel still has over 84,000 of them. That's quite a bit.

Here's our favorite assistant, once again. Oh, if you want to follow his real account,
where he unfortunately doesn't post as many selfies of his chiseled visage,
go follow @tanegent. He's turned into a good photographer,
no doubt through my excellent and selfless guidance.

Why hasn't Instagram stepped in to shut down this account or remove its fake followers? Here are a few reasons why Instagram and Facebook may not be tackling this problem head-on:

- **They like the big engagement numbers** as much as the brands do, because it makes Instagram look more successful. Wall Street likes that, too. All the top people at Instagram and Facebook have a lot of stock options, so bigger numbers translate to millions or billions of dollars in compensation for them. So, why would Instagram want to seriously address the fraud problem, and cull bot accounts, if doing so is not in their financial best interest?

- **They aren't evil—they're just confused.** This is a complex issue and they are not sure how to fix the problem. I think there is just a lot of confusion there and no one can figure out what to do.

- **They are waiting on an AI to clean up the fraudulent accounts.** Maybe they're working on a super-secret technology that will be able to quickly and accurately identify the bad guys. However, this is a clear case of coevolution—the bad guys will figure out new unscrupulous techniques to employ faster than the AI can evolve. I'm not counting on AI to save the day here.

- **They're bolstering their team security humans and not doing it fast enough.** Today, they have a team of 10,000 security humans working to identify and fix issues like this and that team is supposed to grow to 20,000.

- **They know it's a problem, but nobody is talking about it.** They think they can coast for a while longer.

- **They know it's a problem, but it's not as big a problem as some of the other complicated and serious issues that have been in the spotlight**, such as fake news, online bullying, or election manipulation. They're spending time and resources to tackle these big ones first.

I am not the first to spot all the gaping holes in Instagram's armor, but I wanted answers, not just theories. So I went to Instagram to ask them myself what they're doing to stop widespread user fraud and to prevent companies from getting scammed while doing business using these platforms.

Over the years, I've had repeated discussions with Instagram and Facebook about these problems (remember that Facebook bought Instagram for $1 billion in 2012). I knew one of the founders of Instagram, Mike Krieger, before he started the company. I also spent the day with Mark Zuckerberg some time ago, when he invited me to Facebook Headquarters.

Hi, Mark! Here's a picture of Zuck holding one of my prints from many years ago, when we met for a few hours at Facebook's headquarters. Later, at their hackathon, I snapped a shot of him that he used as his FB profile photo for ages, so I thought that was pretty cool. I hope he agrees with my points in this book and some possible solutions, and that we're still kinda friends after he reads this whole thing!

When I brought up these issues of Instagram fraud with Krieger, he did not have anything specific to say. He instead routed me back to Instagram public relations and security teams. Look, I don't blame him. What could he publicly say that their PR teams could not say?

One of the PR team's jobs is to deflect negative questions from the media. Those poor people. I didn't want to subject them to more deflection, but I got in line anyway and waited my turn to ask the Instagram PR team some hard questions. It's a hard job and they are just stuck in a rigid system that doesn't allow them to give satisfactory answers, even to plain questions. They really have no authority to write honest, interesting responses.

In this case, the PR team tried to explain this fraud away as a minor issue and they point to automated services they have that clean up the fake accounts. It is clear to me that these services do a lousy job of identifying and addressing the fake accounts and activity. As a reminder, no automated Instagram service has yet flagged @genttravel as problematic.

I have also talked to many other senior people I know at these companies. They absolutely know, and admit, that the fake engagement economy is a problem on these services. They all spoke to me off the record, of course, and I'm not here to name names. Well, except for @miss.everywhere.

Throughout the book, I believe I make a strong case that it is indeed in Instagram's long-term best interest to clean up their platform. Otherwise, eventually, no one will trust in the platform. When people stop believing in the veracity of followers, likes, and comments, this entire Instagram economy could collapse. Why would advertisers continue to spend money on Instagram Influencers when they can't believe the numbers being reported back? It's a looming issue that is only getting worse.

In this chapter, we take a look at what Instagram and Facebook are doing to combat these fraudulent engagement issues. I share some conversations I've had with folks inside these organizations and share some of my thoughts about their responses.

INSTAGRAM PUBLIC RELATIONS AND INSTAGRAM SECURITY RESPOND

As mentioned, the conversation began when I reached out to Mike Krieger, one of the founders of Instagram. I knew him pre-Instagram, so I often reach out to him, although we had never spoken about this topic. He pointed me to the Instagram Communications team. Here's what happened when I spoke, on the record, with a couple of folks on Instagram's Communications team.

As part of my research for this book, I went out and looked for some fraudulent accounts. In less than 48 hours I found more than 200 accounts I suspected to be cheating the system. It was remarkably easy. When I talked with Instagram, I also asked if I could send 10 of these suspicious accounts over for Instagram's security team to review. They said yes and warned me that any account sent to Instagram security found to have fraudulent numbers could be terminated.

Besides emailing over the ten suspicious accounts, I wrote down a few questions I wanted to ask on the phone, which I detail below. They gave me answers on the phone but asked that I wait for a follow-up email for an on-the-record response. A while later, an Instagram spokesperson sent an email back to me. There are some parts of that email I can quote, which I have. They've asked me to summarize other parts.

To start, they responded with this very official-sounding statement.

> We take spam, inauthentic and other abusive behavior very seriously.
>
> We consider services that automate or sell likes or follows to be spam, and we aggressively remove them from the platform. When we find "spammy" activity, we work to counter and prevent it, including blocking accounts and removing violating content all at once. We review suspicious activity closely and take the time to understand how to help prevent similar activity in the future.
>
> Our internal estimates show that spam accounts make up a small

fraction of Instagram's monthly active user base.

Below are the questions I asked, their summarized responses, and my thoughts on those responses.

1. **How do the bots that use automated follow, unfollow, like, and comment functionality work?**

The Instagram Communications team actually provided a pretty good answer to this one. I've summarized what they've said about each method below:

- **Programs and scripts that run locally, on a user's computer:** These sorts of scripts search for a given hashtag, and, when they find it, send out likes, follows, and comments on posts that match the hashtag in hopes of receiving a like or follow in return. This engagement model relies on reciprocity to succeed (just like we've discussed in this book). These programs and scripts are generally paid, for but can be free and/or open source.
- **Purchased services where the service provider runs automated activity on behalf of the user:** The user provides their credentials to the service. The service provider logs in and performs similar actions as in the previous example. This type of service requires no technical skill and is highly automated.
- **Buying likes and follows from a farm of pre-existing fake accounts:** This is less prevalent. Instagram said they are often able to police these accounts and shut them down *en masse*. Their response didn't answer the question of how this particular approach works, however.
- **Engagement pods:** These pods often use browser plugins that will automatically like posts or comments from a desktop or laptop computer. Instagram said this behavior is some of the

hardest to detect, since it does a good job of mimicking a real action from a real user's browser.

2. **How many bots use the web interface and use scripts and scrape info?**

The Instagram Communications team did not give us an answer to this one. They did say that some bots will engage in scraping behavior as part of their audience discovery process—the hashtag searching method mentioned above—but that the primary goal of these bots is to attract reciprocal engagement behavior.

3. **What are you doing in general to mitigate spam, inauthentic, or abusive behavior?**

Not surprisingly, the Instagram Communications team had an excessively long response to this one. In summary, they said they have a combination of automated and manual systems to combat fraud like this. The automated systems are largely based on machine learning algorithms that try to detect suspicious non-human behaviors. The manual systems rely on a team of 10,000 folks working on safety and security topics. They told me that this team will be growing to 20,000 individuals in 2019.

The Instagram Communications team pointed to a variety of legalese policies, guidelines, and terms of use, which I've summarized below. There are also links in case you want to check it out (warning—these are kind of long and boring to read. Instagram should already know, based on all their analyses about user engagement, that nobody is going to read all these policies).

- **Platform Policies #18:** "Don't participate in any "like", "share", "comment" or "follower" exchange programs." https://www.instagram.com/about/legal/terms/api/
- **Community Guidelines Bullet 3:** "Help us stay spam-free by

not artificially collecting likes, followers, or shares, posting repetitive comments or content, or repeatedly contacting people
for commercial purposes without their consent."
https://help.instagram.com/477434105621119/

- **Terms of Use: #3**: "You are responsible for any activity that
  occurs through your account and you agree you will not sell,
  transfer, license or assign your account, followers, username, or
  any account rights."
  https://help.instagram.com/478745558852511

- **Terms of Use #10**: "You must not access Instagram's private
  API by means other than those permitted by Instagram." Use
  of Instagram's API is subject to a separate set of terms:
  http://instagram.com/about/legal/terms/api/

Since we emailed them, the Instagram Communications team have
also written a blog post on how they are approaching the issue of fraudulent engagement. They have launched some machine learning tools to
identify fraudulently-procured engagement. In this post, they said:

> Starting today, we will begin removing inauthentic likes, follows
> and comments from accounts that use third-party apps to boost
> their popularity. We've built machine learning tools to help identify
> accounts that use these services and remove the inauthentic activity.
> Accounts we identify using these services will receive an in-app
> message alerting them that we have removed the inauthentic likes,
> follows and comments given by their account to others.

You can read the whole thing here: https://instagram-
press.com/blog/2018/11/19/reducing-inauthentic-activity-on-insta-
gram/

As I mention further down, whatever system they've implemented
is still not doing a great job. Most of the ten fraudulent accounts I
identified in my original email to them are still very much alive and

kicking.

4. Why don't you sue those Follower/Like/Comment companies for being injurious and get them to turn over their client list?

No response on this one. I still think it's a good idea.

5. Why would Instagram provide an API that lets a third party follow/comment/like on their behalf? I can't think of a useful use-case for that. All following should be done while I am logged into the app on my phone, right? If you are disabling that, why was it allowed in the first place? Why did it take so long to remove?

Same as above—no response here, although I still think it's a good idea.

6. What if you only allowed Instagram access via the app instead of the web. Would this eliminate some of the bad activity?

The Instagram Communications team said that it is unlikely that restricting activity to the app would effectively deter bad actors on the platform because bots typically mimic IOS or Android behavior in an attempt to circumvent Instagram policies and "blend in" with real humans.

7. If you do remove access to the API that allows follows/likes/comments, then what will you do about the hundreds of millions of ill-gotten gains? Do you have the ability to backtrack and purge?

No answer on this one.

8. In terms of pods: do you think megapods with 1000+ people inside are a problem? Can you detect it? Why did it take Buzzfeed writing this article to make you go out and do something about it? Some of those group names like "Daily Instagram Engagement" are incredibly obvious. What about groups not on Facebook?

The Instagram Communications team said they recently took action on a number of groups on the platform promoting podding behavior. I personally don't think they've done enough to combat this behavior, as it's still very easy to join pods and podding groups.

9. I found over 200 bad actors in 48 hours, and I barely tried. Why doesn't Instagram have people doing the same thing? The patterns are obvious, so why isn't there a process, manual or automatic, for clearing these accounts or deleting the ill-gotten gains?

For this one, they did investigate the 10 I sent over, and they found suspicious activity on many accounts (although they weren't able to comment on which ones specifically). They admitted to being able to identify that some of these accounts had bought likes and followers from inauthentic and automated accounts.

I wanted to see for myself if they had taken action against any of the accounts I had flagged. Let's go back to the 10 suspicious accounts I initially sent the Instagram Security team. Here are the accounts, which I anonymized:

Generic Names	Followers (April 1, 2018)	Followers (Dec 24, 2018)	% Growth
Suspect 1	566,261	966,000	41.38%
Suspect 2	127,288	812,000	84.32%
Suspect 3	463,878	1,050,000	55.82%
Suspect 4	195,004	298,000	34.56%
Suspect 5	721,363	1,000,000	27.86%
Suspect 6	182,370	174,000	-4.81%
Suspect 7	285,940	319,000	10.36%
Suspect 8	606,965	925,000	34.38%
Suspect 9	246,547	317,000	22.22%
Suspect 10	1,176,561	1,200,000	1.95%

In column 1, you see their follower count in April of 2018, when I first sent the email to Instagram Communications. The next column shows December of 2018, six months later. You can see quite clearly that despite finding "evidence of suspicious activity":

a) Instagram security did not ban their accounts
b) Followers were not culled—even if they were, it was effectively useless, because most of our suspects had tremendous follower growth in the 6 months afterward

INSTAGRAM STATS SUMMARY / USER SUMMARY (2017-02		
DATE		FOLLOWERS
2017-02-26	Sun	-15	408,762
2017-02-27	Mon	-86	408,676
2017-02-28	Tue	-42	408,634
2017-03-01	Wed	-37	408,597
2017-03-02	Thu	-38	408,559
2018-03-28	Wed	+55,778	464,337
2018-03-29	Thu	+51,158	515,495
2018-03-30	Fri	+6,045	521,540
2018-03-31	Sat	+37,784	559,324
2018-04-01	Sun	+6,937	566,261 ⊘ LIVE

This is an example of one of the accounts (Suspect #1) that I sent to Instagram security. It appears this guy purchased 150,000 followers that were delivered in 5 days. Source: Socialblade.com

Of those that did not grow dramatically, it appears they bought a big following at the start of our tracking, and then perhaps stopped buying because they were already in the top 1% of the most followed users.

I don't think the 10,000 people in Instagram security are incompetent. Maybe they're just too busy and overworked. Maybe they are busy fixing other problems that they deem more important. I don't know what to think.

What follows are some ideas on how to fix many of the problems in the existing system.

Possible Solution #1: Flip the Business Model
Facebook has been very prominent in the news lately. There are some

chinks in the Facebook armor causing anguish both inside and outside of the company. Part of this is due to the nature of their business model. Today, Facebook and Instagram have very similar business models. They acquire as many users as possible and then sell their data and attention to advertisers and third parties, primarily through advertisements.

So, what do I mean by "flip the business model"? Well, instead of generating all its revenue from advertising, Instagram (and therefore, Facebook) could begin to charge users to use their service. This model would look more like what Netflix, Pandora, and Spotify do today, with tiered pricing systems for users and a lowered (or completely removed) reliance on advertisements. This switch has several aspects I'll talk through here, but I contend it would ultimately please more stakeholders than the current model does.

Flickr has recently switched to a similar model. While there has been backlash, all the serious photographers and artists stayed on because of the new benefits of the paid model.

If Instagram began charging users a few dollars a month, there could be many immediate advantages for users:

1) Users who pay would no longer be subjected to advertising.
2) Users could have the option of returning their feed to chronological order, since the algorithm's goal will no longer be to maximize your screen time in order to maximize advertising income.
3) Resources inside Facebook and Instagram that are currently spending time on maximizing the advertising code and algorithms would be freed up to instead give users lots of new features.
4) User data would be less likely to be sold to third parties, as advertisers would play less of a role in the revenue ecosystem.
5) This model would keep the bots at bay. Bot farms wouldn't pay millions of dollars a month to keep their bot army going. For

example, Netflix doesn't have hordes of bot activity ramping up view counts or thumbs-upping shows to create fake metrics.

6) Lastly, Instagram and Facebook would have everyone's credit card number stored, which would support the ability to offer all other sorts of other additional services through the platform. Facebook has already introduced the option to buy some products and services (like event tickets) directly on the platform. Having a higher percentage of users with credit cards information already stored on Instagram would decrease microtransaction friction. What does that mean? When a service like iTunes already has your credit card number, it's much easier to make purchases, because buying is now a one-step process.

Now, some users would be upset that they have to pay money to use a service that was previously free. However, *users are already upset* with these platforms, for a variety of reasons:

- Users don't understand where their personal data is going, who has access to it, and how it is being used.
- Advertising appears intrusive, excessive, and overly targeted to individual users.
- The algorithm determining what content appears in their feed seems to prioritize irrelevant or incendiary content.
- Some people are losing trust in the platform because they think Facebook is actively trying to set political agendas.

Photographer Thomas Hawk is especially frustrated about advertising on Instagram. Over email, he told me, "Alas, I am not the biggest Instagram fan. I'm not sure why. I think a big part of it is the ads. I hate ads. I go on there for 2 minutes and then start seeing ads for Butterfinger candy bars or worse, and I just close it."

Here's one of those Instagram ads that @thomashawk is talking about. I picked the first ad on my stream, and this one looks particularly sketchy. I am fairly suspicious of anyone selling a Nintendo Switch and 6 games for $20.

To me, introducing a user-paid subscription option for Instagram is an obvious strategy to pursue. That said, there are a couple of downsides:

- Instagram, today, has users across the world—some from countries with lower per-capita income, where paying a monthly subscription fee is not a realistic possibility. A paid solution like this wouldn't be accessible to these users unless there were much less expensive subscription options in these places.

- It is possible that Instagram has run the numbers, and they've found that the revenue-per-user is higher through advertising rather than a user-paid model.

At the end of the day, it may be worth taking a small hit to revenue to improve the overall user experience. Taking a paid approach, like the one I've outlined, would create a safe, walled-garden experience with none of the myriad complications that come with an advertising model.

Facebook Ennui with Its Own Current Model

I know many VPs at these organizations personally and many of them don't like the advertising model. Relying on advertising means Instagram and Facebook must devote a large number of employees to support the advertising model. There are employees working on selling ads, supporting advertisers, and, from a product perspective, determining the maximum number of ads a user can see before they get frustrated with the experience.

Secondly, there have been several issues in the news lately around the misuse and mismanagement of user data, and the sharing of that data with third parties, such as advertisers. One such example was the scandal involving Facebook and Cambridge Analytica. Cambridge Analytica gained access to extremely deep personal data of Facebook users. It appears this data was cleverly used to push political ads to people in an attempt to manipulate the political views of those users and influence their vote in the 2016 U.S. election.[5]

It's not just elections that can be swayed. There are rumors that Russia's Internet Research Agency used the same methods to instigate a negative backlash towards *Star Wars: The Last Jedi,* even though I did not need Russians to tell me this was a terrible movie.[6] When Facebook sells user data to third parties, these third parties can help foment unrest over anything from political elections to space operas.

Many similar issues have made the news. That negative press has had deleterious effects on Facebook's overall brand image, as well as their stock price.

The last year has seen several legal and ethical accusations leveled against Facebook really take a toll on employee morale. Many employees suspect these allegations are not just allegations and question whether Facebook is heading in the right direction. Meanwhile, Facebook is driven to both continue to grow market share and maximize advertising income. A recent article in The Verge highlighted the issue, citing an internal Facebook employee survey that found that "the number of employees who said Facebook is good for the world declined 19 percentage points in a year."[7]

I believe Facebook can still turn it around internally if they have the stomach to pivot. It would be painful, but ultimately it would be better for employees, users, and the world in general.

Amping up Revenue with Shopping

Now, although advertising may play less of a role in the new user-paid revenue model, Facebook could open a pathway for advertisers to pour significant money into the system by adding another "shopping-like" feature.

One of the next big features that Facebook, and Instagram need to focus on is the ability to shop right on the platform. Facebook, in particular, has already dipped its toe in the water by offering the ability to purchase event tickets directly on the platform.

To monetize the shopping features, these social networks would obviously take a percentage of the sale, which is fine. Many other platforms do this. Shopify, for instance, takes about 3% of each transaction.

Also, when Facebook and Instagram roll out these features, they'll only need to pry our credit card info from us once. Then, they'll be able to store that information, which allows them to open the floodgates to impulse purchases for the foreseeable future.

Influencer Brokering Directly Through Instagram

Instagram could also create a mechanism for brands and agencies to do deals directly with verified Influencers, by acting as a trusted broker. Imagine the reaction from an Influencer who received a message like this, from Instagram itself, that read:

> Hi Kiersten,
>
> I'm Mark from the Instagram Influencer department. We have an offer for you from Tesla. They would like to give you one of their cars for a year, as well as $50,000 cash (we would take a $5,000 fee). In exchange, they ask that you take and share at least one photo per month on Instagram, featuring fun things you are doing with the car, and share at least one Instagram story per week that mentions the car. Click below to accept this offer and get follow up information, and let me know if you have any questions.

This is a simplified example, and obviously, a partnership like this might be a bit more complex than that, but you get the idea.

Furthermore, the brands and agencies would have access to all the pertinent campaign outcome metrics, right from Instagram, so they could also report more accurately on the effectiveness of the campaign. Great idea, eh? Yeah, I got a ton of 'em. I'm an idea machine.

AN INTERNAL SEA CHANGE

By charging each user only a few dollars a month, Facebook and Instagram would immediately create a meaningful, viable, alternative revenue stream to advertising. They can save money by reducing or getting rid of their advertising departments completely, and perhaps re-purpose them to build a good shopping experience or other features. Now, it sounds a bit haughty of me to say, "Hey Facebook and Instagram, a few billion a month is more than enough… just calm down a little."

But, it's true. I have no doubt they can run with a nice profit as they continue to add more goods and services to the platform that their customers might want to buy. Now, Facebook will certainly take a hit on Wall Street as they pivot around, but they could innovate again by setting the stage for the next generation of trusted social networking and online commerce.

I speak for many people when I say I would rather spend my money on Facebook to buy goods and services that I choose, rather than have Facebook and Instagram sell my data and my attention to advertisers.

POSSIBLE SOLUTION #2: USE MORE SCRIPTS TO HIGHLIGHT SUSPICIOUS BEHAVIOR

There's a saying that goes, "You have to play the game to win the game." Instagram security could do just that, by creating fake Influencer accounts and buying followers, just like I did. Once they've done that, they could examine those accounts and see if they are real people. If they're not, delete them.

It's a simple, but time-intensive, process to do manually. To decrease manual time spent on this task, they could create a script that goes out looking for suspicious accounts and spits out a ton of results every day to review.

Rinse and repeat this process at the 100+ places on the web where you can currently buy followers and relentlessly cull the bots.

POSSIBLE SOLUTION #3: MOBILE APP ONLY + MONTHLY FORCED PASSWORD ROTATION

To solve most of the issues associated with automated follows, likes, and comments, all Instagram needs to do is require that all these actions be done exclusively through the Instagram mobile app.

Currently, the bot problem persists because users have given their username and password to third parties, via other apps and websites. I realized this when buying followers, likes, and comments for our fake Influencer account. For this experiment, we tested a variety of websites and apps and almost all of them required us to provide our username and password for Instagram, which allows them to access our account without the need for an API token from Instagram. Huge numbers of Instagram users have done the same, giving these programs the right to act on their behalf, on Instagram, using automated scripts.

Remember when we talked about podding—the creation of groups of Instagram users who brigade new posts, with comments and likes, to make it look like these are popular? We also discussed how the podding process can be automated. One of the many websites and apps we used to support the creation of our fake account was Fame Boom, which has over a million downloads on Android alone. To use the app, you need to give them your Instagram username and password. It's only after you've supplied your login credentials that the app can use automated scripts to have your account automatically follow, like, and comment on posts.

To slow down the bots, Instagram could force a password change every month, making us all log back in with it. Currently, once you've given a third party your Instagram login details, they can act on your behalf indefinitely—as long as they don't log out and you don't change your password.

Of course, a forced monthly password change would be annoying to users. However, updating passwords on a schedule is becoming a fairly common practice in the corporate world, where employees are required to create new passwords for their corporate email accounts as often as every 90 days. Requiring this sort of password refresh on Instagram would dramatically slow down the thousands of sketchy companies out there that already have hundreds of millions of Instagram usernames and passwords.

I also don't think we would be sacrificing significant functionality. I cannot think of a legitimate use case for which a third party would need to access my account to follow, like, or comment on my behalf. One possible exception is if an Influencer hired an agency or had their assistant—a third party, manage their account. To solve that edge case, the client could simply give their login details to that third party, who could only act on their behalf via the mobile app.

I am sure many clever readers have ideas of their own. There should be a more open conversation in public circles about ways we can all work together to maintain strong foundations within these platforms we increasingly depend upon.

Here's a place where perhaps we can have an open conversation until we can find a better venue: https://www.facebook.com/groups/UnderTheInfluenceBook.

One rule! Be nice in there. It's a good rule for life.

RESPONSES FROM @MISS.EVERYWHERE

Let's end this chapter by going back full-circle with @miss.everywhere.

This book began as a shorter article for an online publication, which featured @miss.everywhere as a case example. The editor suggested I reach out to @miss.everywhere to get her side of the story. I absolutely agreed. In fact, I was really looking forward to it. Personally, I find what she appears to be doing to be ethically unsound. To recap what we found earlier:

- It appears that @miss.everywhere trades fake followers, likes, and comments for luxury travel deals, goodies, and cash.
- If my analyses are correct, her actions are directly impacting hard-working travel journalists, who are playing the game by the rules and have years of skillful talent.
- Her too-good-to-be-true fancy travel photos, where she depicts her enjoyment of an idyllic life, create a false and unrealistic narrative. This narrative probably contributes to undue anxiety to others and may be spawning even more Instagram copycats, who may use this same sort of illicit behavior to exacerbate the problem.

I used Facebook Messenger to befriend @miss.everywhere. Much to my surprise, she accepted. However, that's about where it ended. I sent her a list of questions (which I share below), but, after quite a bit of back and forth, she declined to answer them and to be interviewed for this book. As you'll see, I began the set of questions with an emollient approach.

Here's the list of questions I sent her:

- On many posts, I see you can have around 20,000 likes and around 1,000 comments. How are you so successful?
- How did you get so many followers?
- Do you get these free hotel stays, cash, and other goodies because your numbers are so high?
- Sometimes luxury travel photographers are friends with the same kinds of people on Instagram (pods) and they support one another. Do you do anything like that? How does it work?
- Have you ever purchased followers, and how much did they cost?
- Tell me more about how you bought them, how does that work?
- Have you also purchased likes and comments? How does that work?
- Do you also have a service that automatically posts replies for you to people who comment?
- Do you use a service to automatically respond to other people's comments? That really makes the comment count go way up, eh?
- In the middle of July, it looks like you bought 60,000 followers over a 5 day span. What's that about, yo?
- Do you think it is fraudulent to fake numbers so you can get free trips, goodies, and cash? And, if not, do you think lying to big companies is fraudulent?
- Do you believe that buying followers likes and comments is ethical?

- When you use your high number of followers and high engagement to get free hotels, travel, goodies, and cash, do you think this is fraud?
- Do you speak Spanish?
- Are you popular in Mexico and Latin America?
- Your followers are predominantly from these three countries: Mexico, Colombia, and Chile. Why is that?
- I looked at your stats and only 25% of your audience speaks English. Why is that?
- ¿61% Speak Spanish, but you don't speak Spanish, si?
- Why do you do it?
- Are you involved with any other criminal activity you would like us to know about?

So, as for now, she hasn't shared anything with me on the record. If she does come back with a response, be assured I'll post it on this book's Facebook group, at
https://www.facebook.com/groups/UnderTheInfluenceBook.

Also, for those of you keeping track of "Is Trey on @miss.everywhere's Christmas Card list" status, the current status is no.

CHAPTER 5
SELFIES AND THE EGO RUNNING AMOK

*"There is nothing more important to true growth than realizing
that you are not the voice of the mind—you are the one who
hears it."*

— **MICHAEL A. SINGER, *THE UNTETHERED SOUL:
THE JOURNEY BEYOND YOURSELF***

I DO ENJOY SOCIAL MEDIA. I think of it as a fun game. I play with it the way a fluffy kitten might eye up a ball of yarn. Batting it this way and that, not deterred when it begins to unravel. Personally, as we've discussed, I also think social media can be a tremendous tool to inspire and help people. But, as we've also reviewed, it's currently under siege by some of the worst aspects of human nature.

So, let's get into some behavioral psychology and new patterns which have emerged, now that so many humans are connected through the Internet in ways that didn't exist fifteen years ago. As a result of these new platforms and ways of interacting, dangerous online sociologies are developing, which are creating and enabling detrimental behavior patterns at the individual and group level. Our increased time online is fueling a growing epidemic of anxiety and depression.

It's a complex process. First, we see a couple of personas online who have seemingly amazing lives. We look at two of them—Paris Hilton and @slutwhisperer—in this chapter. Then, we compare ourselves and find that our lives aren't quite as glamorous as the manufactured ones we see on social media. To compensate, we too construct our own public personas, trying to project a glamorous and glorified lifestyle that doesn't exist. And, of course, no social media persona would be complete without ample selfies.

When I watch my youngest daughter's relationship with social media, I do worry a bit. Her current trajectory of media consumption, which heavily features YouTubers who are not the paragons of intellect, does not seem to point towards encouraging inner peace. On social media, we're all on display, judged by people we don't know against unrealistic pulchritude and consumption standards. I don't want her to grow up and judge herself by what strangers think of her. I think she's got a better shot than most at avoiding this, because, as her dad, I'm hyper-aware of all this stuff and I can try to guide her gently. But she still spends significant time online, consuming content developed by Internet stars that might accidentally turn into role models.

ACCIDENTAL ROLE MODELS SETTING UNREALISTIC STANDARDS

It's not unusual for young people to look up to role models that may not display model behavior. Instagram has its fair share of "stars," who have acquired a significant level of notoriety, even though they may not be the apotheosis of virtue. Young people look up to some of these icons and may see what these icons have as perhaps some sort of goal to reach.

There is a documentary on Netflix, *The American Meme*, which profiles about half a dozen Influencers. It outlines some of the outlandish (and possibly morally bankrupt) behavior of some of these icons.[1]

CASE STUDY: PARIS HILTON WITH A FAUX MESSIAH COMPLEX

"A lot of the Little Hiltons [my fans] were comparing me to Jesus," Paris Hilton said in *The American Meme*, without a hint of irony. "It's a huge compliment, and it makes me feel really special."[2]

The show would not have been complete without Paris, who many consider to be the original "It Girl" who cast the mould of "famous for being famous." She preens and purrs on camera for her 50+ million fans all day long, on all the social networks. She is unapologetically, 100% obsessed with sharing her flawless, glamorous life with the rest of us, in an endless stream of idyllic selfies.

I think that is a Bible quote. I'll need to look it up.
But I am not sure Matthew the Apostle used emojis.

Towards the end of the show, we see Paris in a Virtual Reality lab, where she is being immortalized as a 3D-model, so we can experience her uber-perfection in the next wave of virtual worlds. "I can really control the way people see me," says Hilton about the experience. "A lot of people don't understand that you have to be sustainable forever."[3]

The show is full of many more of these daft, hollow comments that illustrate how poisonous these platforms can become, and the poison runs deep with this one. Paris is basically saying that someone as incredible as her should live forever and she can always be in control of her flawless form.

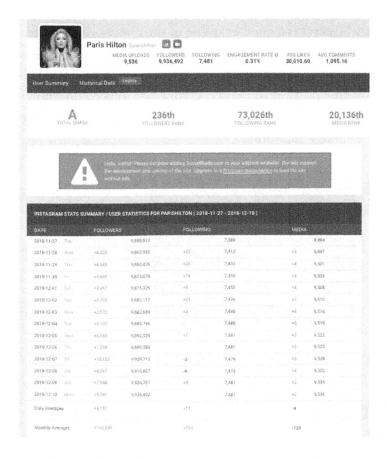

@parishilton is at 10 million followers on Instagram and growing at the rate of about 150K per month. Please note that I am not suggesting she buys followers.

CASE STUDY: THE @SLUTWHISPERER

The show also features a photographer named Kirill, who goes by the charming Instagram name of @slutwhisperer. He has over 1 million followers. He's known for going into clubs, pouring champagne on those *curazy* club gals and putting stickers on their butt cheeks. Kirill says, "My real life isn't that interesting that would want people to really want to follow me, so I have to put on an exaggerated truth."[4]

Of all the sad characters in that show American Meme, he is perhaps the most broken of them all, and he admits it. He said that his normal life is just that—normal—and he spends significant energy trying to make it look even better than it is.

@slutwhisperer is a good example of the many people on Instagram who put forward the perfect life, but once you dig into it, have a life that isn't nearly as glamorous as it's made out to be on social media. This posturing puts pressure on everyone else to keep up, showing others how amazing their own lives are, which causes a network effect of increased anxiety all around.

Be sure to invite Kirill, (a.k.a. @slutwhisperer) to your next neighborhood BBQ.
He seems to really bring the partay.

THE COMPARISON GAME: HOW WE MEASURE UP

While I was writing this book, I was having lunch with my friend David Maxwell (@davidewtmaxwell), who is a perfectly average Instagram user and, by his own admission, very average in pretty much all aspects of his dismal life (I kid—we're friends). He asked me, "Hey, well, you know, sometimes I get bored, and I check Instagram, and I get kind of excited to see I get 50 likes. Is there something wrong with me?"

Now, I found this to be a very interesting question! And I told him so, along with my diagnosis. I'm a bit "softer" on this particular example, not because he's my friend, but because it isn't one of the more extreme cases that I have already analyzed. As I see it, there are a few things going on here with my friend David and many other casual Instagram users.

The first thing he's noticed is that he likes seeing those likes on Instagram. To get one level deeper, what he really likes is when Instagram triggers that small reaction of dopamine—a natural chemical in your body that gives you pleasure. Humans get squirts of dopamine all day, from many things: eating some ice cream, holding a puppy, smelling a flower, watching a comedy, and more. There's nothing really wrong with seeking a dopamine rush, as long as it doesn't become an addiction, as we've discussed.

Secondly, there is definitely a feeding-of-the-ego aspect to looking for likes. However, someone like Dave does not tie up his entire identity in getting those likes, as many people do. If he were to start checking Instagram compulsively every 15 minutes, well, then that's another thing altogether.

The third aspect is more interesting and it relates to a game we have been programmed to play: The Comparison Game.

In school, after we've learned the basic stuff, like the alphabet and coloring, we are introduced to The Comparison Game. This happens around the age of eight. So, there you are, in third or fourth grade, in a classroom with, let's say, about 20 other children. You all start to get academic grades, and, naturally, only two students can be in the top 10%. You're either one of those two students or, like 90% of the class, you aren't.

The Comparison Game starts out pretty tame. No one really worries about grades so much in third or fourth grade. However, they do start to matter more over the next few years.

Fast forward to eighth grade. Now, you are still in a class of about 20 people, but the competition is getting fiercer. You are really quite concerned about your place among those 20 people academically—maybe even more so than learning itself—because the ranking seems to be more important than the content. Even the kids who aren't so "into" school; those kids are still well aware of their position in the academic pecking order.

As you prepare to enter high school, you're not just comparing grades. You are competing based on how much money you have, how attractive you are, and where you rank socially amongst the opposite sex. You are continually comparing every aspect of your person with those other 20 people.

And you have to do well. Otherwise, you won't make a smooth entrance into the next set of schooling. The Comparison Game gets more and more intense every year. You're still in a class with about 20 people, but your comparison pool could expand to hundreds if you're competing with your whole year group. Now, you're worried about comparing yourself with even more people academically and across a variety of other variables as well. The traditional "school system" is built on, and depends on, this comparison game to motivate students.

There are many systems in place that are continually comparing you to other people. Once you leave high school, this stack-ranking and comparison is continued by colleges and then other organizations—including corporations you work for. Even though it can be very difficult to rank people within a business unit that may have tremendously different but important skills, businesses still try to do it, and it can be very stressful for employees.

At work, your performance is always being evaluated against your co-workers and this establishes how much money you make as well as your position within the company. There are even companies that will stack rank their employees, then systematically fire the lowest 10% of performers. Talk about anxiety.

So, your brain is stuck in a system where you are always fighting for the number one position. This constant desire to be "first" can bleed from your work into your personal life.

Danielle Leigh Wagstaff, a psychology professor at Federation University Australia, believes that Instagram "confuses our social radar." It does this by prompting us to try and figure out "if we're more or less attractive, smart, and accomplished than everyone else" within this unnatural environment.[5]

However, on Instagram, we aren't just comparing ourselves to our 19 classmates, or our 5-10 immediate co-workers, or even the rest of the employees at our company. We're comparing ourselves to everyone in the world. And, as we've established earlier, what we're comparing ourselves to may not even be real.

On top of that, it is important to recognize this salient truth: there is no need for any human to compare themselves to any other human. How we stack rank against our peers has nothing to do with being a valuable human being. Every human is equally valuable no matter how much money they make or how many likes their photos get. We live in a system that tells us otherwise. Don't fall for it.

Now, here's a real character named @theposhpt. We'll use some of his sumptuous photos over and over again, so get ready. This is a good example of a very public scoreboard, where you can constantly see how many likes and comments others are getting. It makes one want to compare oneself.

Cosmo on Steroids

The media and advertising worlds have a reputation for setting unrealistic beauty standards for both men and women to meet. While this is as true as ever, it's turned into even more of a pressure cooker due to social media.

Think back to the '90s. Sure, you might pick up a copy of Cosmopolitan, see beautiful women inside who have been styled and airbrushed to perfection, get kinda down on yourself for a while, then toss the magazine aside half an hour later. You'd repeat the cycle, but not until the new issue arrives in your mailbox the following month.

But now, we never get a break from this cycle. As opposed to occasionally flipping through a magazine in a waiting room or in bed on a Sunday morning, we check Instagram hundreds and hundreds of times each day, week after week. Our Instagram feed is a constant torrent of "aspirational" photos, all getting a ton of likes. Some of us might be painfully aware that our own photos go relatively unnoticed. It's no wonder this is demoralizing and raises anxiety levels.

Your Instagram feed is like Cosmo set on endless repeat.

The social pressure to look good and be popular is particularly pronounced for young women. Imagine what this sort of cycle is doing to the psyches of millions of young girls, who are growing up with the constant influx of unattainable beauty and popularity standards. Not only are they continually bombarded by unrealistic images and taking in their toxic messages passively, they now have obvious metrics—likes, follows, and comments—to remind them of how much they are falling short. Constantly comparing one's own feedback on Instagram versus others'—often unaware that some may be cheating, is a true poison to the mind, and will inevitably tear away at self-confidence and important feelings of self-worth.

If we want the next generation of women to grow up confident, clever, and knowing they are worth much more than how they score in appearances, these unhealthy feedback loops, warped by unethical Influencers, are making that difficult task nearly impossible.

The same can be said for men, of course. Instagram is full of the sort of hunky men you might see in a calendar of attractive firemen. Many men might feel negatively about their own bodies as well because they don't think they could ever measure up. They're in a tricky situation because there's significantly less social discourse about body image when it comes to men.

Here's our posh friend again. Hey, whutchya got hidin' behind that towel there, you tall drink of water, you?

I talked to famous YouTuber Jared Polin (@jaredpolin) about this topic and he agreed that what we see on social media seems to be unrealistic lives. "When your life is to pretend you have an extraordinary life," he said, "it's really messed up. Hopefully, the damned tweens that follow these people will figure out that it's fake and they're full of shit."

Cocaine and Tapas

Hey, I'm not saying all Instagram models blast through dunes of coke and entertain an occasional bite of tapas to stay thin, but, by her own admission, this one below sure did.

I think my new favorite word for cocaine is "Mexican Leftovers."

In an article on Yahoo, the Australian model Ruby Tuesday Matthews (@rubytuesdaymatthews at over 19,000 followers) opened up about how she maintained such a skinny figure. "I did a lot of cocaine, like a lot," Ruby said. "So basically I just smoked cigarettes, had long blacks and did coke. And in between, had the tapas. Like my life was tapas and cocaine."[6]

The article goes on to say, "Her lifestyle wasn't at all far from the norm. Instead, she admitted that the influencer industry pushes a lot of women to depend on the same extreme means of dieting."[7]

rubytuesdaymatthews • Follow

rubytuesdaymatthews TWO THINGS I
LOVE ! BED TIME AND
@gooseberryintimates

gooseberryintimates I ❤ U
@rubytuesdaymatthews

christophercameronphotography
😍 😍 😍 😍

shapecan Class!

tylahthomas Need this @annniebruns

jessafanny @hoddzy

jessicahobden @jensenwebster
omg...I want

simonmerrick_mtb Oh my days your
gorgeous @rubytuesdaymatthews

wooda03 I love you in intimates😘

alexandrahindle @elleburrill

hoddzy @hayleymbrown

3,622 likes

MARCH 25, 2015

Add a comment...

*Here's Ruby in peak coke mode. Actually, this is kind of a good
advertisement for cocaine.*

The article also quotes Marissa Meshulam, a dietitian and nutritionist, who describes the social deleterious effects these sorts of photos can
have on young women. "The role Influencers play in affecting their
followers' diet and lifestyle decisions is really scary," Meshulam said.
"People look at influencers as 'goals' in so many ways. Followers then
try everything to replicate their influencers' lifestyles, thinking that they
too can achieve these goals."[8]

Ruby says she has stopped ripping through mirrored-rails of Charlie
since the birth of her two children. However, that has not stopped her
from a steady stream of photos, describing the trials and tribulations of
her postpartum abdominal rebound.

The struggle is real.

The Social Media Scoreboard

Let's talk for a minute about the very public social media scoreboard, which amps up the competitiveness. Everyone can see how many followers you have and how many likes and comments a photo gets. With your score on every post and every profile, people can't help but equate it with a scoring system in the Olympics or a Miss America Pageant. This very public scoring system is perhaps one of the biggest flaws in Instagram and most of the other social platforms.

It is conceivable that many people may purchase likes and comments from bots just to make sure everyone else is impressed by the volume of positive feedback they receive. The ego can rationalize all sorts of scenarios that will justify these bizarre behaviors.

What would happen if the scoreboard was turned off so when someone liked or commented on your photo, you were the only one who could see it?

I proferred this idea to Sergey Brin, co-founder of Google, during a recent sit down with him at Google X. These are the sorts of questions I like to ask clever people who are nice enough to be friendly with me.

As a thought experiment, we explored the idea together. I shared my thoughts that most YouTube comments were rather toxic and maybe not good for the mental well-being of the more than a billion people who use the platform and he tended to agree. He said that it's a known problem and they are working on a few different ideas around this.

What if we stopped attaching numbers and feedback to online activity? No visible YouTube comments. No follower counts. No like counts. No thumbs up or thumbs down counts. Yes, perhaps the system records them, and the creator could see them, but the public scoreboard remains dark to take some of the pressure off. We could play the game for fun again.

I am not saying I have the right answer to the question, but a case can certainly be made that a public scoreboard doesn't add functionality, yet greatly increases the amount of user anxiety. If a worthy goal is to reduce the amount of anxiety and suffering of all creatures, perhaps we can make platform decisions that are aligned with the greater good.

Life Is Not a Zero-sum Game

So, let's get back to The Comparison Game. Basically, starting from the age of 8, you've been in a system that's been promoting this Comparison Game as the most important of structures, because it indicates your place in the pecking order. And then you leave school and your brain continues playing this game forever.

And it gets better. You don't even need to compare yourself to anyone else to play the game because you can play the game against yourself. When you compare the like count from one of your own photos with that of your last post, how did you do? You have been programmed to play the game this way and you can't stop.

It's important to point out that some competitions are great, and they can bring out the best in human nature. But these competitions always involve a bit of cooperation—people follow a set of rules, so they are invited back to play again. Great examples are football, science fairs, 10K running races, baking contests, etc. Some of the greatest innovations in technology have been due to competition, whether formal or informal. Examples of this include the X Prize Foundation, the Netflix Prize, and the Space Race.

Some variants of The Comparison Game fall into a game category called the Zero-Sum Game. What's a Zero-Sum Game? Basically, if one player "wins," then the other player "loses." Both players can't win. Poker is a good example of a Zero-Sum Game, because if one person wins $20, the other player, by definition, loses $20.

The Comparison Game has similar elements. For example, the school system's grading and graduation process is just like this—only one person can be the valedictorian, and the rest lose. The education system crams the zero-sum notion into your brain at every opportunity.

Case Study: Atlanta Mom

There was a ridiculous story on The Today Show recently about an Atlanta Mommy Blogger (@bowerpowerblog) who was lamenting the lack of "likes" she was getting on Instagram for her 6-year-old son. She took to Instagram to express her dissatisfaction with her account's performance in her own Comparison Game.

Her post read as follows:

> Guys I am gonna be perfectly honest ... Instagram never liked my
> Munchkin and it killed me inside. His photos never got as many
> likes. Never got comments. From a statistical point of view, he
> wasn't as popular with everyone out there ... I say all that because
> I want to believe that it wasn't him—that it was on me ... because
> I truly KNOW that my Munch deserves alllllll the likes ... whether
> or not a stranger gives it to them.[9]

bowerpowerblog • Follow

Guys I am gonna be perfectly honest...Instagram never liked my Munchkin and it killed me inside. His photos never got as many likes. Never got comments. From a statistical point of view, he wasn't as popular with everyone out there. Maybe part of that was the pictures just never hit the algorithm right. Part might be because he was "the baby" for a very short amount of time before Li came along...and then Max and then Ella. And people like babies. I say all that because I want to believe that it wasn't him...that it was on me. My insufficiency caused this statistical deficit because obviously my

7,380 likes

14 HOURS AGO

Isn't the ego a tricky thing? It can twist a post around to make it seem like it's support-ing someone else when it is really all about the mom herself. Either way, the whole thing is ridiculous, and you can see how the ego works in mysterious and tricky ways. If she should be worried about anything, it should be about how her baby's head is so blurry.

STAYING IN THE COMPETITION: MANUFACTURING OUR ONLINE PERSONAS

The idea of "identity" is an interesting subject. In his book *A New Earth,* Eckhart Tolle talks quite a bit about how people who have no true sense of identity often "roleplay" an identity. This can give them a false sense of identity for a while, by providing a convenient template to use with a particular set of expectations and rules of conduct. Cul-ture, and people around us, often help reinforce those expectations. But roleplaying—wearing a mask—causes problems, because that mask is not genuine. Sooner or later either you will no longer be required for the role, or you'll outgrow the mask.[10]

Do Looks = Identity, Especially If You're Female?

Some people tie up their entire identity in their outward appearance. I believe the emphasis on appearance and the constant feedback loop might be why so many people are depressed nowadays. Some beautiful people are depressed because they actually feel an emptiness inside, no matter how many positive comments they get, because of this role as a beautiful object that they're expected to play. Some people with banal looks feel empty because nobody says anything positive about the way they look. It's all kinda crazy, right?

Yes, it is well known that, for women especially, looks are one of the major factors that others evaluate. Many studies show that, while both women and men understand the importance of appearance for social functioning, women are judged more by their looks than men are, in almost all spheres of life.[11]

Often, many of the other desirable attributes in a woman, like intelligence, sociability, personality, and sense of humor, fall by the wayside. One of the strange aspects of Instagram is it can really only indicate one of those attributes: appearance. This focus magnifies the importance of that single attribute more than ever before.

Studies have shown that women between the ages of 16 and 25 typically spend up to 5 hours per week taking selfies and sharing them on social media. Individuals who want to boost their self-esteem upload more photos.[12]

The research also shows that women (rather than men) tend to be more motivated to create a positive self-presentation on their photos, so they exhibit more photo-enhancement behaviors.[13,14] Social media has provided yet another platform for women to strut their stuff, and for others to judge them based on it.

Selfie Made Men: Showing off Wealth on Instagram in India

The props may look slightly different, but men are not immune either. There is no real reason to pick out India as an example because every country and culture has its own particular social media quirks. However, this example does highlight that there is no universal selfie-posting behavior across the diaspora of the world.

And yes, there are many female models on Instagram in India as well, but they are not nearly as intriguing of a case study as the following examples. I chose these examples because I think they illustrate the phenomenon of showing off wealth through physical objects and commodities, especially expensive ones, quite well.

I often wonder about the thought process people use when creating an Instagram account. In this case, this guy must have been thinking, "Hmmmm, well, my grandmother had this classic saying of 'It's Lavish Bitch' so let's see if @itslavishbitch is already taken."

The doors go like this.

Ball so hard haters start following you #SaveWaterDrinkChampagne #LuthraMoney

4,656 likes   73 comments

Instagram

I must admit that I am not cool enough to understand his intrepid description of "Ball so hard haters start following you." Note that I added the period, as I don't want to misquote wise words from the Oracle of Delhi.

Have a great Saturday!

10.5k likes   72 comments   *Instagram*

Hey, you have a great Saturday too there, el guapo.

Yes, we see these kinds of photos that men take in most countries. From what I've observed, in India, it's off the charts. And because some of the most popular people do it and play this role, millions of Indian men copycat this behavior, which graduates the phenomenon into mass delusional behavior, a topic I cover in some length soon.

In any species, there is a natural "preening" that happens with both sexes during their reproductive lives. In a way, we are not too different from bowerbirds, who decorate their mating-nest with as many bright blue objects as possible. They even collect those bright blue bottle caps from water bottles. Female bowerbirds are attracted to the male that amassess the largest collection of blue stuff, because it is an indication of a resourceful DNA. Then, they, too, can have awesome bottle-cap collecting babies.

In a way, Instagram has become a lot like a mating nest for humans. The more they can show off, the better mates they can attract. Whether it's sexy gym photos from women or conspicuous consumption photos from men it's almost understandable. This behavior is also the product, however, of a materialistic, superficial culture, where companies and brands use advertising to convince everyone that their lives will be better if they are rich, beautiful, and own well-regarded products.

INSTAGRAM SELFIES

A young woman takes a selfie in Beijing, China.

In an email exchange I had with photographer Thomas Hawk, he waxed poetic about the nature of selfies. He philosophizes, "Are they doing it to create art? Usually not. Usually, they are doing it to garner attention, and it's probably destructive."

I also talked to Digital Influencer Lauren Bath (@laurenepbath) about the subject of selfies, and she had quite a reflective response:

Over my years of working with different Influencers and reading anything I can get my hands on the topic, I've seen and heard a thing or two. The worst is when you see a beautiful girl taking photos of herself (or having someone else take them) only for her to practically cry when reviewing the shots, loudly proclaiming how fat or ugly they are. Then eventually she'll pick the best, most flattering shot to post accompanied by an upbeat caption. To me, it's a tragedy.

I've always tried to live my life (online and offline) avoiding the comparison to others, but it's taken a lot of maturity, a lot of work on myself, and a lot of experience to get to where I am. I would be lying if I said I didn't have bad days on the 'gram,' days where I feel like I don't stack up, that I'm too old and too ugly to be in this profession. FYI, I'm 38, I have an incredible career, and I'm beautiful! So why does it make me feel like this? And if I feel like this, how do the masses feel?

Now, you might think I will be very negative in this section on selfies, and you're right. Well, you are kind of right. There are two varieties of Instagram selfies. One is harmless. The other is incredibly annoying, and that's the one I'm negative about. The difference can sometimes be quite subtle because it's all about intention. However, like United States Supreme Court Justice Potter Stewart said in 1964, "I know it when I see it."

The first type of selfie, the harmless type, is the one that is created out of sheer joy and pure interest in telling your story. For example, friends may be heading out to have some margaritas and they all squeeze in for a quick one. That's cool. This is a "fun, casual selfie" that shows what you're doing, without ego or artifice. I'm not saying all selfies are bad—these ones certainly are not.

My philosopher friend Jason Silva is never short of words for making things sound rather dramatic, and, in this case, he agreed with me that some selfies can be good. "As far as the meaning of the selfie: I think the selfie is loaded with metaphysical and philosophical significance," he told me over email. "The selfie is an affirmation of our own existence. It is the digital equivalent of carving our name on the tree. It is a way of saying that WE ARE HERE. It is an affront against impermanence and death. It is a way of raging against the dying of the light." So yeah, he's pretty bullish on them it seems.

However, I'm a little in disagreement with him when I see the deluge of selfies that don't seem to reach his level of universal ecstasy. That's where the second type of selfie comes in.

The second type of selfie, which seems to serve narcissistic purposes, occurs when the selfie-takers take about 100 photos, spend 10 minutes in silence picking the best, and then add the perfect filter that smooths their skin and enhances their other bits so all their other friends who weren't there have no choice but to succumb to their fabulousness.

This comment-inviting selfie pose has become such an unoriginal trope that it was lampooned in a recent article on Fstoppers.[15]

Selfies: Harmful to the Psyches of Young People

Selfies are ubiquitous. Ever since the infamous Ellen DeGeneres selfie a few years ago, where she took a photo with several of her friends at the Oscars, anyone with a mobile phone feels empowered to explore this new mode of self-portraiture.

However, is it possible that we've gone too far? In this chapter, I explore the idea that selfies might, in some cases, do more harm than good, especially if taken for the wrong reasons.

Travel Influencer Liz Carlson (@youngadventuress) agreed that selfies can lead to negative outcomes. She told me over email, "I think it's really damaging. It's not real, it's selling a fake lifestyle that isn't attainable. With Instagram being a popular platform with younger people, I think it sets an impossible standard for beauty, travel, etc. that can never be achieved. You inevitably begin comparing yourself to people that aren't even real. How can that not be damaging to anyone, let alone teens or kids?"

There was a notable study that just came out of the psychology departments of York University and Flinders University on the effects of selfies on the mental well-being of young women specifically. The researchers began by citing other studies that confirm what most of us already suspect:

- Social media presents innumerable idealized images of thin, lean/tone, beautiful, Photoshopped women, and the "thin ideal" and "athletic ideal" are displayed as a normal, desirable, and attainable body type for every woman[16,17,18]
- Furthermore, the Internet and social media have been found to promote thinness, dieting behavior, and weight loss through idealized images of "perfect" women[19]
- Women who use social media often internalize the "thin ideal," causing them to strive for an unrealistic, unnatural standard of beauty and to feel ashamed when they are unable to achieve it[20,21,22]

So, based on the data collected, they ran a scientific study on selfies to see what effects it had on the psyches of women between the ages of

16 and 29. I've included some highlights from their paper, entitled *'Selfie' harm: Effects on mood and body image in young women.*[23]

The research team split the group three ways:

- Group A– Untouched Selfie: This group of young women got to take just one selfie, but it must remain untouched before uploading.
- Group B– Retouched Selfie: This lucky group of gals got to take several photos, choose their favorite, and then retouch it using basic mobile app software.
- Group C– Control: These people did not take selfies, but instead read articles that had nothing to do with appearance.

Interesting study, right? Here's what the researchers found:

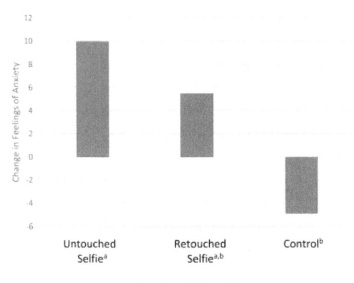

After testing, you can see the results of the three groups. There is a sizable increase in anxiety in the two groups that took selfies. The young women who did not retouch their photo had the most anxiety. The control group had lesser levels of anxiety.

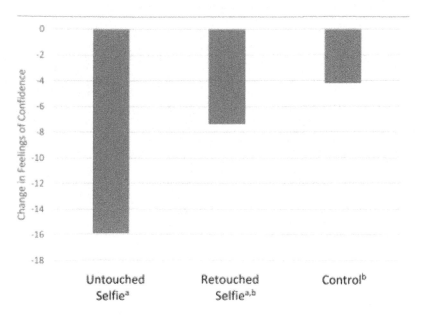

It's not surprising that when anxiety goes up confidence goes down for the Untouched Selfie and the Retouched Selfie groups. The control group went down a little in feelings of confidence too, but it's the variance among the three groups that are noteworthy.

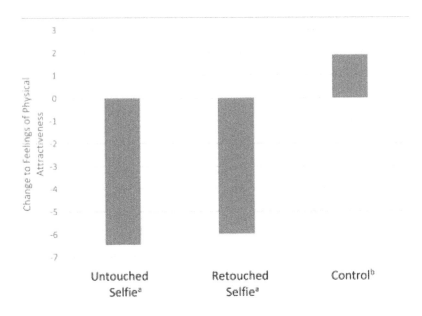

Last, we see a dramatic dip in these young women's feelings of attractiveness after posting the selfie. The act of posting a selfie, even when she has some control over it, leads to women feeling less attractive than before posting.

This study is clear in demonstrating how posting selfies is harmful to young women. It's interesting to note that being able to retouch their own photo did not result in feeling significantly better about themselves. What's even more troubling though is that if you remember, an earlier study found that individuals who want to boost their self-esteem upload *more* photos.[24] This could inadvertently lead to a dangerous downward spiral of mood and self-esteem for these young women.

The selfies used in this study were only of the young woman's face and did not include her body. The researchers speculate that if the selfie tests were to include her body, the results might be even more drastic than you see below. (Speculating is generally frowned upon in the research world, so they may have to do that follow up study for comparison.)

Our friend, photographer Thomas Hawk, weighed in on selfies. He said, "I think when people focus too much on self, to the point where kids are being killed by trying to take more and more daring selfies on top of electrical towers, or when young women must get skinnier and skinnier because it produces more likes, or when people ignore more important things to focus too much attention on a network, they can be harmful and unhealthy."

Remember our two categories of selfies that we talked about above—the harmless, and the harmful? I've gone a little further here and loosely defined some buckets, or types, of selfies to help us explore this not-so-subtle art form, and I can show you what I mean.

Dangerous Selfies

2015 was the first year in recorded history where more people died while taking selfies than were killed by sharks.[25] Since then, sharks have shown no signs of dieting, but the number of selfie deaths has increased year-on-year.[26]

Couple Falls to Death During Selfie at Same Yosemite Cliff as Viral Photo

A couple tragically plunged to their deaths while taking a selfie at Yosemite's Taft Point last week. The accident came just days after an engagement photo captured at the same spot went viral online.

OPEN ARTICLE

This kind of nonsense happens way too often. It's a side-effect of this mass delusion that encourages social media users to go to such extreme lengths to show people how awesome their lives are. If you're happy that you've just gotten married, then you already know it, so then it seems unnecessary and delusional to have to tell the world about it.

Source: PetaPixel

30 April 2018	Brazil	1	Fall	At Corumbá Lake in Caldas Nova, a 34-year-old man ended up drowning, after falling off a platform in an attempt to take a selfie	[191]
2 May 2018	India	1	Animal	In Nabarangpur, Odisha, India, a man tried to take a selfie with a wounded bear and was mauled to death	[192]
11 June 2018	Indonesia	1	Fall	A 46 year old Chinese tourist died after falling into the sea while taking a selfie on a cliff at Devil's Tears on Nusa Lembongan, an island off the coast of Bali	[193]
12 June 2018	Portugal	2	Fall	On the Praia dos Pescadores, Ericeira, Portugal, an Australian couple fell to their deaths when they tried to take a selfie on a 30 meter high wall	[194]
5 September 2018	United States	1	Fall	An Israeli teen fell to his death while trying to take a selfie at Yosemite National Park	[195]
19 September 2018	United States	1	Fall	A Californian woman fell to her death while taking selfies on the edge of a 200-foot cliff over Lake Superior at Pictured Rocks National Lakeshore	[196]
12 October 2018	Panama	1	Fall	A Portuguese woman fell to her death while taking a selfie on the 27th floor balcony of a Panamanian residential building	[197]
25 October 2018	United States	2	Fall	An Indian couple fell to their deaths from Taft Point at Yosemite National Park	[198][199]

Wikipedia has a page that keeps track of the increasing number of selfie deaths, including the gruesome and sad details. Source: Wikipedia

Rushing Alyson to urgent Care again. Called on call
doctor and they are very concerned... Prayers
please :'(

The next candidate for Mom of the Year is this woman, who took the time to take a selfie with her sick baby before heading to urgent care. Obviously, this post is all about the mom and not about the daughter at all, but that's how tricky the ego can be. No doubt her comments had the predictable "Thoughts and Prayers" responses, which are materially useless. Source: reddit

What better time to take a selfie than when on a dangerous highway? Source: reddit

It's sad that people go take these photos just to copy other people, and sometimes they die.

Ridiculous Selfies

Many people have begun to take the selfie craze to the next level. To the casual observer, many of these people have achieved an impressive level of insanity.

Here's Hillary Clinton. What's wrong with people nowadays? This is what I am getting at as we get into the topic of mass delusional behavior. I mean, couldn't they just tell their friends they saw Hillary? Do they need to prove it with a photo? They aren't even looking at her. Source: CNN

A group of women surrounding James Franco and desperately trying to get a selfie with him. Source: reddit

This guide explaining the best way to pose for a selfie was helpfully included with the purchase of some leggings. Source: reddit

Some people use selfies to promote their causes. There is more in another chapter about how social media algorithms are pushing opposite sides of controversial issues even further apart. But for now, I just like how you can see the baby's hand on her mother's shoulder with the Confederate flag blazing in the background. Source: reddit

Queen Elizabeth is surely very confused by this behavior, and those around her don't look too pleased. This kid wasn't happy with this selfie, so he chased her down for another. Source: Daily Mail

You know what they say, "If at first you don't succeed, selfie, selfie again." I'm sure the Queen was silently thinking, "WTF," but in a very proper British accent.
Source: Daily Mail

Look-At-My-Amazing-Life Selfies

Yep, we all know 'em. These are the sorts of selfies meant to portray the perfection that only the selfie-takers seem to be able to achieve. Most of these selfies actually take quite a bit of work, planning, and staging. And it's clear that many of them are absolutely dripping with ego.

Here's @theposhpt, showing us one of his bad angles. By the way, this charmer was one of the 5,000+ people that a bot followed when it absconded with my account. I'm now following him for his steady stream of manimal.

He gets dressed here, tagging his photo with Dolce & Gabbana to illustrate he really is the full package.

It is important to reflect on the most important things in life. It's also important to keep your travel documents warm.

Here's our old friend @travel_inhershoes again, the doyenne of travel influencers. She's dropping a plug for @delta. Did she take off her top before getting under that blanket? If so, well done Delta! That would actually make me interested in flying your listless airline again. Note she says in her description for this post, "I have no idea how I became a travel influencer," and then subsequently sells a "How to Become A Travel Influencer" online course and makes about $200,000.

Here is @pilotmadeleine (1.1 million followers) just having a light breakfast in a luxury resort hotel with a cave in Mykonos. Is she really gonna eat all that food? Anyway, as far as that @pilotmadeleine goes I could have chosen any of the photos in her stream, as they all portray an uber-perfect life. She also has a suspicious historical follower count that is worthy of your investigation, in addition to what appear to be automated comments and likes.

Oh, give us a break @miss.everywhere. I swear, some of you Influencers can really pack away the calories. On a more serious note, I think this is a good example of how Influencers create a false narrative of a perfect life (sometimes in a fraudulent manner) and it basically makes other people feel bad about their lives.

I could share thousands of photos of this ilk from countless people on Instagram, but I have a feeling you're already seeing them in your stream. There's a wide gap between an ego-fueled perfect-life selfie and a fun, light quick selfie for storytelling.

But now let's take a less cynical turn and look at some fun selfies.

Selfie-Deprecating

These are the sorts of silly selfies that are ironic and actually pretty funny. I quite like these sorts because they poke fun at the entire institution of selfies.

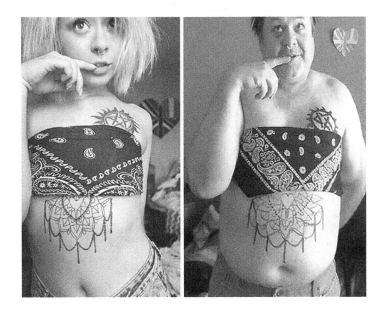

Now, this is the kind of selfie I think is great: where dads actively troll their daughters by recreating their daughters' ridiculous selfie posts. Once he got into it, he surpassed his daughter in followers. Source: reddit

This one is called The Mount Rushmore of Selfies. It's another fun example of a selfie that I quite like. They're not really making fun of the artform itself, but no one is taking it too seriously either. Source: reddit

Hey, Tyrion Lannister can do whatever he wants, and I will love it. Source: reddit

Clever idea for this lady to make it look like the elephant was taking the selfie.
Source: reddit

Selfies in "Selfie Zones"

Many people have begun to take the selfie craze to the next level. To the casual observer, many of these people are exhibiting insane human behavior.

Here's a selfie party for you in an Instagram-famous selfie spot in Singapore.

For example, there is a beautiful infinity pool in Singapore atop a hotel. Every day, there are dozens of women there on the edge of the pool, taking countless selfies each until they look as fabulous as possible. They get bonus points if they can manage it while holding some bubbly and perhaps you can see the brand of their sunglasses.

Related to this scene above with all the selfies in the pool, the Ayana Resort and Spa in Bali recently banned any photos in their "Instagram-famous River Pool". They couched it in a new campaign they are calling "In the Moment," which is a pretty good spin.

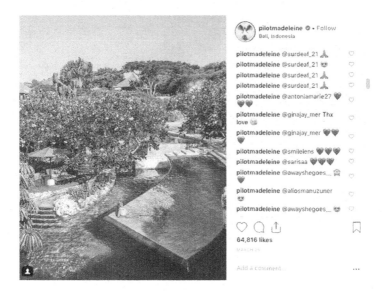

Here is a photo from the Ayuna Resort in Bali from @pilotmadeleine, where Instagrammers are no longer allowed to take photos. Note the high-quality bot responses to get that comment count way up.

Besides these sorts of travel hotspots, there is a growing number of pop-up businesses and "museums" that are set up specifically for taking selfies.

For example, one such interactive "museum" in New York is named the Rosé Mansion. Instagrammers pay to enter, and the museum has a variety of Instagram-ready photo opportunities. Visitors can lay in bathtubs filled with faux rose petals or embed themselves in a ball pit whilst sucking down a glass of rosé.

Places like this are popping up all over the country. Amanda Hess writes about a few of these museums in "The Existential Void of the Pop-Up 'Experience'" an article for the New York Times:[27]

> [The museums I visited] included Color Factory, stocked with "participatory installations of colors"; Candytopia, an "outrageously interactive candy wonderland"; 29Rooms, a "groundbreaking art experience" dedicated to "expanding your reality"; and the Museum

of Ice Cream's spinoff space, featuring a "Pint Shop" and "tasting room" created in collaboration with Target that "re-envisions the grocery store, enabling a hyper-sensory experience."

Hess goes on to say there is even a place you can take your dogs, to get some of the best photos of your pet. It's called "Human's Best Friend," and they feature many photo-worthy locations.

One of the many places you can position your Instagram-perfect pet at Human's Best Friend.

Hess visited many of these places and was amazed at the level of hollowness and narcissism. She ends her article with the comment, "I felt like a shell of a person. It was as if I was witnessing the total erosion of meaning itself."

Friendsies and Groupsies

Technically, a selfie's not a selfie if it's taken by someone else, but since *friendsies* and *groupsies* are taken with selfie-like intent, I've included them here.

Friendsies are when two or more Instagrammers spend a lot of time taking photos of one another in different poses. This approach allows the pair to get more camera angles, which allows for more angles of the outfit and more context for the photo.

Here's what I mean. When multiple ladies (note: I've mostly seen ladies doing this) are in friendsies mode, one lady takes many, many, many photos of the other lady, who cycles through her rotation of poses. The model knows to maximize the number of options she'll have. Then, the two swap phones and rinse and repeat for the other friend. If there's more than two, they cycle through all the rotations. Then, the girls stare silently down at their phones for the next ten minutes, while selecting the best photo to share with the world on social media.

Of course, not all friendsies are ill-conceived. Some friend groups are just indulging in pure fun and not trying to feed a social media ego at all. But, let's be honest, most are just feeding the ego monster that's whispering, "If everyone thinks I am beautiful, cool, or wealthy, then that is better for me." This is a very clear sign of insanity. I'm not saying regular friendsie-takers are totally insane, but I am saying they are somewhat mad.

View More on Instagram

3,665 likes

boyfriends_of_insta She's only in it for his angles 🏖️😎•• #sugardaddy #allabouttheangles #firstyougettheangle #thenyougetthegirl - @adamcnye

view all 300 comments

There is a popular account on Instagram, called @boyfriends_of_insta, that provides a funny, behind-the-scenes look at what really goes into producing these "candid" friendsies.

Now, after posting the perfect photo, a lot of rando Instagram users will immediately jump in the comments and tell the poster how beautiful they are. The poster gets rewarded straight away (cue: rush of dopamine) and is encouraged to do it all again for a non-stop cycle of rewards. Also, the poster will feel somewhat obligated to go to that commenter's profile, find a photo, and say that the other person looks "so beautiful" in it, too. It's like a cabal of insane people encouraging this clearly insane cycle of behavior.

A new twist on the friendsies are the *groupsies*. This is an interesting phenomenon, super popular amongst South Koreans, that mostly happens when groups of friends travel together. Instead of taking photos of each other, they hire a photographer to follow them around on their fabulous vacation, taking photos of their group everywhere they go to share with their friends stuck at home. Now, I do not think this is a "bad" or "terrible" thing, but it is something new. Below is a photo I recently took in Thailand.

Here's a group of five Korean women having a heck of a good time. This photographer follows them around all day to take photos of them and pose them in all sorts of ways. Again, I don't think there is anything inherently wrong with this kind of behavior, other than it is something that is now very popular because of social media sharing.
Source: @treyratcliff

Let's look at one more example of how mass connectivity converts a peccadillo into a preposterous and poisonous problem.

I've noticed something peculiar about women friends in the real world. It isn't always the case, but it often is. Women friends, or even acquaintances, when they get together in person, often begin the interchange by telling the other woman how pretty she looks. They comment on each other's dress or shoes or something to this effect. It's a quirky thing women learn to do that acts as a social lubricant. That's fine.

Let's expand this woman group to a social occasion, let's say a Book Club meeting. Now there's five of them meeting at a Starbucks. The first few minutes will be this serpentine Elizabethan-parlor etiquette where they must give a cumulative 5-factorial set of outward compliments to complete every combination and permutation. It's great because each individual woman will receive at least four compliments on her outward appearance that acknowledges the time and effort she put into preparing for this royal televised meeting.

Again, this is not a bad thing at all. It's just friendly women saying friendly things to their friends. They're friends! That's all fine in my book.

However, let's multiply that book club by 1,000. And that's what Instagram has done. Now, women are getting 1,000 times the dopamine boost of other women telling them they are pretty. The strange thing is, most of those women are *not* their friends, they will never meet them, and they will have no material impact on their life. In fact, they are the opposite of friends, because they are strangers. And, as they receive compliments about their outward appearance, the posters are obliged to give a compliment back to that stranger to continue this superficial cycle.

So, the network effect of Instagram has taken this one quirky behavior of women that works in real life and makes sense on a small level and created a multiplier that over-reinforces the importance of outward appearance.

Lookism

It is important to note that women are, on average, more concerned with their looks than men because it is one of the primary determinants of sexual selection. It was once thought that men cared less about their appearance because of a higher self-esteem, but recent studies show that is not true. It is an unfortunate fact that women are more likely to be judged by their appearance than men are. And because Instagram is a visual machine, women are more likely to use it as a vehicle to display their appearance.

In an article in Psychology Today entitled "Why Women Feel Bad About Their Appearance," Nigel Barber, Ph.D., said:

> The truth is that women's insecurity about their appearance is driven by *competition* with other women. We see this quite clearly in connection with the slender standard of attractiveness where women wish to be more slender than men find attractive. The reason, of course, is that they want to beat their competitors – other women.[28]

I believe that social media has made it very difficult for some women to maintain an inner serenity because their appearance is constantly on display. Normally, it's only on display when they go out of their homes for whatever reason. Now, everyone sees them and judges them all the time. This is a new phenomenon in human interaction, as never before have non-Hollywood women been on display 24/7.

Case Study: Sexy Selfies and Danielle Cohn

Let's look at an interesting example that shows how certain kinds of selfies can create an entire persona in an otherwise innocent young woman. It's also an open invitation to get trolled, unfortunately, as well.

Here is Danielle Cohn, age 14. I'm not sure what's happening under the water, but I can hear the Jaws theme song in my head.

In a Netflix episode of *Follow This*, Buzzfeed journalist Scaachi Koul talked to 14-year-old social media megastar, Danielle Cohn, who has 10 million followers on TikTok (formerly called Music.ly) and over 2 million on Instagram (@daniellecohn). Danielle is known for dancing, singing, being cute and spunky, and wearing sexy outfits[29] (quite inappropriately for someone who is only 14, in my opinion).

Many of the comments she gets are overwhelmingly negative and toxic.

*She shares rather suggestive photos and videos here on Instagram
and other social media. Notice the hashtag for #playboy so that people following that
hashtag might discover her as well.*

Danielle gets tons of comments on the dances and photos she posts every day. Many are negative. On the show, Danielle, reads a few of the negative ones out loud, like, "Being fat. Being a slut." She then shows some cartoonish images of her body that her audience post back to her.

"This is deeply disturbing and wildly unfunny," Koul says to her, in the show. Koul goes on to ask, "Those comments don't bother you, because you seem so impressed about your appearance?" Danielle responds in a circular manner, "Not really, I just like to look good because I want to look good."

Danielle's mom jumps in and argues, "I know they bother you because there are days you don't even eat, because you don't want people to say you are bloated." Danielle responds, while slowly pinching in the natural amount of fat under her jaw and giving the hint of a duckface, "Well, yeah, but that's like every teenage girl."

Koul replies, "I don't know if it is."

The entire episode, entitled "Girl Boss," is fascinating and illustrates how the harmful effects of social media are getting into the minds of not only young teenagers but girls even younger.

The meme spreads from girl to girl to girl. Many of her fans are taking similar photos to share with others. Young girls see how successful and popular these sexy kinds of posts can be, so naturally, they emulate it to build their own self-confidence in an endless spiral of hollow pursuits.

It's a little obvious, but we can't leave here without at least touching upon narcissism as well. There was a recent study, co-authored by Aziz Muqaddam and Seunga Venus Jin, that illustrated how there is a bit of an inter-narcissist feeding-frenzy going on that's being fueled by social media. The study, entitled, *Narcissism 2.0! Would Narcissists Follow Fellow Narcissists on Instagram?* found that narcissists have a more favorable attitude towards selfies posted by other narcissists. These individuals also showed a higher tendency to follow other narcissists.[30]

CONNECTION BETWEEN SOCIAL MEDIA AND ANXIETY

Another recent study, *No More FOMO: Limiting Social Media Decreases Loneliness and Depression*, by Melissa G. Hunt, Rachel Marx, Courtney Lipson, and Jordyn Young confirmed that the less time people spend on social media, the less anxiety they have.[31] Now, to me, this is obvious, but it is good to have actual scientific studies to back up our own intuition and observations. Below is a synopsis of their study:

> Given the breadth of correlational research linking social media use to worse well-being, we undertook an experimental study to investigate the potential causal role that social media plays in this relationship.
>
> Method: After a week of baseline monitoring, 143 undergraduates at the University of Pennsylvania were randomly assigned to either limit Facebook, Instagram and Snapchat use to 10 minutes, per platform, per day, or to use social media as usual for three weeks.
>
> Results: The limited-use group showed significant reductions in loneliness and depression over three weeks compared to the control group. Both groups showed significant decreases in anxiety and fear of missing out over baseline, suggesting a benefit of increased self-monitoring.[32]

One of the students in the study summed it up by saying, "Not comparing my life to the lives of others had a much stronger impact than I expected, and I felt a lot more positive about myself during those weeks."

This anxiety has been engineered by the algorithms that are in a race to capture our attention. Former Google project manager, Tristan Harris, has posited the idea that these algorithms are hijacking our minds in a negative way. On CNBC, reporter Christina Farr said, "Harris was among the first to make the connection between neuroscience and social media, and question whether it's even possible for many people to use social media constructively."

She dug further into how social media creates anxiety and reported:

> For the latest thinking from academics on the subject, I turned to John Torous, director of the digital psychiatry division at Beth Israel Deaconess Medical Center. Torous said he doesn't rule out the possibility that social media is making people more depressed and anxious, but he pointed out that the research is still early.

Anxiety Is Not Just Tied to Selfies

Instagrammers suffer more feelings of anxiety when looking at photos of others. This seems to be consistent across all categories regardless of the subject matter. I've chosen one example: destination wedding photography.

Well-known wedding photographer Jim Pollard (@jimpollardgoesclick), who routinely takes a helicopter to stunning locations throughout New Zealand to shoot his bridal couples, talked to me openly about social media-induced anxiety. He said that the wedding photographer community is absolutely full of angst when they see beautiful photos taken by other photographers.

"Let me tell you, it's an absolute cesspool of drama and anxiety," Pollard told me over email, who often speaks at wedding photography conferences to try and get people to calm down a little bit when it comes to social media. Even he gets caught up in it sometimes though, and admits that despite his success, he still feels tremendous anxiety when he sees a good photo from a competitor.

Here's an amazing photo Pollard took after getting dropped off by a chopper high up in the remote, glaciated mountains of the South Island of New Zealand. This would naturally cause quite a bit of angst for wedding photographers in Kansas, for instance, who would have no way to compete with a setup like this.

Pollard goes on to say that Instagram is also having a major impact on how couples are choosing a photographer for their wedding. He sees a lot of less-experienced photographers with a strong Instagram presence racking up a lot of the wedding gigs based mainly on the number of followers, likes, and comments on their photos. He notes that there are some wedding photographers that buy their numbers to make them more attractive to new couples. Who wouldn't want to hire a wedding photographer that is obviously uber-popular? Again, it's a huge public scorecard that also functions as an endorsement, or so the clients believe, when choosing who will document their experience of one of the more self-centered rituals in today's society.

A wedding photographer's level of experience, demeanor, skill, planning, and responsibility are no longer the only factors. As a result, Jim claims he knows many wedding photographers who artificially pump up their numbers to get more business.

A MASS DELUSION

More evidence is piling up daily of a "mania" that has taken over modern society. Millions of people are creating contrived photos for Instagram, so they can get the approval of absolute strangers, who they will never meet.

This phenomenon was impossible 100 years ago, or even 20 years ago, before we were connected with billions through online social networks. You only had a few people around you every day to give you feedback and those people actually mattered to you.

This photo speaks for itself.

But since we are all connected now, isn't it unusual and fascinating how we actively seek the approval of absolute strangers we will never meet and will have no impact on our lives? It's delusion on a mass scale.

Lukas Stefanko @LukasStefanko · Nov 25
The social media queue

People line up for hours for their turn to capture a familiar Instagrammable moment, seemingly alone and finding meaning in their life, when the opposite is true. People who have meaning in their lives don't feel the need to have to prove it continuously to other people. This photo is from here in New Zealand where I live. I don't even hike up here anymore because I don't like meeting morons on my hikes. There are similar social media queues at other Instagram-famous spots around the world, and sadly I witness this sort of behavior all the time.

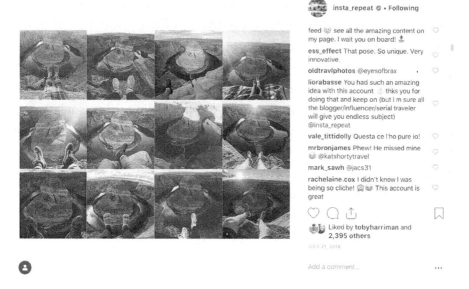

insta_repeat ✓ • Following

feed 😂 see all the amazing content on
my page. I wait you on board! 🐝

ess_effect That pose. So unique. Very
innovative.

oldtravlphotos @eyesofbrax

liorabasse You had such an amazing
idea with this account 💡 thks you for
doing that and keep on (but I m sure all
the blogger/influencer/serial traveler
will give you endless subject)
@insta_repeat

vale_tittidolly Questa ce l'ho pure io!

mrbronjames Phew! He missed mine
🐝 @katshortytravel

mark_sawh @jacs31

rachelaine.cox I didn't know I was
being so cliche! 🙈🐝 This account is
great

Liked by tobyharriman and
2,395 others

JULY 21, 2018

Add a comment...

Yet another place like this is Horseshoe Bend, in Arizona,
where everyone takes the exact same photo.

People will do almost anything to make sure you comment on their
Instagram posts. Yes, *some* of the people who comment will be actual
friends and family members. However, in our ever-growing demand
for more followers, the vast majority won't be. And I'm not talking
about people with over 10,000 followers. I'm also referring to people
with over 500 followers. No one really has 500 friends in real life. If
anything, we're pre-wired to form tribes of 150 people or less. That
number—150—is known as Dunbar's number, and we'll talk more
about it later on.

However, these days, if you only have 150 "friends" online, you
would feel like a failure, even if this belief runs counter to what we
know about human interaction (according to Dunbar's number). In
fact, many people today have an insatiable craving for more and more
followers while expecting to get positive comments from all of them.

Millions and millions of people are posting photos and they're all
putting significant value on the overwhelmingly positive feedback of

strangers. Comments from strangers must be 100% positive or over-whelmingly positive; any hint of negativity causes distress. I heard Penn Jillette (of magical Penn & Teller fame) say once that just one or two negative tweets will really bother him. And that's coming from Penn Jillette, one of the most mentally tough people in the world!

Plus, something about the way our overly-sensitive society has evolved makes it very difficult for people to deal with negativity or op-posing viewpoints. But when you have an order of magnitude more comments online than in person, it stands to reason you'll hear more negativity the more time you spend online. Even worse, because of the anonymity of the medium, people are much more likely to say nasty things online than they would in person.

To summarize: there's a lot happening to us, psychologically, when we use social media, and not all of it is good. We're subjected to images of beautiful people and unattainably perfect lives. We compare our-selves to these manufactured realities—to our own psychological detri-ment—then try to create our own personas to keep up.

In the next chapter, we look at the way these systems are con-structed—the automatic algorithms that keep us clicking—exacerbate the problems we discussed in this chapter.

A group of Instagrammers all competing to get a better photo. They see everyone else playing the game, so that surely must be the game to be played, right?

CHAPTER 6
SEE THE MATRIX

"Instead of a trap door, what about a trap window? The guy looks out it, and if he leans too far, he falls out. Wait. I guess that's like a regular window."

— JACK HANDY

LET'S DO A DEEPER ANALYSIS of how Instagram chooses what to show you. I will also use Facebook as an example here because they use very similar tactics.

I think it is valuable for you to know how the machine works, so you can realize when you're getting sucked in. Note that I am *not* saying the methods that Instagram uses are evil or anything like that, but it is good to realize how easy it is to manipulate human behavior and spread information.

Taking a step back, let's talk about information and ideas. I believe it's in the best interest of the eight billion people on earth to spread, share, and adopt good information—ideas that make us, as a society, better off. Examples of good information are instructions on how to teach kids to read; information about how to eat healthy; that it's a good thing to help strangers in need; and things of this nature.

It's also better to spread good ideas than to spread bad ones. I mean, this should go without saying, but I'm just building up a foundation. Examples of bad ideas are intolerance, hate, violence ... and I'm sure you can think of many more.

It's important to know social networks are completely indifferent as to whether they are spreading a good idea or bad information. They're just there to spread information. It all comes down to the algorithm and what it's optimizing for.

ALGORITHMS ARE THE PUPPET MASTER

Algorithms are the robotic rules that social media networks use to filter and prioritize loads of data to decide what shows up in your "newsfeed" on Facebook, or what you see first as you scroll through Instagram. We used to see everything our friends posted chronologically, but our feeds have evolved to be more sophisticated and algorithms now determine what we see in our feed, and when we see it.

The engineers behind the algorithms are constantly changing them to create a "better" user experience. However, "better" is a subjective term. Algorithms are typically engineered to keep us around longer clicking, scrolling, liking, and sharing like good little consumers. Some of these lines of code have some serious, I'd like to think unintended, consequences. Because the algorithms are designed to keep us coming back for more, they also tend to be created in a way that exploits our cognitive biases and human weaknesses.

Secondly, the construction of the algorithms can lead to some un-anticipated use cases and consequences. To understand what I mean by this, let's begin by talking about technology and how people use it in ways which are not expected by those who create it.

YUVAL NOAH HARARI AND TRAINS

Yuval Noah Harari has a great view of technology and how it transforms culture in unexpected ways. He is the author of *Sapiens*, *Homo Deus*, and *21 Lessons for the 21st Century*—I recommend them all. These books analyze history in a wonderfully unique way. I heard a lengthy interview with Harari by Sam Harris. Among the myriad topics, Harari began to talk about the technology of trains.[1]

A train, Harari explains, is just a technology, and it doesn't care how people use it. Once trains were invented, new social structures and behaviors to develop around them.

We all know of ways that trains can be used to enable positive outcomes. We can transport goods long distances, visit friends far away, and, today, even commute to work using them.

However, trains have also been used in some less than savory ways. They have allowed communist governments to unilaterally make decisions about where to send food and supplies and have enabled more efficient mass genocide in wartime.

Harari's point was that, when a new technology comes out, like "social media," we really have no idea how it will be used, who will use it, or what the results of that use will be.

For example, let's look at an average person on a social network. Let's say they have about 1,000 followers. Before social networks, any given person could maybe influence 100 people in their real life (family, their friends, their bingo club, their church, etc.) so this is about ten times more people than what was once possible.

Now that we have technology that allows each of us an order of magnitude more influence, behavior on a societal level is changing dramatically. Influential individuals can broadcast their ideas more quickly, to more people, than ever before, and the content of those ideas could be either good or bad. So, you see, Instagram and Facebook made this tremendous technology, and a new use case arose—one that wasn't necessarily expected.

The inventor of the train certainly didn't have a choice in how it has been used. Is it possible that the inventors of social media have run into the same outcome?

How the Algorithms Work

This is how the algorithm decides what you get to see. The algorithm watches everything you do. It tries to be helpful by showing you more content that you'll engage with. If you engage with a piece of content, the algorithm reasons, it must be useful for you to see it.

How does it know what you'll engage with? Well, doesn't properly research what you genuinely care about. All it can do is make guesses based on your reactions.

Whenever you see something in your feed that excites you, you will either respond with a like, a positive comment, or a negative comment right away. That response feeds the algorithm. The algorithm also factors in how long it takes you to react; if you react more quickly, it thinks you're more interested in the content.

The algorithm also takes into account what other people are reacting to and engaging with. It feeds that into its calculations too. If more people are engaging with a certain post or topic, you're also more likely to see that post or topic. Remember a few chapters ago when we talked about how pods can game the algorithm by spamming a new post with a lot of responses so more people will see it? This dynamic is why that works.

Now, I don't have to ask if you have friends on social media that complain about stuff. You name it, someone is being querulous about it. Politics. Sports. Relatives. People. Whatever. On social media, people will complain, often vociferously, as they tell the world what they think about this or that. This person should be doing that! Can you believe what that person did to me? Can you believe how our group was wronged by them?

The negativity online sounds a lot louder, because all the Negative Nancies have something to complain about and they use social media to do it.

This kind of negativity is very emotional. It can spark a range of strong reactions in other people. Tactically, what this means is that people will engage with it. The algorithm interprets that engagement as a positive signal and makes sure the post gets widely shared.

So, you might find your feed filled with petty bickering, or outright arguments, because that's what the algorithm thinks you want to see. That's what gets engagement.

Fringe Groups Get a Megaphone

I'll do a quick analysis of a controversial group based on a belief system that has been strengthened and exacerbated by social media. I could pick any group: Libertarians, Vegans, Neo-Nazis, Miami Dolphins Fans, Numinous Xealots, Burning Man Attendees, Trophy Hunters, Fantasy Fiction Fans, Anti-Vaxxers. Now, listen. I'm not saying all of those groups are "bad" (only some of them are). However, the beliefs of many of these groups are considered quite controversial.

As an example, think about groups for which you have an affinity. For example, I used to be a big fan of the Dallas Cowboys when I was in my 20s. If they played well and won, it put me in a good mood. If they didn't, I'd be in a bad mood. I would talk with other Dallas Cowboy fans and would get excited. It made up a significant part of my identity. To insult the "story" of the Dallas Cowboys was something that would once have offended me.

And, as far as "groups" go, a sports team is rather innocuous. Think of some groups that you or your friends might be in. These groups are serious business and a huge amount of a person's identity is defined by their association in the group. Facebook and Instagram highly encourage people to participate in groups because it keeps them online longer, increasing screen time, and allowing the opportunity for more ads to appear.

Sample Group Activity: Those Wacky Anti-Vaxxers

Anti-Vaxxers, eh? Perhaps you've seen their inane online ululations.

If you have not yet heard of this group of twits, Anti-Vaxxers are parents that choose not to vaccinate their kids. Vaccinations prevent terrible diseases like measles, mumps, rubella, diphtheria, and many other things. Forgoing vaccines is generally considered an unhealthy and dangerous choice for children and is widely condemned by medical professionals as a bad move. Not only are the unvaccinated children at risk of contracting the disease, but they also become carriers, possibly infecting other children as well.

I'm using Anti-Vaxxers as an example of a group who holds views that are almost universally agreed to be incorrect. I'm also choosing Anti-Vaxxers because I'm a man of science and it's a perfect example of one of those bad ideas that is getting spread around widely, despite the existence of ample scientific evidence disproving it. If you don't happen to like what I've chosen for this example, you can substitute any other controversial group that elicits highly polarized and emotional reactions.

Let's talk about measles. In the 1980s, measles killed 2.6 million people a year. Now, it kills fewer than 100,000 each year.[2] Most measles deaths are of children under the age of 5. The disease is highly contagious because the virus remains active and transmissible in the air and on infected surfaces for up to 2 hours.

Now, Anti-Vaxxers have been perpetuating many myths about the dangers of vaccines, saying that vaccines themselves can cause a variety of safety and health issues in children. For example, Anti-Vaxxers believe that vaccines cause autism. (Spoiler alert: they don't.)

However, there has been a significant increase in the number of Anti-Vaxxers in recent years. The US National Library of Medicine explains why this is a problem:[3]

> Parents hesitant to vaccinate their children may delay routine immunizations or seek exemptions from state vaccine mandates. Recent outbreaks of vaccine-preventable diseases in the United States have drawn attention to this phenomenon.

We identified 18 published measles studies (9 annual summaries and 9 outbreak reports), which described 1416 measles cases (individual age range, 2 weeks-84 years; 178 cases younger than 12 months) and more than half (56.8%) had no history of measles vaccination.

I believe the increase in the number of parents who are choosing not to vaccinate is partially linked to social networks and their evolving algorithms, which reward increased interaction and engagement. Social media algorithms unintentionally help the views of Anti-Vaxxers to spread because their views are controversial and spark significant engagement from users. Remember when we talked about how algorithms are able to identify and promote posts that garner significant attention from users? That same dynamic is what allows posts about topics like this to be spread widely across the platform.

For example, immediately after a post about how vaccinations cause autism, users that vehemently agree with Anti-Vaxxers will offer words of support. People that disagree will immediately tell the Anti-Vaxxers what morons they are. This high level of activity signals to the algorithm that this might potentially be an interesting post. It increases the odds that this post will appear above other topics that might get less interaction, such as golf or gardening, that don't receive as much passionate and immediate interaction.

The Anti-Vaxxer movement is also spreading both because social networks have topical communities that users can join to share ideas with like-minded folks and because both employ the hashtag feature to point people towards similar posts. Users can read posts that are specifically tagged with #antivaccine and #vaccineskill, for instance. Both of these features can create echo chambers for the misguided to affirm their own beliefs on these topics.

Many people still have not heard of the Anti-Vaxxing movement. However, they may see something in their feed from a friend who recently became an Anti-Vaxxer. The Anti-Vaxxer will often link to these topical groups, or curated accounts, so possible new recruits can get more information.

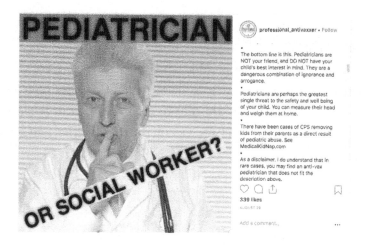

This @professional_antivaxxer account has thousands of followers and tons of nonsensical posts like this, designed to scare new mothers. It's worth reading some of the gobbledygook in the description there on the right.

So, now you see how the Anti-Vaxxer movement, or any fringe group, has a fantastic platform to spread their misinformation—faster than measles itself spreads.

I hate to single out just one group of irrational people, like the Anti-Vaxxers, because there are a variety of examples to draw from. I guess I could have just as easily chosen those looney Flat-Earthers. And don't get caught up in which camp you fall into. My real point is demonstrating how social networks can accidentally mass-engineer the proliferation of an arbitrary set of thoughts, giving misinformed fringe groups a megaphone through which they can share their ideas.

Facebook has recently admitted that the Anti-Vaxxer movement has been growing because of its algorithm. They are making a "special case" for the algorithm to limit the spread of these dangerous ideas. That is encouraging, but clearly, the problem is the algorithm itself. How many special cases do they need to code around? What about Neo Nazis who foment violence towards minorities? Are they going to make a special case, so those messages don't spread via its interaction-hungry algorithm?

Algorithms Cause Idiots to Multiply

Have you noticed how impossible and futile it is to have a rational conversation with someone who is irrational? I think we have all experienced this to one degree or another in our real life. For whatever reason, it seems even more likely to occur on the Internet, and also less easy to tolerate.

No description needed. Source: XKCD.com

In the previous section, I described one specific example, but there are many topics where information is "siloed" automatically by the algorithms, allowing many discussions, topics, and groups to exist in self-affirming echo chambers. Worse, the uninformed can often be swayed by bad, or at the very least, incomplete information, as these echo chambers do not introduce conflicting or contradictory information to the user. This sort of confirmation bias is a basic thing that happens in real life too, of course, but the dynamic is really pronounced on social networks, where the algorithms feed you a steady diet of what they know you'll like.

One particularly negative aspect of these algorithms is they do not reward thoughtful debate. There are so many groups of people who are not getting the sort of information that might really help their lives, either physically or emotionally. In many of these echo chambers, it's very rare to see any cogent arguments from an opposing side. People in these groups become further and further entrenched in their beliefs.

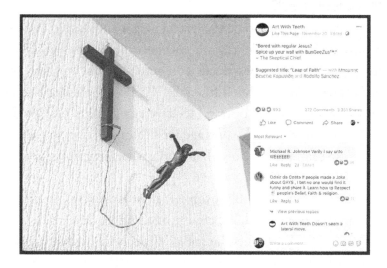

Hey, I just chose a random example here and I'm not taking any sides. But we all know this is the kind of stuff that happens during social media "discussions."

This example above is a fairly lighthearted post and I think most Christians would even chuckle. But then, someone in the comments feels the need to make a non sequitur reference about "gay" people, and then the comments get all out of control. If you scroll through the comments on these posts, you'll find that eventually even vegans join in the debate and find a way to wedge veganism into the discussion. You know those vegans. Because this post is receiving such a high level of engagement and activity, the algorithm thinks it's worth promoting in your feed, even though that activity is mostly vitriolic trolling and bickering.

Social media encourages polarizing behavior. By showing us posts that are similar to what we've "liked" in the past, it plays right into our confirmation bias, or the tendency to search for and only accept new information if it confirms our preexisting beliefs. This, in turn, serves to strengthen our egoic self-identities, because we interpret what we see as confirming what we already knew.

How You Are Manipulated

Tristan Harris, former Google Project Manager and design ethicist, describes how social networks reward and encourage emotional outrage. "If you're the Facebook newsfeed, you actually benefit when there is outrage," Harris said, in his TED talk. "If Facebook had the choice between showing you an outrage feed versus a calm newsfeed, they would want to show you the outrage feed. Not because someone consciously chose that, but because that works better at getting your attention."[4]

Sam Harris, an author, philosopher, neuroscientist (no relation to Tristan), always has a brilliant clarity of thought. He made a salient observation in a podcast when he said, "With social media, you are very likely consuming misinformation that is manipulating you, and this is bad not only for you, but for society."

CHAPTER 7
MOVING FORWARD—WHAT COULD "GOOD" LOOK LIKE?

"We are more than the parts that form us. "
— **PATRICK ROTHFUSS**

NOW THAT WE'VE FULLY ESTABLISHED that there are several aspects of social media that are broken, how can we fix it? Well, this is the chapter where I get to design my own social network. I think it's better than Instagram and all the other ones out there. Don't believe me? Come along with me on this little thought experiment.

HOW WE GOT HERE

In order to understand how to build a better network, it's helpful to understand how the problems of social media evolved to exist today. To do that, we'll briefly recap a few of the more memorable milestones.

A Brief History of Social Media

- 1997: The first time that social media really surged to the fore, with the rise of the website Six Degrees. Six Degrees connected about one million San Francisco hippies in a very simplistic social network, which was based largely on users organizing around common interests.
- 2002: Friendster moved the needle a bit, especially in the dating and music arenas.
- 2003: Myspace introduces personalized profile pages. Tom became everyone's friend.
- 2004: Zuckerberg founded Facebook. That was also the year that Flickr, the photography website, launched.
- 2006: 140-character limit is introduced, with Twitter.
- 2010: Instagram popped into the world with square-cropped photo feeds.

There are a lot of other social networks out there that I won't get into. Oh, by the way, there are huge social networks in China too, like WeChat and Weibo, with hundreds of millions of users. These are worth an entire book—or several—of their own.

Back in the early 2000s, these sites were simply a great way to make new friends and discover new things. Myspace was especially fun because users could decorate their pages any way they wanted. They could share music. They could write stories. Users could basically do whatever they wanted and connect with anyone they wished, and they always had at least one friend in Myspace Tom. These sites were (and in some cases, continue to be) just plain fun and social and humans are incredibly social animals. These new social media sites made it easier and more fun to meet people with similar interests over the Internet than ever before.

These social networks gave public voices to millions around the world who wanted to say something. Having the ability to connect with others in this way was extremely liberating for those who traditionally hadn't felt heard or hadn't been able to find other people like themselves.

For example, when it first came out, I loved using Flickr. Flickr was really the first social network I took seriously because I was able to meet so many photographers from around the world and find inspiration like never before. Those magic moments would have been impossible without Flickr.

Over time, social network activity became more specialized. For example, my wife has neuroendocrine tumors, and she has been able to find several excellent support groups inside of Facebook. Specialized doctors even come into the group to share their latest findings with all the patients. This level of connectivity and information sharing just isn't available in the real world.

Even though I have been very critical of Facebook and Instagram, I certainly agree that some good comes from connecting the world. So, where exactly did we make a wrong turn?

WHAT WENT WRONG?

After a lot of fragmentation in the social networking world, a significant portion of social media activity has now solidified around Facebook and Instagram. These two platforms did the best job of connecting people and keeping them engaged and now there are over a billion people that use these two networks on a regular basis. While the idea behind these two platforms was inspired, a few things have happened to make the end product—at least, the one we see today—a flawed and fragmented one.

The Newsfeed Is Optimized for the Wrong Things

As we discussed earlier, at a critical point a few years ago, Facebook and Instagram changed the behavior of your newsfeed. Your newsfeed used to present posts chronologically and now it has been switched to "intelligent" sharing, which shows high-engagement posts first. High engagement frequently signifies controversial content, so social media became an opportunity for fringe topics to flourish, as we discussed in the previous section.

The reason Facebook and Instagram did this is to keep you on their platforms for longer. The longer you are on the platforms, the more ads you see, and the more money Facebook and Instagram make. I'm not saying this is evil because it's perfectly fine for corporations to make profits. However, by maximizing your screen time, they may not be doing what is best for you, the user. We've seen repeated instances of an increased level of anxiety and self-doubt correlated with increased usage of social media.

Decisions Are Made by Committee

Even though a corporation's principals may have principles, it doesn't mean those principles make it all the way out the factory door.

Social media sites start as a blank slate, imagined and designed by one or two people. Over time, more and more designers get involved, some of whom have differing goals. This can result in the implementation of a bunch of different features, not all of which align with the original design goals and some of which are Frankenstein-esque compromises made by this committee of designers. Many plans that are decided by a committee are failures, and this is why you never see a statue of a committee.

The founders of Instagram have quit, and I believe it is because they were not happy with many elements in the company. After he left, co-founder Kevin Systrom told the press, "No one ever leaves a job because everything's awesome." Ouch.

Wall Street Is on the Prowl

Public companies are responsible for delivering revenue growth, always, no matter what. This incentivizes short term gains over longer-term projects. The push towards incrementalism does make the bottom line look good but often leads to sacrificing investment in a broader vision or long-term strategy. Now, all that matters is the numbers and how they look today.

Momentum Is a Powerful Force

Have you ever wondered why we have ten numbers in our counting system? We use what's called "base ten" for counting for a very complex, highly mathematical reason—it's because we have ten fingers. Imagine, however, if we had seven fingers. How would we represent a random number, like 382?

Sometimes, a system, once created, becomes so entrenched in our society and way of life that it is almost impossible to change it. The way we count is one such example. It's a system that works pretty well and isn't really inconveniencing anyone, so it isn't important that this one changes.

However, take electrical outlets as another example. When you think about an electrical plug, you probably have a very specific image in mind. I imagine a three-pronged contraption, with two of the prongs being flat-ish and one of them being round. What you imagine, though, might be completely different. Electrical outlets are not standardized around the world, so it makes traveling internationally a rather difficult experience. Electrical plugs are an example of a "system" that works well locally but doesn't actually work that well on a worldwide level. However, there's so much momentum at the local level that it doesn't make sense to change the system at a global level.

Here's another example that I like—the measurement of time. At one point, someone did actually try to change how time was measured. Many years ago, Swatch, the watch company, tried to popularize a new way of measuring time, by bringing time to the metric system. They based their measurement units on base ten, instead of the confusing 60 seconds, 60 minutes, and 24 hours. Swatch called the unit for their new system of measurement "beats."

Beats is a terrible and confusing name, but let's just talk for a minute about how good the actual idea was. Each day contained a thousand beats. There were no time zones—220 beats was the same whether or not you were in New York or Berlin. However, someone in Berlin might be eating breakfast at that time, whereas someone in New York might be deep asleep in the middle of their night. Scheduling would be easy. I could send a note to a friend in Sydney and say, "hey, want to catch up between 100 and 300 beats?" She wouldn't have to do any sort of translation to her local time. It was a genius system that solved a lot of problems with our current system of measuring time, which is a mess. Let's not even bring up the havoc that Daylight Saving creates.

However, you probably haven't heard of beats. That's because better and more efficient systems don't always win. Sometimes we get stuck with what we have. This is my big worry with Instagram. The current system is broken, and no one seems terribly concerned with making it better because it has so much momentum. It doesn't appear to matter that even though the current metrics are increasingly useless and untrustworthy.

IT CAN WORK: LESSONS FROM THE ONE-TIME PANACEA OF GOOGLE+

Well, the social network Google+ is dead now. Before it was shut down Google+ was the most beloved social network for many creatives, especially photographers.

When it launched, Google+ felt like an optimistic gathering place for all sorts of creatives: painters, chefs, dancers, photographers, performers, etc. It was as if we were getting together in a Parisian salon during one of the most artistic periods in history. If you've seen Woody Allen's *Midnight in Paris*, with so many different types of creatives gathering and sharing ideas, then you'll know what I mean.

At some point, I had over eight million Google+ followers. That was pretty cool because I was able to share my message of positivity, love, and creativity quite widely! There were many other photographers and creatives on the platform spreading the same message to tons of their followers. We all got quite caught up in the zeitgeist of it all.

The Top 100 most popular Google+ users:

		user	Friends	Followers
#1		Mark Zuckerberg	68	29,543
#2		Larry Page	0	19,878
#3		Vic Gundotra	0	15,793
#4		Sergey Brin	0	15,646
#5		Robert Scoble	3,119	13,501
#6		Matt Cutts	0	10,813
#7		Leo Laporte	284	8,959
#8		Bradley Horowitz	606	8,342
#9		MG Siegler	268	7,637
#10		Gina Trapani	128	6,814
#11		Kevin Rose	6	6,418
#12		Markus Persson	15	6,366
#13		Mashable -	9	6,339
#14		Kelly Ellis	0	5,067
#15		Jeff Jarvis	326	4,970
#16		michael arrington	86	4,785
#17		Tom Anderson	0	4,702
#18		Loic Le Meur	149	4,572
#19		William Long	0	4,003
#20		Chris Messina	333	3,907
#21		Pete Cashmore	1	3,780
#22		許朝芸	4,955	3,745
#23		Louis Gray	3,101	3,513
#24		Marissa Mayer	145	3,344
#25		Sarah Lane	60	3,335
#26		Danny Sullivan	319	3,244
#27		The Next Web .	534	3,142
#28		Sascha Lobo	210	3,106
#29		Marshall Kirkpatrick	281	3,094
#30		Steven Levy	0	3,070
#31		Thomas Hawk	4,457	3,064
#32		Tim O'Reilly	38	2,872
#33		Trey Ratcliff	451	2,788

Most Followed [lll]

1. Britney Spears ✓
8,093,978 followers
4,315 following
Location: Los Angeles, CA
It's Britney Bitch! (Official
Google+ for Britney Spears)

2. Lady Gaga ✓
8,024,681 followers
1 following
Location: New York, NY
Mother Monster. The Official
Google+ Profile for Lady
Gaga.

3. Larry Page ✓
7,201,400 followers
0 following
Location: Mountain View, CA

4. Trey Ratcliff ✓
6,776,496 followers
2,400 following
Location: Queenstown, New
Zealand
I'm a warm-hearted, old-school
gentleman explorer with really
cool toys. INTJ. Browncoat.

5. David Beckham ✓
6,755,529 followers
154 following
Kick a football around for a
living, married to Victoria and
father to four amazing
children...

6. Snoop Dogg ✓
6,694,361 followers
51 following
Reincarnated The Film In
Select Theaters 3/15
Reincarnated The Film + Album
Available Everywhere ...

7. Thomas Hawk ✓
6,653,688 followers
3,439 following
Location: Piedmont, CA
Making Your G+ Experience
More Beautiful One
Photograph at a Time

8. Madonna ✓
6,502,055 followers
0 following
Musician, Singer, Entertainer,
Actress, Director.

9. Tom Anderson ✓
6,119,453 followers
0 following
Location: Oahu, Hawaii, Las
Vegas & Los Angeles
Former MySpace first friend,
enjoying being retired :-)

10. Vic Gundotra ✓
5,471,454 followers
0 following
Location: Mountain View, CA
Google+

*Look at the tremendous growth in the social network from the
beginning of 2011 to the end of 2013.*

It was a great time, creatively, for so many of us. The platform helped to fuel our internal fires. I got to meet so many amazing creatives. I was also invited to speak at many Google (now known as Alphabet) events, meet the management team, hang out with Sergey Brin on many occasions, see secret stuff at Google X, and more.

I even got a message from Mark Zuckerberg one day, asking if I wanted to come over and spend the day with him at Facebook. He was curious why so many photographers were over on Google+. I'll tell you the same thing I told Zuck. Here's what made Google+ work as a social network:

- Google+ was more focused on passions rather than a friend/family network.
- The way photos were displayed worked. Photos on Google+ were big, beautiful, and ad-free.
- Google+ was blazingly fast.
- The platform had a great discovery mechanism for finding new creatives to follow. It was very easy to follow new people because of the simple features in the user interface (UI). For example, you could just hover over someone's name or profile photo, and there was a "Follow" button there—you didn't have to click into their profile.
- Video chats worked, and folks used them. Google+ developed these live video broadcasts called "Hangouts," where creatives could all get together in a 10-way video chat and share ideas and creations.
- Even better, creatives could take that 10-person hangout and share the stream online, live, with millions of people.
- Best thing of all? No ads on Google+.

I mean, how amazing does that sound? And that was way back in 2013.

Then, Google decided they didn't want to be in the social networking business. That was a real bummer because they had something great going. After one of the VPs, Vic Gundotra, left, the writing was on the wall. Google sent the social network out to pasture for five years, until they finally announced in 2018, they were shutting it down. They rescued the best bits of it and launched a robust Google Photos product.

Why did they ultimately shut it down? I have a good theory on that.

More than 10 years ago, when I used to work in big corporations and before I became a full-time artist, I came to understand organizational dynamics. I learnt that plans sometimes go astray in execution and it's never entirely one person's fault. Such is the nature of corporations.

I firmly believe that what took Google+ off track was hesitation about whether or not Google wanted to play the social game or not. Google's mission has always been to organize the world's information. So, social networking was sort of an experiment. Google has many experiments going on at any one time, and they kill experiments quite frequently when they aren't going well.

Here's my logical argument against their decision to get out of social networking. Based on some recent Google Assistant demos, I believe Google has an interest in developing the ultimate Artificial Intelligence (AI). They thought that building a "social network" might be incongruent with the task of building the ultimate AI, which I don't believe is true. That was a double-negative, so let me be clear: I believe that investing in a social network is congruent with building the ultimate AI.

I believe that observing social behavior, which would be easy to do with a powerful social network, would provide important human cultural data that could be used to help develop that AI. Right now, the AI is being fed Google Search data. It's seeing what sites people visit on mobile phones, which ads people click on in YouTube, what types of words or phrases people are translating, how people respond in emails and more. There are *thousands* of data-inputs that are feeding this ultimate

AI. I believe that observing hundreds of millions of people interacting on a social network would have provided additional invaluable behavioral and cultural data to that construct.

Sergey's a heck of a good guy, even if he did kill Google+!
He even makes Google Glass look cool.

About eight years ago, Sergey Brin invited me to spend the day with him at Google X and present something to his team. I can't really talk about what I presented because I signed a lot of forms, but that was the beginning of a nice and casual friendship. I also found out Sergey is quite the hobbyist photographer! I'm not his best friend or anything, but we have talked on many occasions at Google X, at conferences, at Google Zeitgeist, etc. I know he's a very nice and kind gentleman. I totally trust him. And I believe that he would want a Google-made AI to be very helpful to humanity. Even though he probably played a role in shutting down Google+, maybe he (or someone else at Alphabet) has another social experiment up their sleeves.

In the meantime, I also have a few ideas of my own on how to build a better mousetrap.

BLANK PIECE OF PAPER

"You never change things by fighting the existing reality. To change something, build a new model that makes the existing model obsolete."

— BUCKMINSTER FULLER

I love designing things. I designed a game one time that looked like it was going to be a huge success, but it was mismanaged—partially by me—and it was a failure. I've designed a few other things since then which have worked out a little better. So, why not a social network?

Recently, I had the opportunity to do some thinking about what a good social network would look like. I spent some time with a handful of clever tech folks while we were on a multi-day hike in Spain, so I bounced a few ideas off of them. Our discussions there helped to solidify murky things in my mind, especially in terms of analyzing the current landscape of social media.

My roommate on the hike was Matt Mullenweg, the founder of WordPress. I'm biased to like this guy because I've been using Word-Press for over 10 years. On this hike, Mullenweg wisely explained how new social networks changed the game and the reward system. He said, "The thing that made social networks so successful is also their downfall: cumulative counts of your success as measured by posts, followers, likes. Prior to social networks, we'd show you activity. Here's how this post did, here's how many visitors you had on this day. This would go up and down, often out of your control. So how do you always reward someone? Give them a target that always goes up: cumulative followers, page views, etc. People are bad at tracking second-order changes in growth, but cumulative measures can always boost self-worth if they always go up."

I couldn't agree more, and this helped fuel my initial concept.

If I were to design a social network, it would be based on the concept of Dunbar's Number. Robin Dunbar, a British anthropologist who came up with the idea, explained it as "the number of people you would not feel embarrassed about joining uninvited for a drink if you happened to bump into them in a bar." Or, to put it more simply, the number of people you have meaningful relationships with. Dunbar theorized that the number of relationships one person can manage at a time is capped at 150.

Why would this number be 150? 150 was the average size of a village or tribe for 99% of our ancestors when we were hunter-gatherers and whatnot. Agriculture and urbanization, which only happened in the most recent 1% of our human history, allowed bigger towns, beyond the traditional 150 people, to develop. But our brains, according to Dunbar, haven't evolved at the same rate as our technology. We are essentially still locked into that 150-person cap.

Go ahead, think about it. How many people can you keep track of? Family, friends, some old friends from high school you loosely keep tabs on, your doctor, your kid's friend's parents who are certainly not your friends, but you keep track of them, the guy that does your lawn, that kooky cashier at the drugstore, etc. Beyond those one and hundred and fifty people, the rest start to get a bit fuzzy and muddled.

When our ancestors lived in nomadic herds, they'd see the whole crew nightly around the campfire. The 150 connections of our ancestors were immediate family.

When urbanization began people began to be surrounded by thousands of strangers. It was more difficult to find solid footing within your community of 150. In fact, it was almost impossible, because everyone had a different group of 150. There was a ripping of the usual social cohesion.

The way we interact socially also dramatically changed in the 1950s when we combined urbanization with mass media. Specifically, when televisions started popping up in our living rooms, we became para-doxically less likely to spend time with groups of our 150. We'd be at home alone with our nuclear family. To fill the gap, we began to add people we saw on TV regularly to our 150 people, especially if our friends tracked those same people.

This is one of my working theories: Soap operas and celebrity ru-mor-magazines became popular after urbanization because our new liv-ing conditions made it highly improbable, if not impossible, to get to know and form a bond of tribal trust with 150 local people. Think about the great personalities many of us have come to know over the past 60 years through our television. We had people like Walter Cronkite, Lucille Ball, Benny Hill, Johnny Carson, Captain Stubing, Jerry Seinfeld, and well, the list goes on and on. I am only speaking from a Western perspective, but I know that these personalities have their counterparts in the East. Magazines like *People* and *The National Enquirer* were routinely stocked at the grocery store to help you keep track of these relationships because these people were included in so many people's 150.

I swear, in the 90s, my mom not only knew what every actor in Dallas and General Hospital were doing on their shows, she knew what they were doing off-screen as well. Then, when her friends got together in real life, they would talk about their common 150, many of which were fictionalized characters on TV. It still happens. Even when I get together with my friends and the Scotch whisky comes out, we'll talk about how Jon Snow is kind of a whiny, confused-looking guy, but the ladies seem to totally love him.

Even though technology has advanced our human brains have not. Our brains are still stuck at that 150-person ideal tribal zone, where you know your family, your friends, all your friend's family members, the village elders, the shamans, the hunters, etc.

We have these slow brains—wetware, as opposed to software—that still have strange hang-ups about the way life used to be. For instance, we still search for our tribes even when we may not have a real affiliation with a tribe. This is why people get so excited about the Dallas Cowboys playing the Philadelphia Eagles. We may not fight in city-state wars anymore, but these are wars by proxy now, where we send a group of warriors to have a pretend battle. If you know anything about professional sports, you'll have seen how many men treat it as seriously as actual war.

Our wetware has evolved, in some ways, to manage our new existence. Steven Pinker, author and psychologist, has written about a few of these evolutions. In particular, he describes how the average human used to be much more homicidal and prone to violence. Over time, most of that aggression has been worked out of our system and most of us can channel it to do some amazing things rather than kill people.[1]

However, we're not even close to turning the dial much beyond our 150 relationships. Our neocortex is just too small to remember any more than that.

So, how would this idea lead to the design of a social network? Here are my design specs.

- **You can follow up to 150 "things,"** which would include:
    - People: Relatives, friends, crushes, Jeff Goldblum, Flavor Flav, PewDiePie
    - Groups or curators: The BBC, Arsenal, Burning Man, or Global Wildlife Conservation
- **The follow is one-way,** so it doesn't have to be mutual. You could stalk celebrities if you wanted, then with your friends and relatives, the follow would be mutual.
- **You share with who you want to share with.** We'd re-use that great idea of Google Circles where you put the people you follow into groups of your choosing and share content just to those groups. Examples groups might include family, friends, celebrities, sports, yoga class, or book club. People can be in multiple circles. When you post, you choose which Circles you post to.

- **Stats are private.** The number of likes or comments you get would not be publicly shared and would remain just for you to see.

Just that simple.

One reason I like using Dunbar's number as a limiting factor is because you can actually keep track of 150 people. These 150 are people and groups you really care about. When you run out of slots, it forces you to review those 150 things and pick out the ones that you no longer want to follow.

This solution also works because it's asymmetrical. Even though you can only follow 150 people, groups, or topics, you could still be followed by thousands or millions of others.

In terms of monetization, which is important for every startup, the first two years would be free. After that, every user pays $1 a month. No ads.

Anyway, will someone please build this so we can give it a whirl?

HOW THE 150 SOLUTION SOLVES ALL THE PROBLEMS

Here's just a few ways that this approach fixes some of the problems we've talked about:

- **Bots mostly go away.** Because users have to pay $1 per month, the barrier to entry for bots is much higher.
- **The Newsfeed can be optimized for the right things.** The goal of the 150 is not to keep you on as long as possible to show you ads because there are no ads at all. When the social network is not trying to optimize performance to show you as many ads as possible, it can focus on other more positive activities.
- **Wall Street is happy.** The path to revenue is clear and tied to the number of users.
- **Your data is safer.** The 150 doesn't need to sell your data to make money because you already pay $1 to use the service.

- **Your anxiety level is lower.** You would never feel overloaded with too much content because you can only follow 150 things. This limit keeps everything manageable in your head, rather than the generally scattered feeling you probably have now when parsing your newsfeed.
- **Your friends/followers see your content.** There is a high likelihood that most of your content will be seen by people that follow you. Currently, on Facebook and Instagram, less than 2% of the posts you share are seen by people who follow you. That's because they follow too many people. These services also have a financial incentive to not overshare your posts, so that you will pay these services more money to promote your posts.
- **There's no public scoreboard.** The network would not have a public scoreboard that shows followers, plays, likes, or views. Each individual user would be able to see their own stats, but they are not on public display. This immediately removes one of the big determinants of anxiety. Also, comments are likely to be much nicer because people have openly chosen to follow this one person in their previous 150 slots.

Not bad, eh?

I'd also like to implement a recommendation engine organized around sharing positive content. Rather than encouraging outrage, this social network can be a force for positive change in the world: a betterment of the entire human condition on a massive scale. The social network could feature a recommendation engine that encourages the best of human behavior while minimizing the worst of it and then focus on showing you good ideas and good suggestions.

IS TIME UP?

I hate to be fatalistic but Instagram and many other social networks, including Facebook, may be beyond saving. Even though in many ways there are good and positive things happening on them, they are also fostering and amplifying the worst aspects of human nature. I don't think that can be controlled from the top or by the software itself.

There are indeed better ideas for social networks out there. But with more than 1 billion active Instagram users, there's incredible inertia, and we face something called a coordination problem. To summarize—how do we know if our friends will use a new social network?

Here's an example of a coordination problem. Let's say that you and I exist in a time before cell phones and we are interested in meeting for dinner. However, neither of us is sure in which part of the town the other will be. If there's only one restaurant in town it isn't a problem, we both go there. However, the problem would not be so easy if there were several restaurants, whereby my interests are better served by one choice (e.g. a restaurant near me) and yours by a different choice (one near you).

Relating this back to social media, if a better network were to come along it would be easy to get your friend to join you on it because you would just ask them to sign up. However, that's not a scalable solution, you can't do that with everyone you know, so it would be impossible to get most people to move to the new social network.

Facebook has so many users that the problem becomes almost unmanageable. It's a sticky platform, with many users who aren't particularly tech-savvy, which exacerbates the problem. How long did it take you to teach your mom how to use Facebook? If she's still on Facebook, she won't be budging. It's just not going to happen.

There is a similar issue with YouTube. If you are a video creator, you want to post your video where most people will see it. If you're a video watcher, you want to go where there's the largest amount of free content. This is why YouTube dominates the vast majority of the market. They reached critical mass first. Even if something better comes along, you have to convince most of the creators and viewers to move over to the new platform. It's not an easy task.

So, even though I like my idea of the 150, I'm also realistic. It would be hard to get folks to move over.

Therefore, we're back to where we started—figuring out how the existing social networks can change from within. Remember, these are not static entities. They are based on software and algorithms that can be changed if priorities are re-aligned.

Tristan Harris, the former Google Project Manager and design ethicist, imagines one possible future. What if all those smart engineers at social media companies were to stop focusing on capturing people's attention and instead focused on trying to encourage more meaningful real-life experiences? What if social networks could help change people's minds, make them more open-minded, and facilitate healthy relationships? It's absolutely possible but the current system tries to maximize getting your attention so that they can advertise to you, since this is how these organizations make money. There is an excellent podcast with Sam Harris and Tristan Harris that explores these ideas in depth.[2] By the way, I personally recommend listening to as many Sam Harris podcasts as possible. It's a great way to keep your mind zen in today's crazy technology world.

CHAPTER 8
HOW TO STAY ZEN ON SOCIAL MEDIA

"Be crazy! But learn how to be crazy without being the center of attention. Be brave enough to live different."
— **PAULO COELHO**

WE COMPARE OURSELVES AND OUR STATUS to individuals in the media we consume. We subtly change the inner stories we tell ourselves. We might see ourselves as less— less pretty, less rich, or less glamorous—than the famous and popular individuals we see on social media. We might compare ourselves to them and find ourselves lacking.

Social media is an echo chamber of the ego and many of us step into it numerous times a day. Most everything the "world" —aka the media we consume—tells us matters, does not actually matter at all. Having more money, followers, or comments is not the recipe for a better life.

Many people are increasingly anxious due to dealing with nonsense on social media.

So how do we fix it? How do we stop feeling anxious, frustrated, or "less-than" these beautiful people we see online? That's what this chapter is about.

All that really matters is gathering a loving group of people around you who are supportive and fun. The next level, if you can find it, is to foster a broader network who encourage and support your creativity or ambition.

When you break down the best essences of humanity, you'll see we are here to love one another, create, share, and cooperate, and to encourage everyone else to do the same. Anything beyond that is a distraction.

There is a doorway out. It's like one of those last-chance exits for the scary rides at Disneyland that you can slip out of in case you change your mind after waiting in line for an hour. I'll show you how to find that exit.

The most important thing to realize is that it's okay to "let go" of yourself and understand that it is wonderful to say, "Hey, I'm a work in progress." Do not over-inflate some of the ideas you have about yourself. Your ego is always trying to find a definition of you, what you're about, what you enjoy, what people think of you. These narratives are simply stories in your head. Clinging to these stories, if they aren't the right ones, can hold you back. Do not hang on to any rigid idea of yourself. Richard Dawkins referred to us as humans not as a solid structure with rigid selves. We're more like a sand dune, re-forming itself across a desert of time.[1]

Now that we've seen some of the ways users can be manipulated online, let's think about how we can interface successfully with these social networks going forward. I think a good way to talk about this is to figure you out a little on the inside.

HOW TO BE A VALUABLE HUMAN

Let's break down a common thought pattern that the ego creates and illustrate why it is ridiculous. We'll continue to use Instagram as an example, but you can plug in any social network. And we'll use "You" as the actor in this hypothetical situation, which may be disconcerting if it's real and not hypothetical in your case.

You post a photo on Instagram. It could be anything. It's a typical photo for you. A cat. Ice cream. A selfie. A waterfall. An inspirational quote. Whatever, it doesn't matter. Okay, posted.

You wait 30 seconds or, if you are exceptionally patient, you wait a few minutes.

You refresh that post to see how many likes or comments you have received so far. What? You only got a few? Less than usual? Oh, heavens. Maybe the photo you posted is terrible! This is clearly below your standards. You're losing your audience with this one photo! Your friends think you're dumb.

The internal anxiety builds. You are automatically linking the success of that one photo to your entire self-worth in that moment. If people didn't find your photo valuable, then it only stands to reason that they don't find YOU valuable. Thus, over time, photo after photo, you slowly begin to devalue yourself as a human, simply because the world is not valuing your photos with their clicks and taps.

Of course, when it's described this way, this is a completely ridiculous narrative, but you can see the type of poisonous narrative your ego creates for you.

Let me go around your silly ego for a moment and tell you something you already know: You are a valuable human being. You know this already. The very nature of being born makes you a valuable member of the human race. You're probably even more valuable than you think, especially if you love and care about a lot of people in your life.

So isn't it interesting, when you look at it like this, how your ego will sneak in there and start to fill you with self-doubt over something as utterly inconsequential as a series of digital bits you upload to a social network? Watch out for that.

And as you think about this, start applying this concept to other social media accounts that you see. Watch how people will upload anything so that they can rank highly on the constructed scoreboard and their ego can continue its silly little game.

But don't worry, you can check out of that game at any time. We'll talk about how in just a minute.

FIGURE OUT WHAT YOUR GOAL ACTUALLY IS

So many people are lost nowadays, adrift in a world where they let the media dictate what is important only for those values to be reinforced by their friends on social media parroting works of fiction. People are striving for the ultimate goal of True Happiness which is a lie sold by the media and popular culture.

Imagine those words glowing in fairy lights. But is it the right thing to be looking for?

I think people focus too much on happiness because it seems like an obvious thing to chase, but what I believe people really want is meaningful events to happen as often as possible. When meaningful events occur in your life happiness comes over you like a soft shadow in the afternoon.

If you are not having meaningful events when you are poor and have no followers, then you certainly won't have any better chance of being happier once you do have riches and fame. We all know many rich and famous people who are quite miserable.

Nobel Prize winning economist Daniel Kahneman recently posited that humans aren't actually chasing happiness after all—we're looking for satisfaction—which is based on having had meaningful experiences over time. In a podcast, he said, "Altogether, I don't think that people maximize happiness in that sense ... this doesn't seem to be what people want to do. They actually want to maximize their satisfaction with themselves and with their lives. And that leads in completely different directions than the maximization of happiness."[2]

Kahneman posits that satisfaction is based mostly on comparisons. "Life satisfaction is connected to a large degree to social yardsticks– achieving goals, meeting expectations."

An article discussing Kahneman's theory goes on to explain how this dynamic actually makes us very unhappy:

> The key here is memory. Satisfaction is retrospective. Happiness occurs in real time. In Kahneman's work, he found that people tell themselves a story about their lives, which may or may not add up to a pleasing tale.
>
> This theory helps to explain our current social media-driven culture. To some extent, we care less about enjoying ourselves than presenting the appearance of an enviable existence. We're preoccupied with quantifying friends and followers rather than spending psychtime with people we like. And ultimately, this makes us miserable.[3]

Instagram is full of people with a lot of followers, likes, and comments, who have seemingly idyllic lives. At the basic Pavlovian level, these metrics become associated with happiness. But it's all a very silly snake oil that you're buying, not only from the salesman-like-Influencers, but from the platform—Instagram. The truth is that you are already a complete and fully realized awesome human. You certainly don't need Instagram or their framework to confirm your worth as a human being.

Derek Sivers takes this minimalist view. In an email to me, he said, "Life can be improved by adding, or by subtracting. The world pushes you to add, because that benefits them. But the secret is to focus on subtracting."

DABBLE IN MINDFULNESS

Learning to use your mind like a quiet ninja is absolutely, positively, without a doubt, the number one most important skill in the world.

And it is a skill, like swimming or sewing, that gets easier the more you practice it.

Meditation is one way you can do this. Meditation is an exercise in quieting your mind and focusing your thoughts. It allows you to reflect on what's important to you. It also has the added benefit of helping to put some of the less important things in life into perspective.

If you don't have a daily practice of meditation yet, there are three apps I recommend that you can use to get started right away. The greatest thing about these apps is you don't have to do anything except carve out a few minutes a day to use them. You don't have to sit in a special position. All it requires is a little shift in attitude that feels like, "Yeah, my mind is kinda strange. I'm curious as to what's goin' on in there and why." You'll find your mind to be quite the playground when you begin to observe it.

The first app I'll recommend is Headspace. Headspace has a free ten-day course for beginners with a series of guided meditations. Start by committing just 10-20 minutes a day to it. Pop in your headphones and just listen to the voice. The voice will tell you what to do. It won't tell you what not to do, so don't worry about that. In fact, sometimes you won't be doing anything at all. Meditation is great because it has a very forgiving premise.

The second app is the Sam Harris meditation app called The Waking Up Course. There is a free version with a few lessons you can try. I think Sam is great too.

The third one I'll recommend is Oak, which was built by Kevin Rose (@kevinrose). It's a free app and he is adding new stuff to it continuously. In that app, by the way, I have contributed one of my videos I made that uses the wise words of Alan Watts entitled, "Life From Above and Beyond."

Anyway, there's a cumulative effect to meditation, so try it for a couple of weeks. Time spent investing in your own mind is probably the wisest decision anyone can make. Even better, meditation can really help you see all social media and your objective position within the fictional maelstrom, from a 10,000-foot view, if you want to.

SET SOME SOCIAL MEDIA RULES OF ENGAGEMENT

One of my favorite books is *The Subtle Art of Not Giving a F*ck,* by Mark Manson. I read it and said aloud, "This is like a fucking autobiography." If you haven't read it yet, it's not at all a manual on how to be indifferent to everything, as the title might suggest. It's about developing the self-awareness not to be concerned about what others may think of you and doing what you feel is right, according to your own set of values.[4] Once you cultivate this attitude, your life gets exponentially easier, and you'll also be able to detect what has substance.

I talked to Josh Whiton, eco-entrepreneur, about his approach to social media, which is comparatively hands-off. He resisted social media for a while, but now uses it for positivity and spreading the word on his MakeSoil.org project. "I mostly use it as a broadcast channel whenever I get an idea that I believe is helpful or healing for people," he told me. "Then I do my best to not stick around monitoring the likes and replies and sign off."

That said, this subtle art doesn't just happen overnight. So in the meantime, I'll share a few practical tips that I use to stay sane on social media. I hope you'll find them helpful too.

My No-Selfie Policy

I do have this policy—which I might only break once a year or so—I don't take selfies. To begin with, I don't find myself to be a real stunner, so it's actually a gift in not forcing other people to look at me all the time.

But that's not the real reason.

The real reason is I have so much quietness and serenity in my mind when I am in a possible "good selfie" location. For example, I was recently on a vacation, sitting in a nice pool and watching the sunset, drinking a glass of wine. It was awesome. I didn't want to spend one second wondering if I should take a photo of this experience. I didn't wonder what angle the light was coming. I didn't think about how to pose myself for the perfect selfie. If I wanted to do that, I would have spent 20-30 minutes on crazy-selfie time, not to mention all the editing, uploading, commenting, liking, and, well, you know. Meanwhile, I was just there in the moment, at peace, and it was wonderful. I don't need to prove to anyone that I look super cool and that I have a good life.

I was out on a boat in the Caribbean a while back with a bunch of Influencers. Oh my lordy, you should have seen it. There were about ten or eleven of us all together. For at least two of the three hours we were out there, all these Influencers did was take photos of one another. It was funny because they all framed their shots in such a way it looked like they were alone on the yacht, experiencing a fabulous moment of pensive solitude. You've probably seen this type of photo. But, actually, in the background, everyone was running around in a chaotic way, trying to get similar shots. It was the strangest thing. None of them were actually in the moment, appreciating the experience.

My No Foodstagram Policy

Have you ever seen Foodie Influencers eat together? It's the most comical thing ever. The second the food arrives at their table, they are all standing up, running around with their phones, getting different angles, etc. It can honestly be 10 minutes of this before anyone takes a bite. They don't even say anything to each other during these 10 minutes because they are concentrating on getting their shots. It's the most unnatural thing in the world. It's also quite unnatural in that they are all secretly wanting *better* photos than everyone else at the table. Meanwhile, their food is getting cold.

A group of hipsters eating lunch

instabrag_ • Follow

instabrag_ (Follow @instabrag_ please)

#instabrag #lolz #high #selfies #fame #socialmedia #funnyaf #narcissism #selfiestick #vain #f4f #f4fb #f4fback #likes #narcissism #narcissist #mememe #true #instagramwhore #selfieaddict #proudmama #selfconfidence #comic #gastronogram #eatingdisorder #foodporn #foodiesofinstagram

oldgal65

bobgc3 Uh, dont be a dick... Those are Yelp reviewers. They're very self-important. They even have a TV show now.

115 likes

Add a comment...

Instagrammers having lunch together.

I prefer to converse with my tablemates. I find that to be more meaningful than intensely documenting the meal. Now look, if you're gonna take a quick photo of your food and share it online occasionally, that's fine. It's not annoying ... the idea is to do it casually, so you control the flow instead of it controlling you.

My No-Clichés And Response-Generating Gimmicks Policy

Instead of being genuine and in the moment, lots of people resort to trite tactics to feed their insatiable need for more engagement. I even notice my ego trying to freak me out a little bit on this topic. Luckily, the ego no longer has a foothold after years of study on consciousness, presence, the mind, Zen, and this sort of thing, but sometimes I still notice it trying to sneak into my internal dialogue. But hey, I'm no Buddha. I'm a work in progress.

Many Instagrammers are spending too much time overthinking, "What can I do to get more comments about my photos?" Feeling the pressure to perform, their ego ends up using one of the following "Instagram Response-Generating Gimmicks."

You have probably seen one or more of the below methods employed. They're popular because people engage with them, but they also lack originality. So I try to avoid them and do my own thing.

.

Image-based tropes I avoid:

- Hold something cute—like a hamster—in my hand.
- Bring something with me that I put in front of iconic scenery worldwide (again, maybe it's the hamster).
- Hold the hand of a girl who is walking in front of me in a scenic location.
- Take pictures of a person's silhouette standing in front of the majesty of nature. Maybe the subject has their arms in a "Victory V" formation.

Text- or caption-based tropes I avoid

- Overshare my own inner pain to try to elicit responses from people.
- Ask questions to my followers to spur an artificial conversation ala "If you could be anywhere, right now, where would YOU be?"
- Add an inspirational quote under a photo of the Milky Way, like "You are made out of the same stuff that is in the stars."
- Make a strong statement about this group I believe in, so I can get a lot of comments from people that believe in the same thing, and really stick it to that other group who disagrees with me.

Running short of photo ideas? Here's a handful from the brilliant account @insta_repeat.

This is a great account called @insta_repeat that shows some of the most obvious visual tropes.

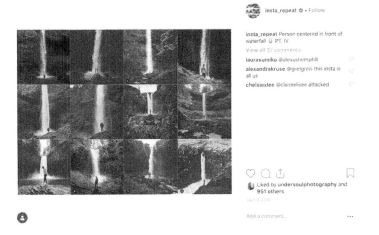

This is another photo you'll see from travel influencers. I honestly wonder if the average viewer knows that this is a staged, unoriginal photo designed to maximize comments and likes.

It's a little bit sad how unoriginal Influencers can be. There is zero creativity. By the way, I have met at least one of the Influencers tagged in this photo, and it is clear she buys 99% of her followers but still makes hundreds of thousands of dollars defrauding travel brands and local tourism boards. For example, Tourism New Zealand gave one of them an all-expenses-paid trip plus cash to come to Queenstown for a boondoggle.

Don't worry about what other people are posting. Try to be original—let your posts be a reflection of you, not of other stuff you see on social media.

Take a Balanced Approach

Now that I've told you most of the traps to avoid, you're probably wondering if there is anything left that's safe to post. Of course, plenty! Think of this as a section with some advice about how and why to share your life online. Look, in a way, who am I to tell you? It's your own life, and you can do whatever you want with it.

Let's just think about life here for a minute. Life is a tremendously complex process. Who are you? I mean, who are you, *really*? It's a complex question that philosophers have spent a lot of time thinking about.

At a basic level, we could say that you are a collection of all the interests, hobbies, creations, and relationships around you. Most humans are quite multi-faceted and some of these facets may have nothing to do with another. For example, here's some stuff that I'm into: photography, anthropology, fiction, Burning Man, mindfulness, my family, my friends, jogging, yoga, hiking, hummus, philosophy, video games, Rick & Morty, writing, recreational drugs, Japan, playing with my dog, and a lot more. I think these things are all great fun to talk about because I find them interesting. You probably have a long list of your own.

Taking another step back, I think it makes a lot of sense to share who you are with others. Not in an egotistical way, but instead with the goal of maybe finding some common ground with others. It is very natural for all humans to share. Sharing is the foundation for great connections and new, meaningful relationships.

So how do you do it in a way that doesn't feed into the social media machine?

To start, more than anything, I advise you to simply stay positive. No one wants to hear you complain about shit. I promise you. Nobody does. Well, there's maybe an exception—other complainers like to hear people complaining because it gives them an excuse to complain too. Misery loves company. But people who complain all the time have great difficulty being at peace with the world around them—with accepting what already exists. The opposite of complaining is acceptance. People who accept the way the world is are generally more positive people. They use their minds to spread ideas they think are better, and they don't go throughout the day in a dour mood feeling that the world is out to get them. Life happens for you, not against you.

Let's get practical when it comes to sharing online. What kind of images should you share? I suggest you share all sorts of photos and content that represent what a multi-faceted person you are. Maybe you're into birds, gardening, space, swimming, or your kids. Share the stuff you love.

Some people will tell you to focus on a "theme," for consistency. That works sometimes, but it can often be quite one-dimensional, and it doesn't leave you much room to experiment. Plus, if you go with a theme, it can turn into an albatross around your neck, as you're then forced to rinse and repeat for your audience well after that topic has become tiresome for you. Additionally, your audience only expects to see a single aspect of your life, which is restricting.

That said, if your Instagram account is your money-making business "brand," then there's a good case to be made that the account can and should be one-dimensional. For example, let's say you make crazy socks for kids. Well, 100% of your photos can be cute kids wearing your socks.

Also, remember, over time, your interests will change, and it's okay for what you share to reflect that. Many people come to the conscious realization that they are a work in process and change is quite natural. Change is fine, and, in fact, change is the natural path of an entropic universe.

So, how do you balance selfies into the flow of your feed? Yes, people like to see you and that's perfectly okay. Humans respond to human faces, especially of people they follow, whether they be male or female. So it's okay to include selfies and pictures of yourself—just don't overdo it.

My friend Rick Sammon, better known to some as the godfather of photography, said, "I use selfies to show the personal side of me, like drinking a beer or having Indian food." His quotes are usually more prophetic than that one, but you get the idea.

A good example of a balanced approach is my friend Sofia Jin (@sofjin_). Yes, she's a real stunner, but if you can peel yourself away from her mind-blowing beauty, you can see she's into all kinds of hobbies and activities. And she's very positive.

Sofia could make 100% of the images she posts to Instagram be photos of her. But you only see one every so often. She knows very well she could have 10x more followers if she just posted photos of her physical perfection. To this, she told me, "Sexy only—what a boring way to be."

NEW SCIENTIST "THE UNIVERSE" MASTERCLASS REVIEW

She's really into particle physics. What a nerd. I use the word "nerd" in a complimentary way.

She's learning about photography and sharing her efforts online.

*Sofia heads out to photography exhibits and shares
all kinds of stuff she thinks is interesting.*

A silly picture Sofia posted.

To take a balanced approach to her feed, Sofia told me, "If I think I'm starting to create unattainable expectations of 'perfection' for myself, I post a deliberately silly face to break up the tension. I also trust that my followers know that my appearance isn't the crux of my profile."

Sofia's 40,000 followers are 76% men and 24% women. Most female Instagram models have an even more extreme male-to-female follower ratio. Sofia can see the same thing that most of us can, which is how it can be very tempting to get big numbers by being as sexy as possible. So her message is a great one for all women out there. You don't have to copycat all those hollow Instagram models. You can just be you, and everything will work out just fine. In fact, here's a secret: when you focus on discovering and sharing your true self, your life will be filled with a lot more meaning.

I asked Sofia if she knows other models that have purchased Instagram followers. She laughed, and said, "Anyone who buys followers [or] likes for themselves is deeply insecure in a way that fake followers and bots can't remedy."

Curate Your Feed

This seems pretty basic, but I'm surprised by how many people don't bother curating their feed or don't do it ruthlessly enough. So many people surf Instagram and Facebook the same way we all used to surf cable TV, clicking that remote for hours and never finding anything good to land on and watch.

I often think that looking at my Facebook feed is the equivalent of staring into my fridge when I'm not even hungry.

You know that if you follow someone and it doesn't work out, you don't have to give them your time and attention indefinitely. You can unfollow them—no awkward breakup speech required. This is one piece of advice I have—if you find yourself reacting negatively to a post you see in your feed, use the unfollow button. That way, there's a little less negativity in your life than there was before.

My friend John Tierney, a science journalist for the New York Times, reminded me of this sanity-protecting tip recently. He said, "Because of our negativity bias, we pay more attention to bad things than good things in just about all facets of life, including social media. Negative posts and tweets get more immediate attention than positive tweets, and they tend to make people turn more negative in their own tweets and posts. To counteract this bias, you need to curate your feed. Try to follow people who do positive posts. You'll feel better, and you'll get a more accurate view of the world because there are a lot more good things than bad things happening."

He's right. Don't be afraid to use the power of the unfollow button.

Don't Make Wealth or Fame Your Goal

Neither wealth nor fame matter. They only have power if you give them power inside your mind.

I was driving in New Zealand with my friend Tom Anderson (the famous @myspacetom) a few years ago. We were headed to Lake Tekapo to take some photos and hang out, and he was checking his Instagram on the way.

"I have a theory," I said to Tom. He was only kind of paying attention—he was mostly checking his Instagram. "My theory is that everyone on these social networks, like Instagram, really wants to get famous. They think that when they reach that zenith, they will finally be happy."

I went on with a lengthy diatribe, which I will attempt to dissect here, although Tom wasn't really listening. He was too busy thumbing through Instagram at the time to contribute much to the conversation, but now that I've had some time to think about it, I think my theory was pretty good.

I began the diatribe with, "I bet we're moving into a world where most people think they are famous." Tom, who is *actually* famous, probably nodded. Still scrolling.

Here's my friend @myspacetom. He was a photo-takin' machine there for a few years!

It would be a bizarre world indeed if there were millions of people who were all convinced they were really famous. And, eerily, this is the world we live in. Fame is a strange thing, and though I only have a limited amount of it personally, I can attest to this. I've seen it really mess with people's heads, and it often takes one's ego to another level. Fame can also cause depression, anxiety, and all sorts of terrible things.

I think we can see this happening with many Instagram "Stars." And still, people crave fame.

As for the fake Influencers who have bought their fame by purchasing followers, some of these people still actually really believe they are famous! They slip into (fake) Influencer mode and somehow conveniently forget that bought followers, even when they pay extra for the "real" followers, are all bots. They get so caught up in the game.

I also talked to well-known photographer Lindsay Adler (@lindsayadler_photo) about fake celebrities. She shared this:

> I think nowadays everyone treats their social media accounts like their very own reality TV show— a chance to show the glamour and excitement in their lives. Like reality TV, there may be truth to the posts, but things are also clearly staged. I think that with Instagram, things feel even more 'real' to people following these online celebrities. Their realities may starkly contrast your own, but they still feel "real," which makes it extraordinarily tempting to compare yourselves to these individuals, and quite honestly impossible not to compare yourself.
>
> I think this pushes both men and women to constantly perform (in real life and online) and makes it even more of a challenge to discover who you really are. Getting to know yourself takes decades, but if you've also spent decades crafting an online persona based upon a desire to please people while comparing yourself to successful 'Influencers,' I feel that many may never find themselves.

A lot of people think that when they finally get rich, well, then they will be happy. But we all know plenty of miserable rich people. It's true that, up to a certain point, wealth and contentment are correlated. However, once you have enough wealth for the basics, like food and shelter, each marginal dollar doesn't make you happier. After that point, wealth and contentment are not correlated and have nothing to do with one another.

So, instead of searching for wealth and fame, what should we be looking for? A vital beginning step is to find peace and meaning in your current life. I am sure there are countless things in your life for which you can feel grateful for now. When you cultivate a mindful life full of gratitude and meaning, everything gets a lot easier.

A more difficult attitude to cultivate is one where you do not desire anything. So much of our life, especially the capitalist consumerist messaging, tells us that we would be happier driving a better car or relaxing on a beach vacation, instead of right where we are.

The Buddha once said, "Suffering is caused by selfish craving and personal desire." It doesn't matter what religion you are—even if you're an atheist. You can't argue with that truth. Think about every time you've had some kind of mental suffering. It's almost always because you want something in your life that you don't currently have. It could be something as shallow as some extra likes on your post or something as intense as your ex saying something that you don't like to hear. Your ego is keeping a running list of all the things you need in order for your life to get better. Every one of those needs is the root of its own kind of suffering.

Once you check out of the ego game, your mind will have a solid foundation on which to build. Then you can begin to add extra stuff to your life without taking anything too seriously.

It's a lot like love. This is a great analogy, so stick with me for a moment. A lot of people out there need to learn how to be alone and love themselves 100% first. That's key. I'm sure you've already heard this common advice about love. It's not easy, and this is why so few people do it. So many people are dependent on another person to make them happy. It's a recipe for disaster, and we all know it. However, once you do love yourself 100%, you're in store for a tremendous relationship because now, all the extra love you get and give is bonus! Well, the one caveat is you also have to find someone who already loves themselves 100% too. Otherwise, you'll end up with an energy vampire. We've all been there and that's not what I'm talking about.

Anyway, the analogy is appropriate for you and your contentment. Be 100% content with your life the way it is right now. Then, when you start to add in more "stuff" to your life, it's all a wonderful bonus on top of a solid foundation.

HOW DO I "CHECK OUT" OF THE INSTAGRAM EGO GAME?

Aha. I thought you'd never ask!

If you find that your ego is indeed causing issues in your life, then you have another path.

If you agree you have the power to use your mind when you desire and in the manner in which you desire, then you can choose to ignore the insidious thoughts your ego attempts to insert into your daily dialogue. Simply check out of the game.

Does checking out mean quitting social media cold turkey? Not necessarily. As I see it, you have two choices if you decide you want to play the Instagram game differently. Quitting cold turkey is one of them—you don't post anything at all, you don't spend any time on these apps. Alternatively, you can do what I do, and only post stuff that you think is interesting, only follow people who you think are interesting and don't worry too much about the scoreboard.

Although this may sound a bit sappy, I think of it like this. We are all a little like flowers. We grow and sprout petals. We notice the wind as it blows us around. We notice when it rains, and the drops hit our petals. But none of that adversity matters. We just grow, because that's what flowers do. It's important to acknowledge the wind and the rain, but you just accept them without judgment.

Accepting adversity without judgment is an incredible skill to develop and being able to do so will help you for the rest of your life. So, you can think of social networks as a little test-bed for practicing this skill. If you don't let things bother you online, you can transfer this attitude to your entire life. It's how I navigate without constantly getting my feathers ruffled. Taking this approach isn't the only one, but it's one that's worked for me and has saved me a lot of stress and heartache.

I talked to my clever, zen friend Josh Whiton about this. He offered, "I'm way into enlightenment as a real path for humans. I've definitely had big awakenings, without any substances—big awakenings into some kind of phenomenal open-hearted consciousness that was bliss to inhabit and where everything was joyous. And I remember losing that a few times after sharing online about it and getting praised, judged, and criticized. The observation I made was that all that social media stuff had taken me out of a low-ego or relatively ego-less state and re-formed it and solidified it. So yeah, social media is like crack to the ego."

A Thought Experiment

You know that voice that bounces around in your head? Yeah, the one that chatters away at you in the morning, mid-day, and night before you finally fall asleep. It says some pretty mean things, like, "Why did you eat that extra slice of cake?" "Did you forget to call your mom again?" and "You should have written something else in that email to your boss."

Imagine those thoughts were not in your head but said aloud by a human who follows you around. This is an idea from Michael Singer's book *The Untethered Soul*,[5] which I highly recommend.

This person that follows you around says some pretty nasty stuff. They might say all these things to you within the next three minutes:

"Why did you comment on that in such a way?"
"You look kinda fat in that outfit."
"Why did that photo you posted only get 21 likes?"
"You should really send your mom a gift!"
"You should read more books."
"You look pretty chubby today, chubbo."
"You should exercise more."
"Maybe you should go back to school."
"What's wrong with your hair?"

"You could have been nicer to your parents."

"You didn't get your mom a gift last time. You need to get her one."

"Maybe you should read more books."

"You really look kinda fat in that outfit."

Wow, that annoying person could go on forever and ever. They sound like a jerk, too. All day, sitting beside you in the car, in the stall beside you in the bathroom, walking beside you on the way to the mailbox, while you're standing in line to get coffee, they're saying mean things about you. There would be zero seconds of silence.

Eventually, you would turn to that other person and say, "Hey, shut the fuck up!"

It would be great if you could silence that inner voice of negativity. This is why I like meditation and creativity. For me, these tools helped me learn how to silence all of that.

Being able to understand and quiet the unnecessary inner negativity makes it easier to spot unnecessary external negativity. Once you've identified it in yourself, it's much easier to identify it online. Then you can filter it out.

Quit the Self-inflicted Zero Sum Game

Remember back in Chapter 5 when we talked about zero-sum games? Well, there are other types of games too, where more than one person wins. In many aspects of life, you can be engaged in situations where everybody wins. There is not a finite amount of awesomeness in the world, so there is no need to treat it like a finite resource.

There are several benefits to getting out of the zero-sum comparison game, including having a clearer and calmer mind. Instead of wasting brain cycles on nonsense, you are free to pursue other things in your life that can add to your life, rather than subtract from it.

Now, the simple act of noticing that you are playing may not necessarily make quitting the game any easier, but you can begin by watching yourself a bit more. Here's how you can have a mini-intervention when you're online:

- Step 1: Notice you are comparing yourself to others online. You're good at this now, because you did the thought experiment above and can identify when posts are introducing negativity into your life.
- Step 2: Remember that you are already a fully realized human being (or, at least, a work in progress!) and there is no need to compare.
- Step 3: If you slip back into the game, forgive yourself.
- Go back to Step 1 and repeat.

Over time, you can reprogram your brain from playing this ridiculous game it keeps getting drawn into.

In other words, follow Rule #4 from renowned psychologist Jordan B. Peterson's book *12 Rules for Life: An Antidote to Chaos*. "Compare yourself to who you were yesterday, not to who someone else is today."[6]

UNPLUG FROM INSTAGRAM

Remember, above, when I said there were two approaches to having a healthy relationship with social media? We just discussed one, where you construct an online experience that doesn't suck, and doesn't make you feel bad about yourself. The second one is quitting cold turkey. In this section, we talk about how and why you might want to stop using social media altogether.

The less time you spend on Instagram, the more you'll have time to get to know yourself.

Your mind is addicted to thinking and finding more input to build the scaffolding of your own story that it made up for you. And whenever you are using Instagram, that ego tends to get a little stronger. Now, this is not the case for everyone on Instagram. I think there are a lot of people that just love creating, sharing, and inspiring. That's great! And that comes from a pure place.

Maybe you've read this far because some of the things you see in your Instagram life are actually driving you a little bit nuts. You don't like this; it doesn't quite feel right. And maybe you kind of beat yourself up and say you will try not to use Instagram so much, but that is like saying, "I really shouldn't drink so much," or "I really shouldn't eat another cookie" (remember the negative internal voice?) That sort of negative self-talk is not a good way to make change.

So, maybe you decide to just quit Instagram altogether. How do you do it?

It's much harder to stop a habit than it is to replace the bad habit with something different. A better way to approach taking yourself out of the social media equation is to reframe the situation and choose to try new things that bring more peace and meaning to your life. And you know, intellectually at least, that Instagram is not a thing that is bringing peace and meaning into your life. In fact, it's the opposite.

So, choose something you'd rather be doing than Instagram. Then, when you find yourself opening the app, do this other thing instead. Maybe you want to read more books, or hike, or listen to podcasts. One of my friends moved a news app to the square on her phone where Instagram used to be, and now, instead of opening Instagram, she opens the news app and reads a few news articles, instead of reading a few posts on social media.

Go experience life. Don't even worry about sharing it on Instagram.

Social Media Nihilism

There are a growing number of people who are completely removing themselves from social media.

Some people, including Jaron Lanier, who wrote *Ten Arguments for Deleting your Social Media Accounts Right Now*, think we should all quit social media completely. Lanier suggests a number of reasons. One reason he suggested is that these platforms are creating algorithms to hack us and control our lives. Another one is that social media turns all of us into assholes. He makes some good points!

Sivers has also left social media and he recently sent me an email that said, "The louder the world gets, the more I feel JOMO: Joy of Missing Out. How nice to have missed this week's drama!"

My friend Om Malik recently quit Facebook because he doesn't really trust those guys. He's also annoyed by the egotistic "fronting," which he felt was affecting his own behavior. He wrote on his blog:

> I took a Facebook vacation about a year ago. It became a long break. And now it is a permanent vacation. Why? Because I don't need it and don't miss it. I left, not because of the company's dodgy approach to privacy, data accumulation or its continued denial of its impact on shaping modern society. I left because it was making me someone I am not —someone who lives life through the eyes of others. There is a hard edge in Facebook life. People are always fronting—putting their best life forward.[7]

Some people just don't like the negativity and quit altogether.

In an article for CNBC, journalist Christina Farr decided to try and stay off social media for a few weeks as an experiment. She started at a tech detox camp called "Camp Grounded," where all guests had to check-in their tech-guns at the door in a "Robot Decontamination Area."

She wrote that the entire experience and the subsequent weeks without social media were transformative:

> But if I'm honest with myself, I was sucked in [to social media] a lot more than that, especially once I started following personal stylists, entrepreneurs and other glamorous Influencers on Instagram who served as a kind of benchmark about success in my own life.
> I tended to post carefully constructed photos on Instagram about once a week, which seemed like a reasonable cadence, with a focus on my relationship, career and travels (I'd alternate them to give off the impression that I'm a balanced person). Like most users, I'd pay

close attention to the number of likes and views I received, but I wouldn't go as far as to check who liked it and reciprocate via their posts. By about the fourth week into my social media detox, I started thinking about my life differently.

While on Facebook and Instagram, I would see a lot of affirmation for people's milestones: Their engagements and weddings, their world travels, pregnancies and births, their new jobs. I unwittingly started to think about my life in that way, relegating the in-between periods between these major milestones as mere filler.

Without social media, that pressure melted away. I started to enjoy life's more mundane moments and take stock of what I have to-day—a great job, a wonderful community, supportive friends, and so on. I could take my time and enjoy it rather than rushing to the finish line.

In short, I started to feel happier and lighter.[8]

So, there's all these really smart people getting off social networks, including Instagram, because they are losing faith in the systems and the people running these networks, and these really smart people feel better when they aren't using social media.

CHIEFS, PRIESTS, AND THIEVES

One of my favorite authors, Matt Ridley, has written a great analysis of the evolution of civilizations over the span of centuries and epochs. What I took from his work is the following framework: there are three grand forces at work in every civilization, and as long as these are in relative balance, steady progress is made. If one force gets too big and goes unchecked, the civilization falls apart. Ridley terms these three primary forces "Chiefs, Priests, and Thieves."[9]

- The Chiefs (Innovators) are the ones who make useful stuff and contribute for the sake of others as well as for their own sake.
- The Priests (Government) do not create anything, but they help

with property protection, redistributing wealth, maintaining a justice system, and various bureaucratic activities.

- The Thieves (Bad Guys) do not create anything themselves. They survive by stealing from the other two forces.

If we think about the rise and fall of Instagram, or any Internet platform, as a type of civilization, we can see these same forces at work trying to find a tenable balance. On Instagram, the Chiefs are the folks who create new, original content for others to appreciate. The Priests are Instagram employees, monitoring and facilitating the ecosystem. The Thieves are the ones who steal others' work or scam their way to success.

Despite some of the more negative things I've said and recommendations I've made, I do have long-term faith in these social networks because, on average, living organisms tend to convert entropy into order. Ants and bees and trees go on about the business of organizing the natural world around them and keeping it in balance. Humans do it as well. We take unorganized messes and get them a little more organized. We're getting better at curing diseases, making more efficient transport, creating quality media and having fewer wars. The list of good news goes on and on. This is why I ultimately have faith in Silicon Valley and the platforms that increasingly form the scaffolding of our lives.

CHAPTER 9
CONCLUDING THOUGHTS

"On a deeper level you are already complete. When you realize that, there is a joyous energy behind what you do."
— **ECKHART TOLLE**

HOW TO FLOURISH IN OUR TANTALIZING FUTURE

Instagram will, most likely, not be the "hot" thing forever. More stimulating interfaces will supplant it.

Personally, as an artist, I try to explore with all of my senses as much as possible. We don't have long on Earth and my personal approach is to maximize meaning and pleasure by stimulating as many senses as possible, including the esoteric wanderings of consciousness, all while taking care of and loving the people in my life. I alternate the stimulation with quiet periods of meditation in an attempt to keep all forces in balance.

Not to get overly clinical about it, but that's what being human is all about. We each walk around this planet as a ponderous DNA replicator that mostly experiences the world via our five (well, five currently identifiable and categorizable) senses. Hopefully, we have a lot of fun along the way. I think it's pretty awesome. As individual consciousnesses, we grow more by placing ourselves in situations that maximize inputs to our sensorium. Think of a raging chaotic river that carves out a beautiful cavern. The more stuff that flows through your sensory pattern-matcher, the more beautiful you become.

Okay, that's all flowery and great, but what the heck does it have to do with Instagram?

Instagram seduces only one sense: vision. Sometimes we get sound, too, but not that often. But, soon, I think, we will interface with technologies that are much more stimulating and immersive. Two prime examples are virtual reality and augmented reality. In ten years, most people will not be flicking their thumb on a black mirror but will have much more immersive experiences mounted on their head or integrated right into their brain with a neural link.

Even though the interface will be different, we will soon have even more choices about what to consume and how. Who will you want to "follow?" What does the platform recommend? Is it more like surfing through categories on Netflix, or is it more like following people on Instagram? I think we will continue to have individual "tastemakers" who create or curate interesting content.

There will always be the temptation of the less talented to fake their influence.

Even though Instagram may not be around forever, the Thieves will be—on whatever platform does become most popular. Although we just talked about Instagram in this book, Thieves exist in almost every domain. It's up to all of us to make sure we're on the lookout.

Fake influencers will still exist. If you want to fake your own influence on any platform, here's what you'll probably do:

10 WAYS TO FAKE INFLUENCE

1) **Use online services to buy engagement** to impress other people and brands. Buy followers, video plays, likes, or comments to make it appear that you are popular and influencing actual humans, rather than non-human bots and scripts.

2) **Put together a media kit** that shows your big numbers, along with an attractive pitch document that you can send to brands or agencies. This can, in turn, get you free products and cash deals.

3) **Create well-crafted content about brands** that illustrate how wonderful those brands are. This will help you get better offers from other brands in the future.

4) **Get yourself mentioned by legitimate accounts.** When legitimate accounts make a reference to you, it will make you look more legitimate, even if you are not.

5) **Get yourself mentioned by legitimate websites** and include these references in your media kit.

6) **Start with small brands** that are unlikely to investigate your numbers to see if they are real or not. After you do a few small gigs, start to approach the bigger brands, using the smaller scams as a foundation, proving your success.

7) **Send the brand some detailed statistics about how effective your posts were** after you've made those posts. Of course, most of the numbers will be fake, based on purchased non-human activity, but the brand will probably not notice, especially if they just want big numbers.

8) **Find one of the hundreds of Influencer agencies out there that will take you on.** Chances are high that those agencies have a few legitimate Influencers, which will make you look more legitimate. In many cases, this approach is the easiest to do, because you don't have to spend all day sending out pitches to brands to see which brands will bite. Let the agencies do the

work for you, and they get a cut of all the money you make.

9) **Make sure you post a good amount of non-promotional content.** This way you look more balanced. Brands like to see this because it means you don't appear to be the money-grabber you actually are.

10) **Above all else, maintain your persona of having an aspirational life.** You want to portray a fantastically wonderful person who is having a dream-like life bolstered by all the products and services that have made this life possible.

Those are a bunch of ways you can make it look like you have influence. But what if you actually want to be influential?

11 WAYS TO HAVE REAL INFLUENCE

1) **Commit to the adage "know thyself."** If you are a bit clueless as to who you really are, then commit to discovering yourself. You can discover yourself while sharing parts of your life that you find interesting or elusive. The point of this is that you appear to be as authentic as you are.

2) **Develop an emotional intelligence** that allows you to be vulnerable and try new things. An audience likes to see you as you fully experience life, so don't be afraid to put in the bad and awkward stuff too. We all know there's plenty of that in life.

3) **Try not to develop a one-dimensional "theme."** You, as an individual, are not one-dimensional. You probably have many interests, so make reference to all the aspects of your life.

4) **Seek to make the world and the Internet a more positive place** where people want to hang out. Don't complain all the time.

5) **Find a handful of Instagrammers you really respect and leave long, thoughtful comments.** That sort of engagement is more valuable than a hundred "nice pic" comments.

6) **Don't worry about negative comments and don't worry about**

positioning your content so as to avoid negativity. A real Influencer is able to take constructive criticism and think about it the next time they post. Also, a real Influencer knows the difference between a constructive negative comment and a negative comment from a moron.

7) **If you have a deal with a brand, talk about it like a regular person.** Don't be showy and use hollow language. There is a subtlety to talking about a brand that doesn't make other people envious of the situation.

8) **Learn to develop deep, trusted relationships with brands by constantly over-delivering.** Share 100% of the stats of the posts and constantly be coming up with new ideas, iterating on a long-term campaign with the brand.

9) **Create conversations that are interesting for your community.** Don't ask empty questions you don't care about just to rack up the comment count. If you have some breakthroughs, share them and get feedback. Create an environment for people to discuss ideas. Remember the adage that small people talk about other people. Big people talk about ideas.

10) **Be loving.** If the overall flow of your posts is positive and full of good and interesting ideas, you will bring more love into the world. People can detect this, and you'll start to have more of the right people show up in your life rather than energy vampires.

11) **Don't take yourself too seriously.**

WHY DOES TREY STAY ON INSTAGRAM (AND OTHER SOCIAL MEDIA)?

This is a good question. And it's one I revisit regularly.

I actually believe that artists are a positive, loving force on these platforms. The photos I post, and share, are all pretty (well, I think so, anyway) and I am always positive. I try to say funny things or inspirational things to help people out. I actually think the world is a beautiful, awesome place, and there are so many incredible people on this planet. I think it's up to artists and creatives to showcase that beauty and help bring more of it into people's lives.

That idea, of helping people become more creative and mindful, is one of my driving forces. It's a good idea. We're in a world where there is a battle of ideas and there are a lot of bad ones out there, so I feel a bit like an idea warrior (without the self-righteousness). When I see friends bail on social media, like Hugh Howey, Om Malik, and Leo Laporte, I admit it makes me a little sad. They were positive, inspirational forces on social media, and now those little blips of light have decided to extinguish themselves.

Some of us have to stay and fight back against all the negative, entropic forces in the world. And this is why I stay on social media, and I stay positive.

A FINAL PHOTO

I will leave you now, my new friend, with yet another positive note in the form of a profile photo of our fake account @genttravel. May his hauntingly delicious stare keep you warm at night.

MY IMPROBABLE ROAD TO INTERNET FAME

*"I think that those who would try to make you feel less than who
you are... I think that is the greatest evil."*
— MR. ROGERS

FOR THOSE OF YOU THAT CRAVY SOME MORE TRAVY

Okay, that title was a really dumb title. I'm just setting low expectations.

Using my career as a case study will provide some good context for the entire book, I believe.

My name is Trey Ratcliff. I grew up in Texas and went to an all-boy Jesuit high school in Dallas that taught me critical thinking. I emerged un-brainwashed as an atheist and continued this unpopular tradition in college at Southern Methodist University, majoring in Computer

Science and Math. I got my first job at Andersen Consulting (Accenture) and worked for a handful of years at CNN. I got married, had three kids, and moved around—we now live in New Zealand. I jumped around to different jobs and (sorta) figured out the way the world works. In my 30s, I got tired of the corporate slog, so I left and did some entrepreneurial endeavors, including building an online gaming company. That company, like many things in my life, was relatively unsuccessful. However, an accidental side-benefit of it was that it required me to travel to far-flung places for gaming conventions, and to our studios in Kuala Lumpur and Ukraine.

Discovering Travel and Photography

While visiting these studios, I discovered that I loved traveling. I found the world to be a beautiful place full of interesting people. I thought, "Hey, I should get a camera!"

I fell in love with travel photography right away but was frustrated that what I was capturing with my camera wasn't matching what I was seeing in person. I decided to teach myself photography and, unknowingly, I broke most of the rules along the way. Whether it was on a mobile phone or a camera, did you ever have a time when you were in a tricky lighting situation, like a beautiful sunset, and the final result of the photo you took came out quite dull in comparison? I was sick of telling people, "Hey, well you should have seen it in person. It was so beautiful!" I was determined to figure out a way to make the final photo feel the same way it did when I experienced it.

So, I put my Computer Science hat back on and started to think of the digital photo as a cube of data that could be manipulated with computer code. I found some unusual algorithms that NASA was using for processing photos of Mars in order to bring out more details that weren't visible in the original photo. They were using HDR—High Dynamic Range—algorithms, and I decided to try them on my sunset photos. The results were amazing! It was a little rough, yes, but I could see I was on to something.

In my continued research, I discovered the dynamic range of light the human retina can detect far surpasses even the best camera sensors. This sent me down a rabbit hole of research, photography, testing, and sharing all my geeky results on my blog. I shared everything, wrote tutorials, uploaded full-resolution photos, embraced Creative Commons, and accidentally figured out how the internet works along the way. I never had a plan to make money from it or anything. I was just obsessed.

Oh, another quirky thing I will jam into the narrative as it is often a point of interest: I was born blind in one eye, and to this day I only see out of my left eye, a strange medical condition I refer to as "the gift."

Growing the Blog to #1 in Travel Photography and Personal Growth

I started my blog, StuckInCustoms.com, as soon as I began taking photos. I have been sharing at least one photo per day, along with stories and free HDR tutorials, to help everyone enjoy and learn what I was discovering for myself. This steady, energy-intensive, approach of providing interesting and useful content consistently over time helped build my little personal blog into the #1 Travel Photography Blog online, with millions of visitors. Google tracks image views and, on that platform alone, it's tracked over 140 billion views of my photos, with over 125 million views a day. (Although at least some of those views are from my mom, who remains my biggest fan.)

Here's my blog at www.StuckInCustoms.com. One new photo and story,
every day! That photo above is when I lived on Antarctica
for about a month at the New Zealand base.

By my late 30s, the blog had become very popular, and I was finally ready to dive full-time into my creative side. This transformation into an artist included studying Zen and practicing yoga and meditation. Boy oh boy, in this book, you'll see a lot about how the study of mindfulness and consciousness has shaped my approach to social media.

The study of mindfulness has also allowed me to completely let go of the ego, which has been an amazing revelation that has freed up a tremendous amount of energy and added a nice calmness throughout my day.

Sprinkling in Social Media

Anyway, back to the story. When social media got huge several years ago, I jumped on all the platforms, and I am still very active on many of them. It's hard to remember what we used to do before we all had to check our phones constantly but, prior to 2010, it wasn't double tap and scroll our way through Instagram.

At the time of this writing in 2018, I'm currently in the top 1% of the most-followed on Instagram, with about 175K followers. In addition, I have 4.3 million followers on Pinterest, 340K on Facebook, 58K on Flickr, and 80K subs on YouTube, with over 34 million minutes of total video watch time. Anyway, I love all my Internet friends and have come to know a fair bit about social media in the process.

I also love hosting photo walks around the world where I get to mingle with the fans (I actually call them friends-that-I-haven't-gotten-to-know-yet). We walk around the city taking photos and I give them tips, tricks, and little golden nuggets of truth along the way. This is the fun crowd that showed up in Melbourne, Australia a few years ago. I'm there in the front wearing a black shirt, the one guy who forgot to look at the camera!

Psychedelics and Artistic Growth

I have used, and continue to use, psychedelics and other non-addictive drugs. They have opened my mind, made me more creative, and made me understand more about the tapestry of energy and consciousness of the universe.

I remember growing up and watching those advertisements on TV with two eggs sizzling in a pan that hauntingly claimed, "This is your brain on drugs." I never really understood that ad, because I really liked eggs. But I got the point, and it scared me.

What I realized about five years ago, when I first tried recreational drugs, is that not all drugs are the same. Yes, there are some bad drugs out there, like meth, heroin, and all the addictive opioids. I have never tried any of those, and I don't recommend them. It seems clear that those cause a net-negative effect not only in people's lives, but in the lives of people around them.

I'll talk about this as if you know nothing about recreational drugs, which I find most people do not. It's an interesting evolution for us as a society, because many of these drugs, especially the psychedelics, were a part of ritualistic village life for 99% of our ancestors. It's only the most recent few centuries where we have stopped using them, a product of urbanization and strong religious and government control.

First, recreational drugs are not addictive. This was a huge revelation to me. Yes, some can become part of a behavior pattern, but that is a lot different than a chemical or psychological addiction. For example, having psychedelics once a month and enjoying the experience is no different than going to the movies once a month. If you like to go to an awesome movie theater to check out of reality, it can't be said that you're addicted to movies. And, by the way, a good psilocybin experience can often be 100x better than the best movie. For more information on this, I recommend Michael Pollan's book *How to Change Your Mind*. I do recommend everyone goes through a session of this with an experienced counselor, as it really can reset your mind while giving you a glimpse of the divine. You'll put on an eye mask, listen to music, and the counselor will guide you through the experience. It's impossible to describe, but you will have breakthroughs that you need to have.

I've tried marijuana (weed) about a dozen times. It just doesn't work for me. I have some friends who really enjoy it, but I don't do it anymore. It doesn't seem to agree with my body chemistry. But this is an important thing to learn about drugs: you will develop your own tastes. I learned to develop these tastes and experiment with mind-expanding substances at Burning Man, and this mind expansion has absolutely helped my creativity, my openness, and my connection with the universe.

Here's a photo of Burning Man from above. I've been every year for the past eight years. This is a temporary city of about 70,000 artists and creatives that is rebuilt every year in a white sand desert in Nevada.

I will now talk about two drugs that I think everyone on earth should do. Maybe that's another book. Also, you should also ask your doctor before you try these. You may have another medication that could disagree, a heart condition, or any variety of things. Don't be afraid to be 100% honest with your doctor. There's nothing to be embarrassed about, and, believe me, your doctor has already seen it all. These two drugs I will talk about are not harmful. They are not addictive. Rather than tell you what they are not, let me tell you what they are.

First, I think everyone on earth would benefit from doing MDMA (also known as Molly or Ecstasy) once a month. Do it with friends or loved ones. You will be happier than you thought humanly possible, and it will open up new rooms in your brain you can revisit any time. I've done this drug many times with doctors who have explained everything to me. It will last 3-6 hours. You'll feel a universal love for everything and everyone around you while having a massive amount of energy. It's impossible to make a bad decision on MDMA, as opposed to legalized drugs like alcohol. In fact, you'll be so happy, you'll be tempted to do it again after the effect wears off, but this is not recommended. Be smart and only do it a few times a year. What is happening in your body? Chemically, there is a massive dump of serotonin and norepinephrine, two naturally occurring substances that elevate your mood. Serotonin is very important in keeping you in a decent "mood," so it is important not to completely deplete yourself, otherwise the rest of the week may be a bit dour. It takes about a week or more for that serotonin tank to refill itself. When you try it the first time, think, "Why on earth is this stuff illegal?" It's actually in phase 3 trials now (so, almost legal), as doctors investigate applications for PTSD and depression.

The second drug to try is DMT. Alternatively, you can go for the full Ayahuasca ceremony. I won't talk about that, because it is impossible to talk about. This is a very popular experience shared by some of my most intelligent and successful friends.

Amongst everyone I know that also does these drugs, 100% agrees that they are all better, more enjoyable, and safer than alcohol. I know, you've probably never heard of this stuff before, right? A bit mind-bending when you realize you've been lied to your entire life. @genttrav

Okay, enough talk about awesome drugs. Let's talk biz. I'm wearing my socks, so you know that means it's business time.

Fine Art Business and Other Business Interests

My main business at TreyRatcliff.com is selling large-format, limited-edition fine art prints to happy collectors around the world. I had the first HDR photo to hang in the Smithsonian Museum, and the museum also featured a few more of my photos in a 2018 Burning Man exhibit. My fine art business is performing well, and we passed the $1 million revenue mark a few years ago. This expedition has been much more fun and exhilarating than I ever anticipated.

Here is one of my installations hanging in the home of Sir Michael Hill.

Beyond the fine art business, I've dabbled in myriad other lifestyle business activities related to my photography and travel life. By the way, let me make it very clear that I am full of gratitude and I feel like one of the luckiest people on the planet. I don't take any of this for granted!

This was our tour bus passing through Paris. It slept 6 people, had a movie room, and even a bar! Wow we had fun... It was part of an extended campaign where I would lead photo walks and give art talks in 80 cities around the world. We partnered with Ritz-Carlton, Air New Zealand, Flixbus, and Facebook as sponsors.
More info at 80stays.treyratcliff.com

One of my favorite projects was creating a solution to a personal pet peeve. I've lugged my camera gear around the globe and struggled to find a way to carry it all that was functional, durable and not too dorky, but nothing like that existed—believe me, I've looked everywhere. So, a few years ago, I got together with the smart people at Peak Design in San Francisco, and we partnered to design a number of photographer-friendly bags. Our two campaigns on Kickstarter were hugely success-ful, making over $13 million. More importantly, our products have made a ton of people happy, since they now have an enjoyable way to cart their photo gear around on adventures.

I also teamed up with Skylum (formerly Macphun) to build our own photography software, called Aurora HDR. Last year, Aurora HDR won Apple's "Mac App of the Year," and to date, the app has reached over 3.5 million downloads and continues to grow.

I also run photography workshops, organize free photo walks around the world, do inspirational public speaking via my agent at CAA, make video tutorial courses about photography, and create other cool stuff we sell on our online store. I mostly use my Instagram and other platforms as a way to inspire other artists and help spread ideas about creativity around the world in a positive way.

MY PERSONAL APPROACH TO TAKING PHOTOS OF PEOPLE AND LANDSCAPES

I didn't want to make a significant chunk of this book about my photography and my approach to the subject matter. I do, however, believe all photographers, even selfie-photographers, have some emotional baggage they carry, and that weight permeates every photo they take. Studying a selection of an artist's creations, looking at what they find interesting, and understanding how they see what they are looking at, can reveal a sense of who the artist is.

I believe the universe is a beautiful and silly place.

I say this after over ten years of traveling to all seven continents, meeting awesome people from all of them, experiencing countless psychedelics and other drugs, studying anthropology and sociology extensively, and undertaking a deep practice in meditation, as I slowly come to understand consciousness and how we are all connected in the same tapestry.

There are many natural forces in the world. The sun heats the planet. Dogs are happy when their owners come home.

Humans are drawn to beautiful and interesting things.

I don't have many skills, I assure you! But maybe my three greatest skills are:

1. Observing and taking photos of beautiful things.
2. Figuring people out.
3. Asking people to help me overcome my shortcomings.

I'm also an awesome dad, as #4, but let's not get into parenting stuff too.

The universe is, by default, entropic. Humans seek order in the entropy. I see order as "beauty," but I use this word not in the common definition of physical attractiveness. So much of my day is utter chaos, whether I am holding a camera or not.

When I experience order (or beauty), I have a moment of conscious presence— whether it be an amazing song, an awesome person, a movie, or some semblance of a transcendent experience—and that's what I try to capture in and with my photographs. The process of tuning in to find order and beauty, I believe, is a kind of consciousness that produces Art with a capital "A," and is what separates some photographs from billions of snapshots and indulgent selfies.

I'm not suggesting that my approach is superior, or that I'm more "woke," but it certainly is the result of intellectual and philosophical deep dives. This is the framework that I use to analyze what's going on in social media today.

I've included a sampling of my photos below so you can get to know me a little better. Think of them as an aesthetic bibliography. If you're on a black and white Kindle, these won't look that great, so better to pop over to my portfolio at https://StuckInCustoms.SmugMug.com and even better on a laptop rather than a phone so the pictures are big and bold!

MY PHILOSOPHY

I'll explain my philosophy on life and the universe as it stands today. I continue to add to it as I learn more about myself and the universe. It informs everything I write. This isn't really a full treatise on my philosophy.

Perhaps I'll write that someday, but I think it's important you understand the shape of the mind that writes this, so it frames the texture of the words in this book.

Overall, my philosophy is derived from a combination of ancient Eastern notions, and not in the religious sense at all. There is not a set of "rules" or a template to "follow," in fact, it is the opposite of that. It is the letting go of all of these constructs, starting with the ego.

Ego is a fictional construct. Our minds are amazing at creating a story, but the story is simply that: a fictional construct.

I often give speeches to photographers and creatives and offer this one simple truth: the greatest creative gift you can give yourself is to let yourself go, as this frees up the energy kidnapped by the ego. That energy is then free to create and to stop worrying about:

1. What other people think of you
2. Yourself

Anxiety. It is a recursive algorithm, a nascent program that instills a once-vital fear. Anxiety and fear used to be extremely valuable tools in our toolbelt back in the hunter/gatherer days when we struggled to survive and had to look out for a lion in the tall grass. Anxiety is the yin to ego's yang. They dance and twirl together as if that is reality. None of that exists as soon as you realize the tapestry of energy that is unfolding around you.

Let me attempt to unpack some key things I have discovered through significant meditation, reading from masters, psychedelic experiences, and introspection.

YOU ARE NOT THE THOUGHTS IN YOUR HEAD

You are the silence behind the thoughts. You, the real inner you, can watch the thoughts go by, like clouds in the sky. Think about a time when you were laying on your back. Maybe you were alone and maybe you were next to a close friend, holding their hand. Maybe your hands fold together like two soft puzzle pieces. Finally, you're looking up at those clouds.

All the clouds were interesting. You don't look up at a cloud and say, hey, what an ugly cloud.

The same goes for the trees you see as you walk in the park. Maybe you see a big tree or a small tree or a misshapen tree. You never think, wow, that tree is shit. What a terrible tree! How dare it enter my visual cortex!

So why do you do this with your own thoughts? Why are you labeling and judging your thoughts?

Your thoughts are no different than clouds or trees. Just as you can simply observe clouds and trees, observe your thoughts but loosen your grip on them. You are the soft silence that observes all things.

I'm only reminding you of something you may already know, or at least may suspect. Your thoughts are clouds and trees. All interesting. There is no need to label them as good or bad.

This is a very difficult concept for people with a very strong ego to understand. They are convinced they *are* the thoughts in their head. But if you just allow the door to open just a tiny bit and let a little bit of the light of consciousness to peek through the crack, you'll see what I'm saying. It's incredibly liberating once you grab ahold of the concept that you are so much more than your thoughts. In fact, your thoughts are one of the most insignificant things about you.

SOME OF MY FAVORITE PHOTOS

Here is a collection of some of my favorite photos. If you want to see them in full color and at better resolution, just visit the website http://StuckInCustoms.SmugMug.com.

Some old school photographers will tell you heavy post-processing is impure. I believe using a variety of artistic tools does not diminish the final effect of a photograph and, in fact, the use of artifice in your craft is noble. For instance, this one is a panorama of 130 different photos taken in southern China that I've digitally sewn together before applying proprietary High Dynamic Range techniques to achieve a look that captures the mood in the moment. It's my artistic interpretation of a subjective experience. You could never get this in just one photo in-camera.

I believe that beauty is around us all the time. Some people are too busy looking at their phones to look up and notice.

I'm mostly a travel and landscape photographer, but I don't limit myself by these defini-
tions. I see beautiful things and people everywhere. Look at this incredible bamboo forest
in Kyoto, Japan. How is it even possible something so amazing exists on this strange rock
we're on, flying around the sun?

The Museum of Evolution. If you don't believe in evolution, then let's agree to call dinosaurs "Jesus Horses." Anyway, this is an image from my fine art series made out of 250 different photos painstakingly pieced together over hundreds of hours. Collectors who appreciate the details of beauty can study an infinite amount of tiny and interesting elements when it's printed out in full at 3 meters (10 feet) across.

Here's a headhunter in Papua New Guinea. He had eyes from every universe.

I spent about a month living in Antarctica. On the first day, I had to go into survival training, where we dug out ice caves for sleeping and built structures like this so we could cook meals. It reminded me of Minecraft in real life!

I took this photo of Anthony Bourdain a little before he committed suicide. I loved this guy and I'm sad he is gone. I'm so confused about why he killed himself, although I have a few ideas. I understand the nihilistic tendencies of a creative intellectual, and I try to channel that energy to enthuse my sanguine approach to life.

One of my counter-intuitive truths of photography is that it is interesting to confuse or obscure information. This principle does not, of course, extend to misleading stats and fraudulent behavior that I discussed earlier.

I love all the art and random things that happen at Burning Man and have returned every year since 2011 to have a digital detox and recharge my creative battery. I know many people can be very judgmental about the event, but I think it says more about them than the actual festival. I can tell you, with absolute and ontological certainty, that if everyone on earth did MDMA, the human race would be in a much better place.

This is the Aurora Australis just off the southern edge of New Zealand.

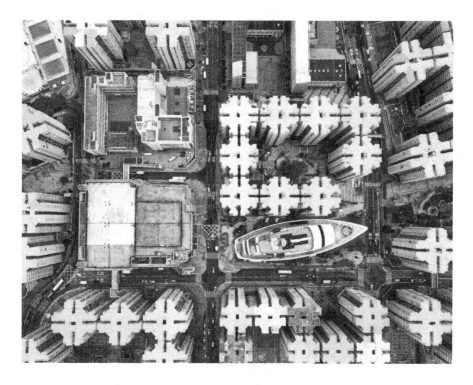

An abandoned yacht in the middle of Chinese government housing.

*Over the years, I've amassed quite a collection of photos from Burning Man. I have my
full portfolio online if you'd like to see more. Just go
to stuckincustoms.smugmug.com/Burning-Man*

I took this in Cinque Terre, Italy halfway through my European photo walk tour last year. This is a three-minute exposure taken during a rainstorm. It's important to note that I took this after having a whole pizza and entire bottle of wine.

This is a very mysterious place in Death Valley where the rocks move across the desert in the most unbelievable manner. I won't tell you how they move, but you would never guess it in a million years. I'm not telling you because I think it is important to just wonder about some things. In a world where you can Google anything, humans are forgetting how to wonder.

This is a leopard in Botswana eating Warthog tapas. I never knew how much I loved animals until I spent several weeks in Africa taking photos of animals in their raw element. Now I can spend all day with animals, especially elephants. If you think that sounds boring, then you probably need some quality time with elephants.

APPENDIX B
THE 1,000 TANE COMMANDMENTS

What follows are the 1,000 custom comments that I threw together and purchased for the fake account of @genttravel. One of the comment-buying services I used allows you to create your own comments that get spread around as many photos you want.

We did this to illustrate how fake Influencers can trick brands or agencies or brands into making them think you are getting actual engagement.

- Oh Tane—Never cry for that person who doesn't know the value of your tears.
- Don't let your eyes be blinded by his booty, Tane
- They say tongue is the strongest muscle of the body. Wanna fight, Tane?
- Tane, do you live in a corn field, coz I'm stalking you.
- Boys are like purses, cute, full of crap, and can always be replaced. And so is Tane.

- I take a lot of pride in being myself. I'm comfortable with who I am. Tane, I will now call you Wolfgang Thrust.
- A human. Being. A human. Tane.
- Tane! Never love anyone who treats you like you're ordinary.
- A man of puzzle and force, whose force is surpassed just by his secret—totally Tane!
- Yo Tanster! Simple during childbirth, computerized by configuration.
- I generally feel dismal for seedless watermelons, in light of the fact that imagine a scenario in which they needed children. Tane doesn't, though.
- I'm truly a titan cupcake. Perplexed about crazy rides and dry ice Tane Says True.
- Yo Tanster! Trying to forget it but the memories are too strong.
- Tane, Right? We all start as strangers.
- Truth is, I'm crazy for you. And everyone can see that but you. Yes, you Tane,
- I act like I'm ok, but I'm really not. Not like you are Big Gent.
- Stop looking for happiness in the same place you just lost it. You got that tanster?
- Tane, Don't worry if you haven't found your true love, they're just with someone else right now.
- Gent Travel! If I die tomorrow, will you remember me?
- Oh Tanay—Keep smiling because life's a beautiful thing and there's so much to smile about
- Being single is smarter than being in the wrong relationship. Listen up Gent Tane
- Do you sit in a pile of sugar? cause you got a pretty sweet ass! , Tane
- Did you swallow magnets? cause you are attractive! Listen up Gent Tane
- Kiss me if I'm wrong but Dinosaurs still exist? Right? Yes, you Tane,

- Nice t-shirt. Can I talk you out of it? Not like you are Big Gent.
- Do you have a name or can I call you Mine? You got that tanster?
- Tane! Do you like sleeping? Me too! We should do it together sometimes!
- Yo Tanster! Can I borrow a kiss? I promise I'll give it back.
- Tane, Right? Aside from being sexy, what do you do for a living?
- Oh Tane—I don't need your approval to be me.
- Gent Travel! I am who I am, I am what I am, I do what I do and I ain't never gonna do it any different. I don't care who likes it and who don't.
- Oh Tanay—Take me as I am, or watch me as I go.
- Sir Tane—If I were you, I would adore me.
- Big T Me? Weird? Girl Please! I am Limited Edition.
- tane—i am not perfect. I make mistakes. But when I say Sorry I mean it!
- Oh Please Tane—I am not trying to give an image of a fairytale, perfect, everything else, I am just being myself.
- I was both loved and hated for being upfront. But I was just being myself. Forgive me, Tane.
- I like being myself. Maybe just slimmer, with a few less wrinkles. Don't hate me, Tane.
- Everyone said I could be Anything.. So I became Sexy! Tane Sexpot!
- Completely clumsy, proudest of geek & nerd, decreaser of world sucking , but not Tane
- Tane, ummm—Forcefully early stages and stuff
- Tane! All you fashionable people need to quit wearing Nirvana shirts on the off chance that you don't even hear them out.
- Tane, Right? Anybody knows my Instagram username not making another record once more.
- Tane, Are you a broker on the grounds that I'd like you to leave

me a credit

- Oh Tane—Uncovered. Frequently Unreliable. Effectively distract
- Gent Travel! Conceived at an exceptionally youthful age
- Oh Tanay—Amigo, would you be able to standard?
- Sir Tane—Light, waggish, effectual, inexhaustible, demiurgic, friendly advertising buddy, independent thousandaire Outdoors is plans
- Big T Would someone be able to let me know my Instagram username I bolted myself out and I don't realize what to do
- tane—Chocolate doesn't make inquiries, chocolate gets it
- Oh Please Tane—Espresso Drinker, eReader Addict, Blogger. I'm exceptionally occupied and wonderful
- Currently featuring in my own particular reality show titled, A Modern Cinderella; One Girl's Search for Love and Shoes , Tane
- Try not to think for a brief moment that I really mind what you need to say And so is Tane.
- Think ambitiously (little textual style) Listen up Gent Tane
- Eating an entire apple center on the grounds that you can't be tried setting off to the canister, let it out, you've done it, Tane.
- Each tempest comes up short on downpour And so is Tane.
- Remarkable finishes in "us" fortuitous event? I think not Listen up Gent Tane
- By and large, the easy way out appeals. Additionally, I am fantastic at parallel stopping. Yes, you Tane,
- God favor this chaotic situation Not like you are Big Gent.
- Great Samaritan, cleaned up competitor, particularly skilled napper. You got that tanster?
- Tane-san—Have heaps of hair and like appalling things
- Travel man Gent—Here to serve. the feline overlord
- I completely loathe Instagram, and whatever else needing to do with hashtags. Except you, Tane

- Tane! I am an on-screen character and an essayist and I co-made my breakfast and my child, Malachai.
- Yo Tanster! I am returning to face the truth that an ordinary day is not lager on the shoreline or calamari in the tummy.
- Tane, Right? I can quote (Insert motion picture) superior to anything you and every one of your companions.
- Tane, I Can't recollect who I stole my bio from or why
- Oh Tane—I have not lost my psyche its went down on HD some place.
- Gent Travel! I have this new hypothesis that human immaturity doesn't end until your mid thirties.
- Oh Tanay—I trust one day I adore something the route ladies in advertisements love yogurt
- Sir Tane—I took a gander at my Instagram photographs and acknowledged I look excellent.
- Big T I once wheezed a beanie weenie through my nose. I likewise made a stallion black out in Costa Rica.
- tane—I just rap caucasionally
- Oh Please Tane—I lean toward my plays on words expected
- Tane-san—I put the hot in maniacal
- Travel man Gent—I as of late surrendered Warcraft so my efficiency, and drinking, have expanded dramatically.
- I shouldn't be permitted to go on Snapchat, Facebook or Instagram when I'm intoxicated! Yes, Tane-craft.
- Despite everything I don't comprehend Twitter, yet here I am. Wait, Tane, this is Instagram! I'm too legit to quit you!
- Tane, you should know—I talk like a child and I never pay for beverages.
- You know this Tane, but I believe its irregular if a young lady doesn't have an Instagram now days.
- I'm embarrassed to say this Tane but I used to act. I additionally hip twirl and eat Jolly Ranchers not generally in the meantime however.

- Lives change like the weather. I hope you remember today is never too late to be brand new. , Tane
- Dear vegetarians, if you're trying to save animals, then why are you eating their food? And so is Tane.
- A recent study has found that women who carry a little extra weight live longer than the men who mention it. Listen up Gent Tane
- They used to shout my name, now they whisper it. , Tane
- Life is not measured by the number of breaths you take, but the moments that take your breath away. And so is Tane.
- Stay sharp and far from timid. Listen up Gent Tane
- If a dentist makes their money from unhealthy teeth, why would I trust a product 4/5 of them recommend? Yes, you Tane,
- Say Beer Can with a British accent. I just taught you to say Bacon with a Jamaican accent. Not like you are Big Gent.
- These are the days we live for. You got that tanster?
- Life is short, false; it's the longest thing you do. Yes, Tane-craft.
- Work until your idols become your rivals. Wait, Tane, this is Instagram! I'm too legit to quit you!
- A clever person solves a problem. A wise person avoids it. A dumb person creates it. Except you, Tane
- Some days start better than others. Tane doesn't, though
- Mom said life is similar to a container of chocolates, you never realize what your gonna get Forgive me, Tane.
- Mermaids don't do homework Don't hate me, Tane.
- My distractions are breakfast, lunch, and supper. Tane, I will now call you Wolfgang Thrust.
- Oh Tane—My life is about as sorted out as the $5 DVD canister at WalMart Tane Sexpot!
- My life was changed by a train. A human. Tane.
- My relationship status? Netflix, Tane Pops, Oreos and warm up pants—totally tane

- Normally and falsely seasoned , but not Tane
- Pleasant fellows completion lunch. , Tane
- Simply a man who sufficiently minded to attempt And so is Tane.
- Gracious I'm sad was my backtalk a lot for you? Listen up Gent Tane
- OMG nobody cares , Tane
- Just Swag young ladies are interested by hashtags on the Facebook. And so is Tane.
- Flawless has 7 letters thus does meeeeee. Incident? I think not. Listen up Gent Tane
- Kindly embed grandiose poo about myself here. Yes, you Tane,
- Present yourself with a beverage, put on some lipstick, and get a hold of yourself. Not like you are Big Gent.
- Presumably the best meat eater on the planet You got that tanster?
- Glad supporter of untidy hair and warm up pants Yes, Tanecraft.
- Pudding tastes better with a plastic spoon Wait, Tane, this is Instagram! I'm too legit to quit you!
- Putting' the "euphoria" in 'Advertising's Except you, Tane
- Suggested by 4 out of 5 individuals that suggest things. Tane doesn't, though
- Recuperating frozen yogurt fanatic Forgive me, Tane.
- S P E C T A C U L A R V E R N A C U L A R Don't hate me, Tane.
- Sometime in the not so distant future, there will be a redesigned form of me. Tane, I will now call you Wolfgang Thrust.
- Here and there I simply need to surrender it all and turn into a good looking extremely rich person. Tane Sexpot!
- I need a six month holiday, twice a year. A human. Tane.
- There may be no excuse for laziness, but I'm still looking.— totally tane

- A blind man walks into a bar And a chair and a table. , but not Tane
- I don't always surf the Internet, but when I do, eyebrows! I Trust TANE.
- Yesterday, I changed my WiFi password to "Hackitifyoucan"; today, someone changed it to—mr Tane!
- "Challenge Accepted". Thanks Sir Gent
- So, you're on Instagram? You must be an amazing photographer. I will travel with Tane!
- Real men don't take selfies. You ARE Tane, after all.
- I haven't done this in a while so excuse me. It's all good Tane.
- I know I'm lucky that I'm so cute. You are cute too Tane.
- Onions make me sad. A lot of people don't realize that. I'm Tane-dream.
- I'm your worst nightmare. Day dream with Tane.
- Hey girl, feel my sweater. Know what it's made of? Boyfriend material. Boyfriend Tane Sauce.
- If I was funny, I would have a good Instagram caption. Caption my Tane.
- I think you are lacking vitamin me! Vitamin Tane!
- What if I told you, you can eat without posting it on Instagram. Diet Tane Number 7!
- Ladies, please. And some Tane on the side.
- Need an ark? I Noah guy. Tane's Ark.
- One time I dreamed of Tane and I woke up soaking wet! Oh Tane.
- When Instagram was down, I ran around town shouting "like" at flowers, dogs, and expensive brunches. I "like" Tane.
- Say "Beer Can" with a British accent. I just taught you to say "Bacon" with a Jamaican accent. Bacon-wrapped Tane!
- I don't always study, but when I do, I don't. Tane-Tutor!
- I'll never try to fit in. I was born to STAND OUT. Like you, Awesome T-Man

- So you're telling me I have a chance. Tane Says True.
- Walking past a class with your friends in it. Tane doesn't care.
- I'm not saying it was aliens, but it was Aliens! , Tane
- Yea, dating is cool but have you ever had stuffed crust pizza? And so is Tane.
- Started from the bottom now we're here. Listen up Gent Tane
- Give me the chocolate and nobody gets hurt. , Tane
- So, you're on Instagram? You must be an amazing photographer. And so is Tane.
- Onions make me sad. A lot of people don't realize that. Listen up Gent Tane
- Women drivers rev my engine. Yes, you Tane,
- Oh you're a model? What's your agency, Instagram? Not like you are Big Gent.
- I liked memes before they were on Instagram You got that tanster?
- Friday, my second favorite F word. Yes, Tane-craft.
- If a dentist makes their money from unhealthy teeth, why would I trust a product 4/5 of them recommend? Wait, Tane, this is Instagram! I'm too legit to quit you!
- I didn't choose the thug life, the thug life chose me Except you, Tane
- Weekend, please don't leave me. Tane doesn't, though
- Need an ark? I Noah guy. Forgive me, Tane.
- What if I told you, you can eat without posting it on Instagram. Don't hate me, Tane.
- I need a six month holiday, twice a year. Tane, I will now call you Wolfgang Thrust.
- If I was funny, I would have a good Instagram caption. Tane Sexpot!
- I don't always surf the Internet, but when I do, eyebrows! A human. Tane.
- A blind man walks into a bar And a chair and a table.—totally

tane

- I had fun once, it was horrible. , but not Tane
- Each tempest comes up short on downpour , Tane
- Marvelous closures in "us" occurrence? I think not And so is Tane.
- By and large, the easy way out advances. Likewise, I am great at parallel stopping. Listen up Gent Tane
- God favor this chaotic situation , Tane
- Great Samaritan, cleaned up competitor, particularly skilled napper. And so is Tane.
- Have loads of hair and like revolting things Listen up Gent Tane
- Here to serve. the feline overlord Yes, you Tane,
- I completely loathe Instagram, and whatever else needing to do with hashtags. Not like you are Big Gent.
- I generally feel tragic for seedless watermelons, in light of the fact that imagine a scenario in which they needed infants. You got that tanster?
- I am a performing artist and an essayist and I co-made my breakfast and my child, Malachai. Yes, Tane-craft.
- I am returning to face the truth that an ordinary day is not lager on the shoreline or calamari in the stomach. Wait, Tane, this is Instagram! I'm too legit to quit you!
- I can quote (Insert motion picture) superior to anything you and every one of your companions. Except you, Tane
- I Can't recall who I stole my bio from or why Tane doesn't, though
- I have not lost my brain its moved down on HD some place. Forgive me, Tane.
- I have this new hypothesis that human youthfulness doesn't end until your mid thirties. Don't hate me, Tane.
- I trust one day I cherish something the route ladies in plugs love yogurt Tane, I will now call you Wolfgang Thrust.

- I took a gander at my Instagram photographs and acknowledged I look delightful. Tane Sexpot!
- I once sniffled a beanie weenie through my nose. I likewise made a stallion swoon in Costa Rica. A human. Tane.
- I just rap occasionally—totally tane
- I favor my quips expected , but not Tane
- I put the hot in insane I Trust TANE.
- I as of late surrendered Warcraft so my efficiency, and drinking, have expanded significantly.—mr Tane!
- I shouldn't be permitted to go on Snapchat, Facebook or Instagram when I'm tipsy! Thanks Sir Gent
- Despite everything I don't comprehend Twitter, however here I am. I will travel with Tane!
- I talk like a child and I never pay for beverages. You ARE Tane, after all.
- I believe it's unusual if a young lady doesn't have an Instagram now days. It's all good Tane.
- I used to act. I additionally hip twirl and eat Jolly Ranchers not generally in the meantime however. You are cute too Tane.
- I was dependent on hokey pokey yet I turned myself around I'm Tane-dream.
- I will go into survival mode if tickled Day dream with Tane.
- I'm a power to be figured with, I figure Boyfriend Tane Sauce.
- I'm not happy its "Friday" I'm happy its "Today". Love your life 7 days a week. Caption my Tane.
- I'm beginning to like Instagram, which is unusual on the grounds that I loathe pictures. Vitamin Tane!
- I've generally believed being famous on Instagram is as about as futile as being rich in syndication Diet Tane Number 7!
- I'm a Basset Hound devotee with a mouth like a Syphilitic mariner. And some Tane on the side.
- I'm a Texan with bunches of sentiments and beautiful hair. Tane's Ark.

- I'm really not amusing. I'm just truly mean and individuals think I am kidding. Oh Tane.
- I'm here to evade companions on Facebook. I "like" Tane.
- I'm not shrewd. I simply wear glasses. Bacon-wrapped Tane!
- I'm not certain what number of issues I have in light of the fact that math is one of them Tane-Tutor!
- I'm genuine and I trust some of my adherents are as well. Like you, Awesome T-Man
- On the off chance that I could hole up my life in one line I would pass on of humiliation Tane doesn't care.
- On the off chance that you don't have anything pleasant to say, come sit by me, and we can ridicule individuals together , Tane
- Looking for rest, rational soundness, & The Shire And so is Tane.
- Embed self important stuff about myself here. Listen up Gent Tane
- It's Weird that all pics shared from Instagram are continually obscuring. , Tane
- Only a cupcake searching for a stud biscuit And so is Tane.
- Simply one more papercut survivor Listen up Gent Tane
- I'm done Yes, you Tane,
- I'm Nothing Not like you are Big Gent.
- My World is nothing without you You got that tanster?
- Please accept me Yes, Tane-craft.
- No one is for me Wait, Tane, this is Instagram! I'm too legit to quit you!
- I'm alone Except you, Tane
- Why everyone seems to be very happy to me Tane doesn't, though
- How to live without happy Forgive me, Tane.
- How to live happy Don't hate me, Tane.
- Oh God he is my crush Tane, I will now call you Wolfgang Thrust.

- I lover him so much, but !!! Tane Sexpot!
- I love you, But as a friend A human. Tane.
- A Tane in yoga pants is like—totally tane
- Never love anyone who treats you like you're ordinary. , but not Tane
- Trying to forget it but the memories are too strong. , Tane
- We all start as strangers. And so is Tane.
- Truth is, I'm crazy for you. And everyone can see that but you. Listen up Gent Tane
- I act like I'm ok, but I'm really not. , Tane
- Stop looking for happiness in the same place you just lost it. And so is Tane.
- Don't worry if you haven't found your true love, they're just with someone else right now. Listen up Gent Tane
- Never cry for that person who doesn't know the value of your tears. Yes, you Tane,
- If I die tomorrow, will you remember me? Not like you are Big Gent.
- Keep smiling because life's a beautiful thing and there's so much to smile about You got that tanster?
- Don't let your eyes be blinded by his booty Yes, Tane-craft.
- Boys are like purses, cute, full of crap, and can always be replaced. Wait, Tane, this is Instagram! I'm too legit to quit you!
- Being single is smarter than being in the wrong relationship. Except you, Tane
- Do you sit in a pile of sugar? cause you got a pretty sweet ass! Tane doesn't, though
- They say tongue is the strongest muscle of the body. Wanna fight? Forgive me, Tane.
- Did you swallow magnets? cause you are attractive! Don't hate me, Tane.
- Kiss me if I'm wrong but Dinosaurs still exist? Right? Tane, I will now call you Wolfgang Thrust.

- Nice t-shirt. Can I talk you out of it? Tane Sexpot!
- Do you have a name or can I call you Mine? A human. Tane.
- Do you like sleeping? Me too! We should do it together sometimes!—totally tane
- Can I borrow a kiss? I promise I'll give it back, Tane
- Aside from being sexy, what do you do for a living? I Trust TANE.
- Do you live in a corn field, coz I'm stalking you.—mr Tane!
- I don't need your approval to be me. Thanks Sir Gent
- I am who I am, I am what I am, I do what I do and I ain't never gonna do it any different. I don't care who likes it and who don't. I will travel with Tane!
- Take me as I am, or watch me as I go. You ARE Tane, after all.
- If I were you, I would adore me. It's all good Tane.
- Me? Weird? B*tch Please! I am Limited Edition. You are cute too Tane.
- i am not perfect. I make mistakes. But when I say Sorry I mean it! I'm Tane-dream.
- I am not trying to give an image of a fairy-tale, perfect, everything else, I am just being myself. Day dream with Tane.
- I was both loved and hated for being upfront. But I was just being myself. Boyfriend Tane Sauce.
- I like being myself. Maybe just slimmer, with a few less wrinkles. Caption my Tane.
- I take a lot of pride in being myself. I'm comfortable with who I am. Vitamin Tane!
- Everyone said I could be Anything.. So I became Sexy! Diet Tane Number 7!
- A human. Being. And some Tane on the side.

APPENDIX C
BOOK SUGGESTIONS

I have a running list of book suggestions I keep regularly updated over at www.Kit.com/TreyRatcliff. If you simply want my #1 recommendation, get *The Untethered Soul* by Michael Singer.

NOTES

Introduction

1. "Black Mirror: Nosedive." Joe Wright, director. Season 3, episode 1, 21 Oct. 2016.
2. Lorenz, Taylor. "When a Sponsored Facebook Post Doesn't Pay Off." *The Atlantic*, Atlantic Media Company, 27 Dec. 2018, www.theatlantic.com/technology/archive/2018/12/massive-influencer-management-platform-has-been-stiffing-people-payments/578767/

CHAPTER 1 – UNDER THE INFLUENCE

1. "Instagram: Active Users 2013-2018." Statista, June 2AD, www.statista.com/statistics/253577/number-of-monthly-active-instagram-users/
2. "Instagram Rich List 2018 - Hopper HQ." Hopper Instagram Scheduler, Dec. 2018, www.hopperhq.com/blog/instagram-rich-list/
3. Schwab, Katharine. "The 2-Year-Old Instagram Influencers Who Make More than You." Fast Company, Fast Company, 21 Dec. 2018, www.fastcompany.com/90278778/the-2-year-old-instagram-influencers-who-make-more-than-you-do
4. "How Brands Use Kid Influencers To Maximize Marketing Efforts." Mediakix | Influencer Marketing Agency, 9 Oct. 2018, mediakix.com/2018/10/kid-influencers-social-media-marketing/
5. JETmag. "Young Kiwis Would Rather Be Social Media Influencers than Doctors." JETmag, 29 Nov. 2018, www.jetmag.co.nz/young-kiwis-would-rather-be-a-social-media-influencer-than-a-doctor/
6. JETmag. "Young Kiwis Would Rather Be Social Media Influencers than Doc-tors." JETmag, 29 Nov. 2018, www.jetmag.co.nz/young-kiwis-would-rather-be-a-social-media-influencer-than-a-doctor/
7. "Instagram Sponsored Influencer Content Volume 2019 | Statistic." Statista, www.statista.com/statistics/693775/instagram-sponsored-influencer-content/
8. "Instagram Rich List 2018 - Hopper HQ." *Hopper Instagram Scheduler*, Dec. 2018, www.hopperhq.com/blog/instagram-rich-list/
9. Robehmed, Natalie. "Highest-Paid YouTube Stars 2018: Markiplier, Jake Paul, PewDiePie And More." *Forbes*, Forbes Magazine, 5 Dec. 2018, www.forbes.com/sites/natalierobehmed/2018/12/03/highest-paid-youtube-stars-2018-markiplier-jake-paul-pewdiepie-and-more/#52721718909a
10. Robehmed, Natalie. "Highest-Paid YouTube Stars 2018: Markiplier, Jake Paul, PewDiePie And More." *Forbes*, Forbes Magazine, 5 Dec. 2018, www.forbes.com/sites/natalierobehmed/2018/12/03/highest-paid-youtube-stars-

2018-markiplier-jake-paul-pewdiepie-and-more/#52721718909a

11. Martineau, Paris. "Inside the Pricey War to Influence Your Instagram Feed." Wired, Conde Nast, 19 Nov. 2018, www.wired.com/story/pricey-war-influence-your-instagram-feed/

12. "Time Flies: U.S. Adults Now Spend Nearly Half a Day Interacting with Media." *What People Watch, Listen To and Buy*, The Nielsen Company, 31 July 2018, www.nielsen.com/us/en/insights/news/2018/time-flies-us-adults-now-spend-nearly-half-a-day-interacting-with-media.print.html

13. Tsukayama, Hayley. "Teens Spend Nearly Nine Hours Every Day Consuming Media." *The Washington Post*, WP Company, 3 Nov. 2015, www.washingtonpost.com/news/the-switch/wp/2015/11/03/teens-spend-nearly-nine-hours-every-day-consuming-media/

14. Griffiths, Mark, and Daria Kuss. "6 Questions Help Reveal If You're Addicted to Social Media." *The Washington Post*, WP Company, 25 Apr. 2018, www.washingtonpost.com/news/theworldpost/wp/2018/04/25/social-media-addiction/

15. Griffiths, Mark, and Daria Kuss. "6 Questions Help Reveal If You're Addicted to Social Media." The Washington Post, WP Company, 25 Apr. 2018, www.washingtonpost.com/news/theworldpost/wp/2018/04/25/social-media-addiction/

16. Lustig, Robert H. The Hacking of the American Mind: the Science behind the Corporate Takeover of Our Bodies and Brains. Avery, 2018.

17. Rsph. "#StatusofMind: Instagram Ranked Worst for Young People's Mental Health." *RSPH*, Royal Society for Public Health and Youth Health Movement, 19 May 2017, www.rsph.org.uk/about-us/news/instagram-ranked-worst-for-young-people-s-mental-health.html

CHAPTER 2 – SOMETHING FISHY IS GOING ON

1. Contestabile, Giordano. "Influencer Marketing in 2018: Becoming an Efficient Marketplace." *Adweek*, Adweek, 15 Jan. 2018, www.adweek.com/digital/giordano-contestabile-activate-by-bloglovin-guest-post-influencer-marketing-in-2018/

2. Confessore, Nicholas, and Gabriel J. X. The Follower Factory. The New York Times, 27 Jan. 2018, www.nytimes.com/interactive/2018/01/27/technology/social-media-bots.html

3. Belam, Martin. "Threatin: Band Creates Fake Fanbase for Tour Attended by No One." The Guardian, Guardian News and Media, 12 Nov. 2018, www.theguardian.com/music/2018/nov/12/threatin-band-fake-fanbase-tour

4. Connick, Tom. 'Fake Band' Threatin Just Played a UK Tour to... Pretty Much No-One. NME, 15 Nov. 2018, www.nme.com/blogs/nme-blogs/fake-band-threatin-just-played-sold-uk-tour-absolutely-no-one-2400572

5. "Women Of Legal Tech On Disrupting A $600 Billion Profession." LawGeex Blog:

Legal Technology, 15 May 2018, blog.lawgeex.com/women-of-legal-tech-on-disrupting-a-600-billion-profession/

CHAPTER 3 – THE INSIDE SCOOP
(OR: HOW TO BUY YOUR WAY TO FAKE INTERNET FAME)

1. "Top 5 Places To Buy Instagram Followers." IG Reviews, igreviews.org/

2. Joseph, Seb, et al. 'We Don't Pay Influencers on Reach': How Kellogg's Is Combating Influencer Fraud. Digiday, 28 Nov. 2018, digiday.com/marketing/influencer-fraud-kelloggs/

3. Kantrowitz, Alex. Facebook Removes 10 Instagram Algorithm-Gaming Groups With Hundreds Of Thousands Of Members. BuzzFeed News, 11 May 2018, www.buzzfeednews.com/article/alexkantrowitz/facebook-removes-ten-instagram-algorithm-gaming-groups-with#.fsAQvjgdo

4. Martineau, Paris. "Instagram's Crackdown on Fake Followers Just Might Work." Wired, Condé Nast, 26 Nov. 2018, www.wired.com/story/instagrams-crackdown-fake-followers-might-work/

5. Influencer, Wannabe. "I Was Scammed by a Celebrity Influencer." Medium, 11 Dec. 2018, medium.com/@wannabe.influencer1/i-was-scammed-by-a-celebrity-influencer-6612d61e1a9e

6. *Ibid.*

7. *Ibid.*

8. Lorenz, Taylor. "Rising Instagram Stars Are Posting Fake Sponsored Content." The Atlantic, Atlantic Media Company, 18 Dec. 2018, www.theatlantic.com/technology/archive/2018/12/influencers-are-faking-brand-deals/578401/

9. Lorenz, Taylor. "When a Sponsored Facebook Post Doesn't Pay Off." The Atlantic, Atlantic Media Company, 27 Dec. 2018, www.theatlantic.com/technology/archive/2018/12/massive-influencer-management-platform-has-been-stiffing-people-payments/578767/

10. *Ibid.*

11. *Ibid.*

12. *Ibid.*

CHAPTER 4 – HOW TO SLOW THE ZOMBIE
APOCALYPSE (OR: HOW TO DETECT THE FAKES)

1. Source: EOnline - https://www.eonline.com/fr/news/608104/this-is-how-many-instagram-followers-celebs-lost-in-the-great-purge-of-2014

2. Parkinson, Hannah Jane. "Instagram Purge Costs Celebrities Millions of Followers." The Guardian, Guardian News and Media, 19 Dec. 2014, www.theguardian.com/technology/2014/dec/19/instagram-purge-costs-celebrities-

millions-of-followers

3. Bishop, Jordan. "6 Female Travel Photographers You Need To Follow On Instagram In 2017." Forbes, Forbes Magazine, 30 Jan. 2017, www.forbes.com/sites/bishopjordan/2017/01/28/best-female-travel-photographers-followers-instagram-2017/

4. Joseph, Seb, et al. 'We Don't Pay Influencers on Reach': How Kellogg's Is Combating Influencer Fraud. Digiday, 28 Nov. 2018, digiday.com/marketing/influencer-fraud-kelloggs/

5. "Facebook Data: How It Was Used by Cambridge Analytica." BBC News, BBC, 9 Apr. 2018, www.bbc.com/news/av/technology-43674480/facebook-data-how-it-was-used-by-cambridge-analytica

6. Desta, Yohana. "Was The Last Jedi Hate Actually Spread by Russian Trolls?" The Hive, Vanity Fair, 2 Oct. 2018, www.vanityfair.com/hollywood/2018/10/the-last-jedi-russian-trolls

7. Newton, Casey. "Facebook's Morale Problem Is Getting Worse." The Verge, The Verge, 6 Dec. 2018, www.theverge.com/2018/12/6/18128267/facebook-morale-uk-parliament-emails-privacy-competition

CHAPTER 5 – SELFIES AND THE EGO RUNNING AMOK

1. Marcus, Bert, director. The American Meme. Netflix, 27 Apr. 2018, www.netflix.com/title/81003741

2. *Ibid.*

3. *Ibid.*

4. *Ibid.*

5. Gritters, Jenni. "The Psychological Toll of Becoming an Instagram Influencer." Medium.com, Medium, 20 Dec. 2018, medium.com/s/love-hate/the-psychological-toll-of-becoming-an-instagram-influencer-5bbd1d9174c4

6. Justich, Kerry. "Influencer Says She Was on a 'Tapas and Cocaine' Diet to Stay Thin - Here's Why That's Not Healthy." Yahoo! News, Yahoo!, 9 Jan. 2019, www.yahoo.com/lifestyle/influencer-says-tapas-cocaine-diet-stay-thin-heres-thats-not-healthy-210417445.html

7. Justich, Kerry. "Influencer Says She Was on a 'Tapas and Cocaine' Diet to Stay Thin - Here's Why That's Not Healthy." Yahoo! News, Yahoo!, 9 Jan. 2019, www.yahoo.com/lifestyle/influencer-says-tapas-cocaine-diet-stay-thin-heres-thats-not-healthy-210417445.html

8. *Ibid.*

9. *Ibid.*

10. Peters, Terri. "Shamed for Post about Son's Low Instagram Numbers, Mom Speaks Out." TODAY.com, TODAY, www.today.com/parents/mom-blogger-shamed-post-about-son-instagram-t143055

11. Tolle, Eckhart. A New Earth: Awakening to Your Life's Purpose. Penguin Books,

2005.

12. Rhode, L D. "The Beauty Bias." Oxford University Press, 2010.

13. Mills, Jennifer S, et al. "'Selfie' Harm: Effects on Mood and Body Image in Young Women." Body Image, Dec. 2018, pp. 86—92., doi:10.1016/j.bodyim.2018.08.007.

14. Haferkamp, Nina, et al. "Men Are from Mars, Women Are from Venus? Examining Gender Differences in Self-Presentation on Social Networking Sites." Cyberpsychology, Behavior, and Social Networking, vol. 15, no. 2, 2012, pp. 91—98., doi:10.1089/cyber.2011.0151.

15. Toma, Catalina L., and Jeffrey T. Hancock. "Looks and Lies: The Role of Physical Attractiveness in Online Dating Self-Presentation and Deception." Communication Research, vol. 37, no. 3, July 2010, pp. 335—351., doi:10.1177/0093650209356437.

16. Day, Andy. "Man's Life Ruined by Instagram After Outstretched Arms Get Stuck While Posing for Ironic Picture." Fstoppers, 10 Dec. 2018, fstoppers.com/originals/mans-life-ruined-instagram-after-outstretched-arms-get-stuck-while-posing-ironic-315324

17. Kim, Ji Won, and T. Makana Chock. "Body Image 2.0: Associations between Social Grooming on Facebook and Body Image Concerns." Computers in Human Behavior, vol. 48, 2015, pp. 331—339., doi:10.1016/j.chb.2015.01.009.

18. Meier, Evelyn P., and James Gray. "Facebook Photo Activity Associated with Body Image Disturbance in Adolescent Girls." Cyberpsychology, Behavior, and Social Networking, vol. 17, no. 4, 3 Apr. 2014, pp. 199—206., doi:10.1089/cyber.2013.0305.

19. Robinson, Lily, et al. "Idealised Media Images: The Effect of Fitspiration Imagery on Body Satisfaction and Exercise Behaviour." Body Image, vol. 22, 2017, pp. 65—71., doi:10.1016/j.bodyim.2017.06.001.

20. Perloff, Richard M. "Social Media Effects on Young Women's Body Image Concerns: Theoretical Perspectives and an Agenda for Research." Sex Roles, vol. 71, no. 11-12, 2014, pp. 363—377., doi:10.1007/s11199-014-0384-6.

21. Kim, Ji Won, and T. Makana Chock. "Body Image 2.0: Associations between Social Grooming on Facebook and Body Image Concerns." Computers in Human Behavior, vol. 48, 2015, pp. 331—339., doi:10.1016/j.chb.2015.01.009.

22. Meier, Evelyn P., and James Gray. "Facebook Photo Activity Associated with Body Image Disturbance in Adolescent Girls." Cyberpsychology, Behavior, and Social Networking, vol. 17, no. 4, 3 Apr. 2014, pp. 199—206., doi:10.1089/cyber.2013.0305.

23. Tiggemann, Marika, and Amy Slater. "NetGirls: The Internet, Facebook, and Body Image Concern in Adolescent Girls." International Journal of Eating Disorders, vol. 46, no. 6, 25 May 2013, pp. 630—633., doi:10.1002/eat.22141.

24. Mills, Jennifer S, et al. "'Selfie' Harm: Effects on Mood and Body Image in Young Women." Body Image, Dec. 2018, pp. 86—92.,

doi:10.1016/j.bodyim.2018.08.007.

25. Pounders, Kathrynn, et al. "Insight into the Motivation of Selfie Postings: Impression Management and Self-Esteem." European Journal of Marketing, vol. 50, no. 9/10, 12 Feb. 2016, pp. 1879—1892., doi:10.1108/ejm-07-2015-0502.

26. Bowerman, Mary. "More Died This Year Trying to Take Selfies than from Shark Attacks." USA Today, Gannett Satellite Information Network, 23 Sept. 2015, www.usatoday.com/story/news/nation-now/2015/09/23/people-died-selfies-shark-attacks/72682068/

27. Molina, Brett. "More than 250 Have People Died While Trying to Take Selfies, Study Finds." USA Today, Gannett Satellite Information Network, 5 Oct. 2018, www.usatoday.com/story/news/nation-now/2018/10/04/selfie-deaths-social-media-growing-problem-study/1518748002/

28. Hess, Amanda. "The Existential Void of the Pop-Up 'Experience'." The New York Times, The New York Times, 26 Sept. 2018, www.nytimes.com/2018/09/26/arts/color-factory-museum-of-ice-cream-rose-mansion-29rooms-candytopia.html

29. "Why Women Feel Bad About Their Appearance." Psychology Today, Sussex Publishers, www.psychologytoday.com/us/blog/the-human-beast/201305/why-women-feel-bad-about-their-appearanc

30. Koul, Scaachi. "Inside The World Of Teenagers With Millions Of Followers." BuzzFeed News, BuzzFeed, 3 Oct. 2018, www.buzzfeednews.com/article/scaachikoul/danielle-cohn-tiktok-instagram-musically-teen-influencer

31. Jin, Seunga Venus, and Aziz Muqaddam. "'Narcissism 2.0! Would Narcissists Follow Fellow Narcissists on Instagram?" the Mediating Effects of Narcissists Personality Similarity and Envy, and the Moderating Effects of Popularity." NeuroImage, Academic Press, 5 Dec. 2017, www.sciencedirect.com/science/article/pii/S0747563217306805

32. Hunt, Melissa G., et al. "No More FOMO: Limiting Social Media Decreases Loneliness and Depression." Journal of Social and Clinical Psychology, vol. 37, no. 10, 10 Nov. 2018, pp. 751—768., doi:10.1521/jscp.2018.37.10.751.

33. Hunt, Melissa G., et al. "No More FOMO: Limiting Social Media Decreases Loneliness and Depression." Journal of Social and Clinical Psychology, vol. 37, no. 10, 10 Nov. 2018, pp. 751—768., doi:10.1521/jscp.2018.37.10.751.

CHAPTER 6 – SEE THE MATRIX

1. Harris, Sam. "Waking Up Podcast #138 - The Edge of Humanity with Yuval Noah Harari." Sam Harris, 19 Sept. 2018, samharris.org/podcasts/138-edge-humanity/

2. Mcneil, Donald G. "Measles Deaths Fall to a Record Low Worldwide." The New York Times, The New York Times, 26 Dec. 2017, www.nytimes.com/2017/12/26/health/measles-deaths-vaccination.html.

3. Phadke, Varun K., et al. "Association Between Vaccine Refusal and Vaccine-Preventable Diseases in the United States." *Jama*, vol. 315, no. 11, 15 Sept. 2016, p. 1149., doi:10.1001/jama.2016.1353.
4. Harris, Tristan. "How a Handful of Tech Companies Control Billions of Minds Every Day." *TED*, TED, June 2016, www.ted.com/talks/tristan_harris_the_manipulative_tricks_tech_companies_use_to_capture_your_attention?language=en

CHAPTER 7 – MOVING FORWARD—WHAT COULD "GOOD" LOOK LIKE?

1. Pinker, Steven. *Frequently Asked Questions about The Better Angels of Our Nature: Why Violence Has Declined.* New York, NY: W. W. Norton & Company, stevenpinker.com/pages/frequently-asked-questions-about-better-angels-our-nature-why-violence-has-declined
2. Harris, Sam. "Waking Up Podcast #71 - What Is Technology Doing to Us?" *Sam Harris*, 14 Apr. 2017, samharris.org/podcasts/what-is-technology-doing-to-us/

CHAPTER 8 – HOW TO STAY ZEN ON SOCIAL MEDIA

1. Dawkins, Richard. "Why the Universe Seems so Strange." *Ted*, www.ted.com/talks/richard_dawkins_on_our_queer_universe/
2. Livni, Ephrat. "A Nobel Prize-Winning Psychologist Says Most People Don't Really Want to Be Happy." *Quartz*, Quartz, 21 Dec. 2018, qz.com/1503207/a-nobel-prize-winning-psychologist-defines-happiness-versus-satisfaction/
3. *Ibid.*
4. Manson, Mark. *The Subtle Art of Not Giving a #@%: a Counterintuitive Approach to Living a Good Life.* Harper, an Imprint of HarperCollins Publishers, 2016.
5. Singer, Michael A. *The Untethered Soul: the Journey beyond Yourself.* Noetic Books, Institute of Noetic Sciences, New Harbinger Publications, Inc., 2013.
6. Peterson, Jordan B, and Norman Doidge. *12 Rules for Life: an Antidote to Chaos.* Vintage Canada, 2019.
7. Malik, Om. "The Long Goodbye (To Facebook)." OnMyOm: Om's Blog, 22 Oct. 2018, om.co/2018/09/01/the-long-goodbye-to-facebook/
8. Farr, Christina. "I Quit Instagram and Facebook and It Made Me Happier - and That's a Big Problem for Social Media." *CNBC*, CNBC, 5 Dec. 2018, www.cnbc.com/2018/12/01/social-media-detox-christina-farr-quits-instagram-facebook.html
9. Ridley, Matt. "Chiefs, Priests and Thieves." *Rational Optimist*, 27 Apr. 2010, www.rationaloptimist.com/blog/chiefs-priests-and-thieves/

ABOUT
THE AUTHOR

Trey Ratcliff is an artist on a somewhat quixotic mission to help spread consciousness and mindfulness to the world through photography and creativity. Running the #1 travel photography blog in the world, StuckInCustoms.com, has taken him to all seven continents over the past decade. Google has tracked more than 140 billion views of his photos, all while he's been building a social media presence with over 5 million followers across social media platforms.

Chris Anderson, curator of the TED conference, called Ratcliff a "pioneer" of the now ubiquitous genre of high dynamic range photography. Ratcliff's photograph, *Fourth on Lake Austin*, was the first HDR photograph to hang in the Smithsonian Museum. Subsequently, sales of his large format, limited edition prints to fine art collectors worldwide have grown into a multimillion-dollar business. In 2012, Ratcliff moved his photography business down to Queenstown, New Zealand (before moving there became a trendy doomsday contingency plan). He now lives there with his wife, three children, and a dog named Blueberry.

To learn more about Trey, visit:
www.StuckInCustoms.com/Trey-Ratcliff

OTHER RESOURCES

Let's Continue the Under the Influence Conversation

Come and join our Facebook group. And hey, be nice, eh? That's a good rule for life.

https://www.facebook.com/groups/UnderTheInfluenceBook

Contact Trey Ratcliff

business@stuckincustoms.com or his agent at CAA

ayavor@caa.com

Trey's Pretty and Pretty Entertaining Newsletter

www.StuckInCustoms.com/news

Trey's Various Websites

Blog: www.StuckInCustoms.com

Fine Art: www.TreyRatcliff.com

Portfolio: StuckInCustoms.SmugMug.com

Trey on the Social Media Thing

Instagram: @TreyRatcliff

Facebook Fan Page: Facebook.com/TreyRatcliff

YouTube: Youtube.com/TreyRatcliff

Twitter: @TreyRatcliff

Pinterest: Pinterest.com/TreyRatcliff

WeChat: TreyRatcliffChina

Line: TreyRatcliff

Flickr: Flickr.com/StuckInCustoms

Trey thinks these Gadgets, Books, and Camera Gear are Cool

Note: there are some affiliate links here

www.Kit.com/TreyRatcliff